UNLEASHING
GOD'S WORD

in Youth Ministry

Barry Shafer

ZONDERVAN®

ZONDERVAN.com/
AUTHOR**TRACKER**
follow your favorite authors

**youth
specialties**

Unleashing God's Word in Youth Ministry
Copyright 2008 by Barry Shafer

Youth Specialties resources, 300 S. Pierce St., El Cajon, CA 92020 are published by Zondervan, 5300 Patterson Ave. SE, Grand Rapids, MI 49530.

ISBN 978-0-310-27497-1

Cover design by Toolbox Studios
Interior design by Mark Novelli, IMAGO MEDIA

Printed in the United States of America

08 09 10 11 12 • 20 19 18 17 16 15 14 13 12 11 10 9 8 7 6 5 4 3 2 1

To Dana,

None of this could have happened without you.

Special thanks to—

My parents, Miles and Bonnie, who lived Deuteronomy 6 in front of my sister, Beck, and me. Seeing Scripture engraved on the doorposts of their lives, I couldn't help but acknowledge God and his Word as something to be trusted and explored.

The students with soft hearts and big ears (Psalm 95:7-8) who've been in my life—and the likes of whom are undoubtedly in yours: Marcie, Sarah (and Sara), Tim, Joel, Gretchen, Karen, Mike, Shawn, Brian, Missy, Amanda, Emily, Wes, Angie, Stephanie (and Stefanie), Jen, Adam, Darryl, Betsy, Chuck, Sue, and many more who've explored with us and applied the wonderful things in God's Word.

The friends and supporters of InWord Resources, including administrator extraordinaire, Kathi Wright. Your encouragement and support have helped plow good ground for meaningful Bible study in youth ministry.

The Youth Specialties team: Dave Urbanski ("Urb"), for his editing expertise, a true gift which has made this a better book. Jay Howver, for giving voice to the vital need of deepening our students' faith with God's Word. Roni Meek, for so graciously keeping this project on track.

My cadre of wise counselors and gracious encouragers: Jim Burns, Rich Van Pelt, Jim Hancock, Chap Clark, Steve and Lois Rabey, Duffy Robbins, Dick and Jeanne Capin, Kurt and Lori Salierno, and the person who took a huge risk many years ago in hiring an inexperienced youth pastor, Vernon Maddox.

My cheerleader-for-life mother-in-law, Sue Buchanan.

Youth workers like you for saying "yes" to the sacred task of pouring your lives into the lives of teenagers.

Contents

PART ONE

GOD'S QUEST FOR US

CHAPTER ONE

Built to Last?

For you have been born again, not of perishable seed, but of imperishable, through the living and enduring word of God. 1 PETER 1:23

They had been in the Presence of God and they reported what they saw there. They were prophets, not scribes, for the scribe tells us what he has read, and the prophet tells what he has seen. A.W. TOZER • *THE PURSUIT OF GOD*

What are you doing in your student ministry that will outlast you?

I remember the first time that question occurred to me. I can't recall where it came from or who asked it. Maybe it was a book. Or perhaps a training seminar. But it made me sit up and take stock.

Looking around at the church youth ministry I directed, I began measuring. Evaluating. Tallying up the "lasting" potential of our hard-fought efforts. The calendar was packed with all the right things: contact ministry in the schools, missions trips, retreats, and the always popular, fun stuff such as ski trips and frozen-chicken bowling.

But in the final analysis, any lasting impact seemed to be measured in months, not decades.

Little did I realize that the one question—*what are you doing that will outlast you?*—was only the first in a series of convictions that would parallel a seemingly unrelated season of preparation, all of which would converge at the place where God was stirring the hearts of students all around me.

It was a fairly amazing convergence.

And it happened like this.

Before Dana and I married, I had been in full-time youth ministry for about three years. Not long after our wedding, we decided to ramp up our personal study of Scripture. Ever since I believed in Christ as a preteen, I've had a curiosity about the Bible. At 14 I spent my own hard-earned money (cash that was earmarked for a 10-speed bike, the rage of the '70s) on a leather-bound Living Bible (the rage of Christian teenagers in the '70s). I just had to have it.

I experimented with approaches and even came up with my own color-coding system, marking Bible themes and highlighting related verses. This led to a better-than-random approach to searching the Scriptures in my early adult years. But it was start-stop at best.

Now in my early 30s and new to full-time student ministry, I knew I wanted to take the Word more seriously. Dana brought a love for Scripture and some great Bible study background to the mix. As our lives and personal approaches to study melded, I began to see that Scripture could deliver a depth I'd never tapped. But the approach called for something more than reading a passage and consulting the nearest devotional commentary.

Picture searching for bedrock by bulldozing off an acre of soil one layer at a time, rather than randomly drilling a few holes here and there. That's the image I had as I discovered the value of going deep, layer by layer, comparing Scripture to Scripture, rather than drilling in fast with a passage and a commentary. Wielding a drill may have gotten me there more quickly, but I had missed too much along the way.

Fascinated with what I was learning and how it was changing my relationship with God, I found that I couldn't get enough. I even became an early-morning Bible person—unprecedented from a sleep junkie who once said, "I could work any job as long as I didn't have to be there before 9 a.m."

My unlikely sanctuary was the local White Castle, where I could count on plenty of solitude (not to mention great coffee), because few go to White Castle for breakfast. There I began to find what I was looking for in Bible study—what A.W. Tozer describes in *The Pursuit of God* as the difference between the scribe and the prophet. The scribe, says Tozer, reads of other people's experiences with God and tells others about them; the prophet goes into God's presence and tells others what he or she *sees.*

Somehow, ever so slightly, I could feel myself shifting realms. And the difference was potent.

As Scripture began to send its roots into more of my life, I started to pick up on the words that those who wrote the Bible used to describe God's Word. *Everlasting. Enduring. Eternal. Imperishable.* Time-sensitive words, too many to count, that credited God's Word with the results I'd only hoped to see in my own youth ministry.

Click.

The light went on.

Dry-Sponge Discipleship

So how would this work? How could I help students experience firsthand the enduring nature of Scripture—or *all* the benefits of Scripture, for that matter—and thus build into them a deeper faith that would last?

It had to be more than saying, "This book is everlasting. Read it."

It had to be more than cajoling them into it. More than memorizing. More than reading a verse and asking, "What does this mean to you?" Hadn't we all had enough of that?

It had to be more than what we could accomplish in Sunday school, a discipleship program, or, in fact, any program.

The way I saw it, there needed to be some metabolizing of the words on the page—an uptake of Scripture's eternal qualities into their lives.

Picture a dry sponge dropped into a bucket of water. That's what it had to be.

More Than a Tootsie Pop

I took a hard look at the discipleship program we had in place, measuring it against my newfound standard for lasting impact.

It didn't fare too well.

So, eager to make some changes, one day in my office I opened a file in my desk drawer labeled "Bible Study."

Except for a lone photocopy of an exercise you could do with a Tootsie Pop, it was empty. Evidently I had a long way to go.

But not as far as I might have expected.

Already I'd been wowed by Scripture in my intentionally ramped-up times in the Word. A few simple hands-on tools of Bible study had worked miracles (and I do mean miracles) in making me "early to rise."

Maybe they'd help our students, too. Not necessarily to be early-risers (that'd be asking for more than a miracle), but to get beneath the surface and tap into the enduring nature of God's Word.

So we threw out an invitation to our entire student ministry. It went something like this: This summer we're having a Bible study at our house. Wednesdays from 4 to 6 p.m.

Bring your Bibles. Don't count on pizza or food, icebreakers or games. We'll be studying Colossians.

And to parents we gave a caution: If your kids don't want to attend, don't make them.

Twelve students signed up. *Twelve.*

I was intrigued by that number for a new "discipleship" effort.

As students filed into our home, filling up our living room, I sensed a level of anticipation I'd never felt from these kids. It was palpable. We'd communicated an atmosphere of challenge, and our students obviously were up for it.

Dana and I handed out the entire book of Colossians, printed on 8½ x 11-inch paper. And then we dove in. Armed with those tools of inductive study that had worked so well for us (more on that later), we gave the students things to look for in Colossians and ways to mark these things once they found them. Then we sent them to different parts of the house for a little mini-retreat with Scripture.

Reconvening after a few minutes, we helped the students process the info they'd seen in Scripture. We asked a few simple questions such as, "What did you find?" "What else did you see?" "What does that tell you about God (or yourself)?" and "What do you need to do now?"

As the weeks passed, we made some unexpected observations:

- Each session ended with a flurry of questions about God, Jesus, the Bible, or theology. Some questions had to do with what the kids were finding in Colossians. Some didn't. It was obvious that our students were getting questions answered in Colossians that they'd never expected would be answered. So they began to bring up all their unanswerables. The discussions were rich, intense, and a good deal deeper than we'd bargained for.

- Many of our students were experiencing personal renaissances before our eyes. Even the kids with attention-deficit challenges managed to stay engaged. Something about the hands-on way we were taking Scripture apart—rather than just reading or listening to it—seemed to keep them connected. (For the record, I was sure I had enough attention deficit to deal with in my student ministry; of course, we all probably think that to be the case in our own ministries!)

- And Dana and I started to notice that we weren't seeing the typical summer drop-off in participation. Our group of 12 steadily grew—in fact, it doubled by fall.

We knew we were on to something, though, when students sent tape recorders and asked for the handouts when they had to miss a session.

Feeding Frenzy

Don't think for a minute that this was a one-shot experience with a group of super-spiritual, exceptionally gifted students. To us they were the greatest kids around. But like the original 12 disciples, their most extraordinary trait was their ordinariness.

Ours was a middle-sized church in a middle-sized town (aptly if not unimaginatively named Middletown) in the middle of the Midwest. Students came from homes representing a cross-section of middle America: Professional, semi-professional, blue-collar. And they varied greatly in terms of spiritual initiative. Some were committed Christ-followers. Others, not so much.

The long and short of it? God had already been moving in these students' lives. They were hungry. Dana and I were only there to help feed the hunger.

What we hadn't expected was an all-out feeding frenzy.

Metabolism

That single-summer Bible study changed the entire landscape of our youth ministry. When the school year began we divided that group into two—middle school and high school. After that our ministry was never the same.

Intentional Bible study became more than just an add-on—more than another program. It was the heart of our work with kids—what kept them, and us, on the leading edge of what God was doing in our midst.

Now, more than a decade later, those same students are teachers, lawyers, pastors, nurses, and missionaries. They are people whose faith we admire, who are having an impact in their families, churches, and fields of influence. We continue to hear from many of them, sharing how a Bible passage we explored is still teaching them—or quoting back to us a truth they've never let go of.

Despite the group's generally high level of engagement, we still sometimes wondered if they were listening. Would they get it? But God's promises paid off. What happened in those years outlasted us—and it will continue to last.

It metabolized.

As a side note, after we moved on from that particular youth ministry, it continued to grow exponentially and remains strongly committed to God-seeking, teenage Bible study. In fact, the ministry currently attracts more than 100 students each week (in a church smaller than 500 in size), and more than 75 percent of those students are involved in the small-group Bible study ministry.

In case you need proof, God packed Scripture with promises of payoff for those who earnestly seek him—not casually or haphazardly but with diligent intentionality. Take a look at Hebrews 11:6: "And without faith it is impossible to please God, because anyone who comes to him must believe that he exists and that *he rewards those who earnestly seek him"* (emphasis added).

God wants us to absorb Scripture into our lives. In fact, God used the metabolism analogy on several occasions, instructing both Ezekiel and John to "eat" his Word (Ezekiel 3:1-3; Revelation 10:9-11). Anything less and we lose the uptake factor—the point at which the Word's active ingredients start to permeate our spiritual composition.

If God's Word is meant to be metabolized, why is it that many of our best teaching and discipling efforts wind up being little more than "spray-ons" that eventually wash off?

The greatest lesson I learned from that seminal question *What are you doing that will outlast you?* is that this was God's way of satisfying a hunger God had already been whetting among the students we were ministering to. Had I remained distracted, Martha-like, consumed with the many activities of student ministry, I'd have missed what God was seeking to accomplish in that ministry.

In fact, in my 20-plus years of doing and observing youth ministry, I've learned that God is constantly creating hunger and is on the lookout for those who will help feed the frenzy.

But are we listening?

Sliding into Biblical Illiteracy

Many observers of modern youth discipleship have noted a decline in the Bible study aspect of youth ministry. Chap Clark, a well-known youth ministry teacher and author, recently shared with me, "One of the blessings and curses of being around youth ministry for three decades is that one is able to witness firsthand where we're moving forward and where we are falling back. I'm convinced that the single most important area where we've lost ground with kids is in our commitment and ability to ground them in God's Word."

The church today, including both the adult and teenage generations, is in an era of rampant biblical illiteracy. And there are consequences.

It's been estimated that as few as 69 percent and as many as 94 percent of teenagers leave the faith after they leave our youth ministries.[1] In fact, the Southern Baptist Council on Family Life reports that 88 percent of kids raised in evangelical homes leave the church by age 18.[2]

Some will return. Many won't. And some return with life-marring scars.

The Barna Group has been actively tracking 20-somethings for several years. In 2006 they reported that of all young adults, 61 percent were churched during their teenage years but are now spiritually disengaged. Only 20 percent have maintained a level of spiritual activity consistent with their high school experiences.[3]

Who among us hasn't experienced firsthand this dropout factor in one way or another? What disheartens me most is that students' decisions to leave the faith are usually based on bad information.

They've observed the adult Word-believers around them operating in ways that are less than Word-true.

They've watched contentious church business meetings, conducted by people who've quoted to them in Sunday school, "Be completely humble and gentle; be patient, bearing with one another in love" (Ephesians 4:2).

They've memorized "Those who consider themselves religious and yet do not keep a tight rein on their tongues deceive themselves, and their religion is worthless" (James 1:26, TNIV)—yet they've listened to adult believers maligning one another.

Or maybe they just want another day to sleep in, thinking unbelief has its privileges.

The point is, most decisions to walk away from the Christian faith aren't based on God or Jesus or anything the Word says about either, but on a poor projection of Christianity.

So what if we could frontload teenagers with a lasting, biblical picture of God? What if we could help them encounter him firsthand in a way that whets their appetites for more?

I believe the race for the exit door would slow dramatically.

It's tough to walk away from things like mercy, grace, and redemption—especially when those terms are infused with new vitality and moved out of tired clichés in ways that only God's Word can accomplish.

Why the Dropout?

In his groundbreaking book *Soul Searching: The Religious and Spiritual Lives of American Teenagers*, Christian Smith examines this dropout factor, asking nonreligious teenagers who were raised in a faith tradition why they became nonreligious. Check out their answers in the following table:[4]

Reasons Nonreligious U.S. Adolescents Raised in a Religion Became Nonreligious, Ages 13-17
(percentages may not add up to 100 due to rounding)

Intellectual skepticism and disbelief	32%
Don't know why	22%
Lack of interest	13%
Just stopped attending services	12%
Life disruptions and troubles	10%
Dislikes religion	7%
Lacked parental support	1%
Vague or no reason	2%

Interestingly, all but the last two reasons could be directly impacted by an effective uptake of Scripture. Scripture is capable of holding up to intellectual skepticism. The concepts of mercy and forgiveness, when properly understood and experienced, always give a reason to follow Christ. Deep exploration of the character and ways of God are practically guaranteed to keep a seeker interested.

When students engage in and investigate their faith, make personal discoveries, and are given opportunities to put these discoveries into practice, they are far less likely to walk away from a life with Jesus.

Why then has youth ministry in general been doing such a poor job of producing lasting disciples?

Gretchen's Story

Gretchen was a middle schooler who helped facilitate her school's Bible club. One afternoon a spirited discussion arose—one that caused another student to grab a Bible for the answer.

After a few moments of futilely fanning the pages, Gretchen's friend looked at the group and asked, "Does anybody know how to work one of these things?"

Pregnant pause.

No one had a clue.

Gretchen was what you'd call a church kid, immersed in our programs since day one. Curious about her personal level of Bible literacy, I later took a few minutes to do the math. And as near as I could tell, by the time Gretchen had reached middle school, she'd heard more than 600 sermons (children and adult), attended more than 600 hours of Sunday school, and as a newly minted youth in the spring of her seventh-grade year had heard roughly 30 Bible talks and logged some 20 hours of discipleship.

Yet she couldn't help her friend navigate the Bible, nor could the other believers in her group.

Regaining Lost Ground

The number one deficiency in student ministry, as I believe research and experience have proven, is good Bible study.

Could there be a link between a teenager's ability to "work one of these things" and an enduring faith in Christ? I can't prove it, but I'll go with what Scripture says.

You see this link in passages such as Proverbs 2:1-15, Psalm 119 (any chunk of 10 verses), and in Paul's famous treatise on the "holy Scriptures" in 2 Timothy 3:14-17, especially when he commended Timothy for knowing Scripture, which could make him wise for salvation. You can also hear this connection in Jesus' words when he explains that the one who hears and understands "the word" is the one who will produce a crop exponentially greater than what was sown (Matthew 13:23).

You and I have embarked on a journey to reclaim lost ground—ground the church has given up by neglecting God's Word. Youth ministry today is packed with opportunities to make up for lost time.

Maybe you have an advanced degree in biblical studies or theology. Or maybe you're an untrained volunteer who was handed your church's student ministry when you raised your hand to ask for a bathroom break.

No matter where you are on the training and experience spectrum, think about what real hunger for God's Word might look like in your ministry.

First we'll look at the *why*. Then we'll tackle the *how*. Chapters 2-5 provide some motivation from Scripture—the Bible's perspective on teaching that leads to metabolism. Chapters 6-17 share principles on how we can practically implement that biblical perspective in our own personal quest with Scripture (it has to start with us) and then in our student ministries.

But before you dive in, think for a minute about the various movements of God you know of that had long-lasting impact. I guarantee you that in one way or another they were driven by God's Word.

In 2 Kings 22 and 23, Josiah found the long-lost Book of the Law and made radical changes to comply. The result was revival in the land and God expressing his pleasure with Josiah.

In 2 Chronicles 17 Jehoshaphat sent Levites and priests throughout the land armed only with the Book of the Law to teach God's people. The result? Judah's foresworn enemies brought grateful gifts to Jehoshaphat. Picture that: Gifts from enemies!

Throughout world history great spiritual movements driven by God's Word wound up being named for posterity (the Reformation) or given a numeric value (the First Great Awakening). Bible translators such as John Wycliffe, Martin Luther, and William Tyndale were catalysts to bringing the world out of the Dark Ages and into the Renaissance simply by championing the translation of the Bible into common language.

What works on the macro level also works on the micro. The same mighty force that can launch reformation around the world can launch a reformation in the hearts of your students.

All God needs is the slightest connection between the hunger he creates and those who will help feed it.

Shall we?

CHAPTER TWO

Priorities

The LORD will again delight in you and make you prosperous, just as he delighted in your ancestors, if you obey the LORD your God and keep his commands and decrees that are written in this Book of the Law and turn to the LORD your God with all your heart and with all your soul.

DEUTERONOMY 30:9-10, TNIV

Every time you teach you launch a process that ideally will never end, generation after generation.

HOWARD HENDRICKS • *TEACHING TO CHANGE LIVES*

Try as I did, I couldn't get Gretchen's question off my mind.

She'd shared it with our group during a run-of-the-mill weekend outing—a trip to a local park for some ultimate Frisbee, food, and one of my riveting devotional moments. After we'd packed up our Frisbees and headed for home, the point of my devotional was quickly forgotten.

But the question from Gretchen stuck with me.

Who knows what topic prompted the question. Maybe Gretchen's Bible club was talking about a friend's depression—or perhaps about sex. Maybe it was a question about the character of God. Obviously the need was deep enough to warrant some kind of search for an answer. Kudos to the guy who reached for the Bible.

But how much was lost when no one—not one kid—had the first idea how to make sense of a Bible? Near as I could tell, Gretchen's friends were asking the right questions and seeking answers from precisely the right source. And the God of the Word was *there*—ready and able to respond directly, personally, and in a way that could satisfy not only their immediate questions, but also their deepest needs. What an opportunity lost.

That's why Monday morning found me back at my desk, fingering the cover of my leather bound NIV and mulling the question: *Does anybody know how to work one of these things?*

Ranking Priorities

I've since realized that the Bible club's question is really the question of an entire generation. Now, perhaps more than ever, teenagers are seeking spiritual depth. And they're looking to us to help them know "how to work one of these things."

Some days I'm not entirely certain we youth workers know how ourselves. And I'm not sure we're convinced we need to.

Search Institute surveyed more than 400 youth workers about the priorities of modern youth ministry. The survey asked respondents to rank in order of importance 16 activities such as "help youth apply faith to daily decisions," "nurture in youth a lifelong faith commitment," and "provide a safe and caring place."[5]

Where did "teaching Scripture" rank in priority? Thirteenth out of 16.

Since the date of that survey, we've had a decade to improve that ranking. But recent data on biblical literacy in teenagers and youth workers indicates that the priority hasn't budged an inch.[6] In fact, Bible study may have dropped even further off the youth ministry radar screen.

What's in a Name?

I realize that when I dropped the phrase *Bible study* above, I may have lost you. Different images come to mind whenever youth workers hear those words. Unfortunately, many of those images aren't too positive.

Maybe you picture a Bible study that bored you to tears when you were a teenager or a failed attempt along your own youth ministry journey. Maybe you picture BSINO—"Bible Study in Name Only"—an hour or so of random discussion that somehow manages to be labeled as *Bible study*. Maybe when you think Bible study, you just assume that you've got that base covered with worship and other Word-centered activities.

Even the words themselves carry some baggage. I mean, who wants to *study* outside of school?

I've experimented with other phrases such as *Bible experience* or *Word journey*, but none sounds accurate or descriptive enough to do the job. So for now we're stuck with *Bible study*. Perhaps we can infuse it with a new set of mental images. In fact, take a second now to erase whatever images you have from the *Bible study* programs, approaches, and methods you've encountered in the past.

Start with a clean slate. And when you hear Bible study, picture a fresh approach that excites God and that teenagers actually enjoy—an approach with the goal of enabling them to assimilate God's Word into their lives.

While you're at it, ask yourself a few questions. Do my students *need* to know how to work "one of these things"? Does student Bible study have a place in the emerging church? Does it have a place in the declining church?

For some insight, let's look in Deuteronomy at the first instance when God told his people what to do with one of these things—God's written Word in their generation.

Orientation Session

You've got to wonder if it was a downer for the people of Israel. They'd just gotten wind that they were poised to move into the Promised Land to take possession of a piece of earth they'd been on a quest toward for a generation.

The days of tents, port-o-johns, and life on the road were about to be history. Now they'd have their *own* land, each family its own little plot.

Finally God's people had paid their dues for the disobedience of their parents and grandparents. They were eager to show God that they were *not* their parents and grandparents, that this was a new generation on the brink of a bold, new era.

Moses stepped up to the microphone as the crowd surged forward to hear the words they anticipated—words such as "Gentlemen, start your engines. People of Israel, it's time to roll!"

Moses cleared his throat, adjusted the mic, and said, "Hear now, O Israel, the decrees and laws I am about to teach you" (Deuteronomy 4:1).

Do what? Anticipation leaked out of the crowd like air from a punctured balloon. Like grade school students counting down the final seconds before the bell as the teacher says, "Take out a piece of paper."

Then Moses said something else: These decrees and laws I'm about to recount. You'll need to know every one of them, so that you will live.

Live? Did he say *live*?

Now Moses had them in the palm of his hand. These people had seen death that resulted from disobedience. The bodies of their loved ones had dropped like carcasses in the wilderness. Moses' words might be worth listening to. These people *liked* life.

How to Follow God

Moses began his sermon in Deuteronomy with a primer on how *not* to follow God, recounting for that generation how the disobedience of their fathers had turned an easy journey from Mount Sinai to the Promised Land, which should have taken just a few days, into a 40-year sojourn in the wilderness. What came next was a lesson on how *to* follow God, infused with plenty of motivation as to why. This teaching makes up the majority of Deuteronomy. And it all hinges on one central phrase: "the words of this law, which are written in this book" (Deuteronomy 28:58).

So what did God say about these words? And more importantly, how do those words written so long ago relate to youth ministry *today*?

In the great pre-Promised Land orientation session that Deuteronomy comprises, God reveals his heart for his Word, the things "written in this book" for the ages.

We learn what God's Word is: *righteous* (Deuteronomy 4:8).

We learn what it does: *Gives life, wisdom, and understanding. People who live it out make following God attractive to unbelievers* (Deuteronomy 4:6-7, 32:47).

And we learn what God expects us to do with it: *Take it to heart, follow it, observe it carefully, keep it, and learn it* (Deuteronomy 4:1-10, 5:1).

If Israel failed to activate God's instructions and use his Word as he commanded, the nation would be of no use to God.

And here's where modern youth ministry comes into the mix. In these decrees and laws, which were meant to be the lifeblood of Israel, the adult generation was given two major responsibilities regarding the younger generation:

1. They were to teach the next generation God's decrees (Deuteronomy 6:6-7).

2. They were to tell that generation of God's ways (Deuteronomy 4:9).

Teach the Next Generation

Moses wasted no time emphasizing *why* the older generation was to teach the younger generation God's decrees: "So that you, your children and their children after them may fear the LORD your God as long as you live by keeping all his decrees and commands that I give you, and so that you may enjoy long life" (Deuteronomy 6:2).

In case you skimmed that verse, read it again. That's a powerful *why*, and it applies to you and your students just as it did to Israel.

God also specified *how* the adult generation was to teach his decrees. God wasn't picturing an occasional devotional moment or a quick pre-meal prayer. God's words were to be intentionally *impressed* on the younger generation as they were woven into the fabric of everyday life (Deuteronomy 6:6-7). The Hebrew word translated as *impress* connotes a repeated action.[7] But the adult generation first had to firmly fix that truth in their hearts so that they could impress the concept creatively and ensure that its repetition never became dry, boring, or rote (Deuteronomy 11:18).

The Hebrew word translated as *fix* conveys the notion of putting something special in a special place with the knowledge that it's going to be used.[8] As a way of keeping these things in their hearts, the adults were to think on them, meditate on them, and respond to them out of conviction. They were to exhibit before the younger generation authentic behavior that showed these decrees ruled their lives.

God's plan was that Israel's behavior would signal to the next generation that his decrees were alive and real—worth selling out to. It was the only way God's words would stand a chance with the youth of Israel. And it is the only way they stand a chance with students today.

With God's words fixed in their hearts, the adult generation of Israel was told to use every means available to make sure their children absorbed those words as well. They were to speak them. Tie them. Write them. Wear them. Some might even say tattoo them. This was to happen during the normal activities of the day: Sitting, walking, lying down, getting up. And the adults were to use all available media—symbols, hands, foreheads, doorframes, and gates (Deuteronomy 6:6-10, 11:18-21).

God told Israel to let the younger generation see that the older generation was willing to go to any length to make sure they knew and obeyed what God had said—"the words that are written in this book."

Stacking the Deck

Think for a moment about the Ten Commandments. What's the one commandment exclusively given to the younger generation? Commandment five: "Honor your father and your mother" (Exodus 20:12).

Remember the promise attached to that commandment? "So that you may live long in the land the LORD your God is giving you."

With the fifth commandment God gave the parents and the significant adults in kids' lives a mechanism to ensure success in their responsibilities to the younger generation. He instructed the adults to teach the decrees in an authentic way in order to show that the Word of God actually impacts life. And then he commanded the children, including teenagers, to honor and obey their parents. Not just because it's a good idea and leads to sanity at home, but also because the parents would be teaching and modeling God's righteous decrees.

With commandment five in play, parents could count on soft hearts among the younger generation—hearts that would receive and honor the things parents were teaching.

Here's the bottom line: If the adults were heeding and teaching the Book of the Law—and if the youth were honoring and obeying what the adults were teaching—these people would exude God's character by walking in God's commands. And God would have a people he could use. And as long as God could use the people, they could live and prosper in the land. For a long, long time.

Tell Them God's Ways

In the future, when your children ask you, "What is the meaning of the stipulations, decrees and laws the LORD our God has commanded you?" tell them: "We were slaves of Pharaoh in Egypt, but the LORD brought us out of Egypt with a mighty hand. Before our eyes the LORD sent signs and wonders—great and terrible—on Egypt and Pharaoh and his whole household. But he brought us out from there to bring us in and give us the land that he promised on oath to our ancestors. The LORD commanded us to obey all these decrees and to fear the LORD our God, so that we might always prosper and be kept alive, as is the case today. And if we are careful to obey all this law before the LORD our God, as he has commanded us, that will be our righteousness." (DEUTERONOMY 6:20-25, TNIV)

The second major responsibility given to adults was to tell the next generation God's ways, sharing vivid testimony of how he had worked in their lives.

Ever noticed what was to prompt this kind of teaching? Questions from the youth. Maybe these came up whenever kids asked about the meaning of something adults were teaching them from God's book (Deuteronomy 6:20). Or when they asked about a funny-looking altar (Joshua 4:6). Or a strange-smelling sacrifice (Exodus 13:13-15).

These were a few of the cues God built into the culture of Israel—cues that caused the younger generation to wake up and tune in to God's ways. That made them ask *why?*

Adults were to use these symbols and occasions to explain all God had done for them and the strength he'd displayed in the past to give the next generation assurance that God would continue to do the same for them. God was exhibiting confidence in the adults. He trusted them to do their part—to teach the statutes, build altars, make strange sacrifices—in a manner that piqued the spiritual curiosity of the youth.

Without the built-in benefit of young people asking *why*, the parents would have had to contrive teachable moments to impart this info. And like most of us, rather than suffering the scathing, eye-rolling sarcasm of a teenager ("There goes Dad again on one of his *things*"), they'd have bailed.

When a child asked about the statutes or the altars or the sacrifices, the adults had to be ready. With God's words fixed in their hearts, they would have been up-to-date and ready to unload all that God had done for them. And as the younger generation heard of the miraculous ways God had delivered, their spiritual appetites would have been whetted.

This in turn would have generated more curiosity. Then the adult generation could confidently *teach* these decrees. As they taught from their hearts and own personal convictions, and as the youth absorbed these lessons into their lives, God was pleased. And God rewarded their obedience with more demonstrations of his presence, protection, and power—not only giving the adults more God-sightings to convey to the youth, but giving the youth more God-sightings to see first-hand. As you might guess, all of this generated more curiosity on the part of the children.

Are you seeing the cycle God had in mind?

Who Broke the Cycle?

Apparently someone dropped the ball.

Despite the perpetual cycle of teaching and heeding God set in place, the remainder of the Old Testament reveals just how miserably Israel failed. Moses passed the baton of leadership to Joshua. And Joshua passed the baton to...well, a committee.

Under Joshua's guidance Israel enjoyed the rich benefits of obedience as they sliced and diced through the Promised Land like Ginsu knives of old. But when Joshua died, a generation grew up who neither knew God nor what he had done for Israel. Then the Israelites did evil in the eyes of the Lord and served false gods, the Baals (Judges 2:10-11).

Some might say it was the rebellious teenagers who stopped honoring their parents. But instinct tells me it was the adults who stopped teaching.

Somewhere along the way the realities of God stopped being real—or relevant—to the adult generation. Their sacrifices became dry rituals. Their encounters with the living God became fewer. They got lazy with their two responsibilities toward the next generation: teaching God's decrees and telling of his ways. Their explanations at the altar became ho-hum. Their teaching became rote.

This may have been the birth of the flannelgraph.

Whatever happened, God's unfathomable ways got reduced to the same-ol' same-ol'. There was no reason for the youth to ask questions or to be curious about God.

When adults lose their diligence in conveying God's decrees—as if the decrees no longer *mean* something to them— and when they become casual in telling of God's ways, behavior that reflects those decrees is the next thing to go.

And if the younger generation doesn't see the things of God making an authentic difference in the adults around them, that's all they need to suspect that those may not be the real deal.

And that's when the Baals start looking good.

Living Outside the Promised Land

From our perspective, it's easy to look back on Israel with some incredulity: *How could they have ignored such a fail-safe cycle, guaranteed to perpetuate a long life in the Promised Land?*

Somehow they did ignore it. And, incredulous or not, we do the same thing today.

It's no secret that many believers today have stopped taking seriously the things "written in this book." You've seen the stats showing little to no measurable difference between the ethics and behaviors (things like lying, cheating, adultery, and the like) of believers and unbelievers.

Church pollster George Barna made an even more startling discovery. Tracking the biblical perspectives of adults for several years, the Barna Group found that only half of adult evangelicals possess a biblical worldview. Presented with a list of key tenets thought to constitute a biblical worldview (such as "the source of moral truth is the Bible," "the Bible is accurate in all of the principles it teaches," and "Jesus lived a sinless life on earth"), only half of those surveyed agreed with every tenet. According to Barna's assessment only 8 percent of Protestant adults possess a truly biblical worldview.[9]

Not only has today's adult generation quit embracing the things "written in this book," they've lost touch with what's in the book at all. Here's another example of this decline in recent years: According to Barna, the most widely recognized Bible verse among American adult Christians is "God helps those who helps themselves."[10]

This is not a verse in the Bible; it's a saying from *Poor Richard's Almanac.*

Thirty-nine percent of American adult lay leaders, people active in the church, believe that Jesus Christ sinned while here on earth.[11] And 37 percent believe that simply being good will earn you a place in heaven.[12] Nearly half of adult believers, 46 percent, agree that Satan is not a living being but merely a symbol of evil.[13]

Beat the Bail-Out

I'm always dismayed when I hear mature Christians bail out of a question by saying, "We'll just have to find that out when we get to heaven," when in reality, God gave us the answer in Scripture.

Some questions may have to wait, but not as many as we might think.

Back in Deuteronomy God asked the adult generation to revere the things he'd "written in this book"—to observe them, heed them, ingest them, and give them a place of honor in their hearts. Then those things could be passed to the next generation with authenticity and passion.

So back to our original question about the place of Bible study in today's youth ministry. Does it really matter whether teenagers know what's "written in this book"?

It mattered to God, and it should to us.

There are no places where quests for things "written in this book" need to happen more than in our youth rooms. Our students are only beginning to experiment with abstract thinking and learning skills. They're asking the *whys, hows,* and *so whats*.

Perhaps more importantly, they're only a few years or months from needing as strong a foundation as we can build into them before they begin navigating the faith challenges of young adulthood.

The kind of teaching we're talking about obviously should be happening at home as the most direct application of Moses' sermon in Deuteronomy. But modern family dynamics place a great responsibility on the shoulders of youth ministry. Many teenagers have one or more parents who aren't believers. Most parents, as the preceding statistics attest, may not know enough of God's Word to impart it.

We can help reverse this trend by cultivating a generation of future parents who will be impassioned about the things "written in this book"—and who know enough to teach them. Consider this shocker: Within the next 10 to 15 years, all of your current students will be deep into parenting age. Your students today may be the shortest path to turning things around.

We can also encourage our current crop of parents to ramp up their personal experiences in Scripture and to let the results spill into their families. And we can create new ways for youth workers and parents to team up in adopting *all* of the responsibilities given to adults in Deuteronomy.

Of course, it's not a matter of memorizing facts or projecting Scripture on big screens. It's a matter of knowing God. It's about paying attention to what's important to God. As we press toward God, what's in his Word will become second nature to us—"fixed in our hearts," to borrow a phrase from Moses.

Let's let our students see how hard we'll work to facilitate their knowing and experiencing God's Word.

Let's help them learn how to work one of these things.

CHAPTER THREE

What You Don't Know Can Hurt You

My people are destroyed from lack of knowledge. "Because you have rejected knowledge, I also reject you as my priests; because you have ignored the law of your God, I also will ignore your children." HOSEA 4:6

Jesus made it unmistakably clear that it is the knowledge of the truth that will set us free.

RICHARD J. FOSTER • *CELEBRATION OF DISCIPLINE*

Sometimes I think of the ancient prophets of Israel and Judah as the youth pastors of the Old Testament.

They were passionate about their message. They had great object lessons. They were more than a little weird. And nobody listened to them.

It was a tough calling.

Hosea was one of those prophets. And he delivered one of the best object lessons of all time: He married a prostitute. The point of Hosea's object lesson? The nation of Israel had cavorted with a prostitute rather than remaining faithful to God.

In fact, by the time Hosea appeared on the scene, Israel's behavior had reached the point of no return. Hosea was charged with prophesying that God would soon invoke the curses first enunciated hundreds of years earlier in the days of Moses, recorded for us in—you guessed it—Deuteronomy.

Israel would soon be removed from the land. Assyria loomed as the oppressor-in-waiting.

Israel's relationship with God had degenerated to this: If there was wrong to do, they did it. Not entirely out of rebellion, but because they couldn't discern right from wrong. There was little if any discernable difference between their way of life and the lifestyles of their decadent pagan neighbors.

How could they have fallen so far? With all the miracles they'd seen, with the many warnings of the prophets, how could they have continued in blatant disobedience?

Hosea's finger was on Israel's spiritual pulse and his ear tuned to the Word of the Lord. He went straight to the heart of the problem: Throughout the land there was no knowledge of God.

Israel had become God's people in name only, walking in utter ignorance of God's truth and his ways. Centuries of judges and kings, prophets and priests, miracles and blessings, victories and defeats would come down to one fatal deficiency: *Knowledge*.

One Glaring Defect

Remember the near-fatal voyage of Apollo 13? About 200,000 miles from Earth, an explosion in one of the spacecraft's liquid oxygen tanks turned the moon mission into a rescue mission on behalf of the three astronauts on board. After five days of nail-biting and problem-solving by Mission Control in Houston and the astronauts onboard, the crew safely arrived home. It was one of NASA's finest and most torturous hours.

The ensuing investigation revealed that, as in many catastrophes of such magnitude, a series of events had contributed to the problem. But the origin of the explosion was simple:

A 28-volt thermostat had never been upgraded to match the vessel's newer 65-volt wiring.

Billions of dollars, countless hours, and the anxiety of a watching world came down to a single defect—one component, the equivalent of a fuse sold for $1.39 at a local hardware store.

During Hosea's day the future of God's treasured possession—the vessel of God's global mission to redeem lost mankind—hinged on one deficiency. Israel's entire saga, which had begun with Abraham, was about to climax in destruction. The bottom-line cause? A lack of knowledge.

For a minor prophet, that's a pretty major point.

So what's the big deal about knowledge? Doesn't it just puff us up? According to Paul in 1 Corinthians 8:1, that's precisely what knowledge does when it's not accompanied by love.

But later in the same letter, Paul writes that the consequences of Israel's actions were recorded in Scripture as a caution for us (1 Corinthians 10:6). Hosea's words aren't just ancient ramblings for an ancient people, but life-or-death warnings meant to spur us into action.

A deficiency in biblical knowledge, sooner or later, will manifest itself in our personal lives and in our student ministries. And this lack of knowledge can have far-reaching consequences.

No Mercy

According to Hosea, the first casualties of Israel's lack of knowledge were integrity and compassion. "There is no faithfulness, no love, no acknowledgment of God in the land" (Hosea 4:1).

The word translated as *faithfulness* is the Hebrew word *emeth*,[14] which carries the idea of truth and faithfulness between people—or, in a word, integrity. The Hebrew word for love, *chesedh*,[15] can be translated as *mercy*. In the context of this verse, the word connotes compassion toward others within the community of God's people.

Integrity and mercy were in short supply among those meant to be God's poster children for the exact same qualities. Israel's interaction with one another—let alone the surrounding nations—was neither compassionate nor scrupulous. As a result the people of Israel were giving the unbelieving nations around them no reason to be attracted to their God.

Hosea's prophecy makes an outright connection between the knowledge of God and godly behavior. Ignorance of God's laws and His ways—the things "written in this book"—had created an atmosphere where godly traits such as mercy and love had been replaced with cursing, lying, murder, stealing, and adultery (Hosea 4:2). Israel's behavior was barely distinguishable from that of her neighbors.

But the next consequence may have been worse: The people of God couldn't keep their hands and eyes off other gods.

Deception

> The LORD said to me, "Go, show your love to your wife again, though she is loved by another and is an adulteress. Love her as the LORD loves the Israelites, though they turn to other gods and love the sacred raisin cakes." (HOSEA 3:1)

There was a second consequence of Israel's lack of knowledge: They turned to other gods and loved their sacred raisin cakes.

Now this might be a consequence you and I can relate to.

Big-ticket sins like cursing, lying, murder, stealing, and adultery aren't so subtle, and perhaps for that reason alone most of us manage to keep them at bay.

But an innocuous raisin cake? Other than a few extra calories, what could be the harm in that?

In Israel's culture raisin cakes were sugary delicacies often served at parties and feasts. David ate them when he was made king over Israel (1 Chronicles 12:40). But over time the sacred raisin cakes became known among the pagans for their supposed aphrodisiac effect and were co-opted for their fertility rites.

Raisin cakes became a forbidden fruit. And Hosea's mention of the raisin cakes strongly suggests that Israel wasn't eating these cakes simply as yummy after-school snacks. They were ascribing a pagan, and probably lustful, meaning to the cakes.

Without knowledge—knowledge of God and his Word— Israel couldn't tell the difference between a party food and the sacred rite of a false religion.

And the same is often the case today.

Temptations common among teenagers today are like the sacred raisin cakes of old. They present themselves as desirable, acceptable, even needed—and with no discernable long-term consequences.

Cheating on a test turns into, I know the answer; I just can't remember it. If I take a peek at my notes, I'm just confirming what I already know.

Experimenting with drugs becomes, I don't want to put a wall between me and my friends; I want them to see me as a player. Besides, this is just a one-time thing. I won't be doing it forever.

As the old saying goes, Sin takes you farther than you intended to go. You stay longer than you intended to stay. And you pay more than you intended to pay. But knowledge, richly supplied by God through his Word, enables believers to see a seemingly innocuous temptation for what it truly is: A stepping stone toward destruction.

REPORT CARD 2002: THE ETHICS OF AMERICAN YOUTH

For the people of Israel, the doomsday clock began ticking when prophets such as Hosea could not distinguish a difference between the behavior of God's people and unbelievers.

Can a similar ticking be heard in the church?

In a survey[16] of 12,000 high school students, the Josephson Institute found little difference between the ethics of teenagers who described their religious convictions as "essential/very important" and of those who said they were "unimportant." When asked about the following behaviors over the preceding 12 months, the students responded as follows:

I lied to a parent.		I stole something from a store.	
Religious Teens	93%	Religious Teens	34%
Nonreligious Teens	93%	Nonreligious Teens	45%

I lied to a teacher.		I hit a person because I was angry.	
Religious Teens	83%	Religious Teens	63%
Nonreligious Teens	85%	Nonreligious Teens	67%

I cheated during a test in school.		I used an illegal drug.	
Religious Teens	74%	Religious Teens	29%
Nonreligious Teens	76%	Nonreligious Teens	49%

I stole from a parent or a relative.	
Religious Teens	25%
Nonreligious Teens	33%

The Church Game

Of all God's complaints against Israel, "playing church" seems to rank at the top of his list.

In Hosea 6:5-6 God speaks clearly about what he really wants from Israel: "My judgments go forth like the sun. For I desire mercy, not sacrifice, and acknowledgment of God rather than burnt offerings." (TNIV) Mercy. Lovingkindness from one to another. Without that heartfelt behavior, God didn't even want their offerings and sacrifices. In fact, he found them repugnant.

Through Hosea God pointed out that while Israel put on a good show of calling on him, they didn't really know him. When it came to worship, they were just going through the motions.

Ironically Israel's so-called spiritual leaders—her priests and prophets—were leading the church game. Hosea laid great blame at the feet of the priests and prophets, observing that whenever the people stumbled, the spiritual leaders stumbled right along with them (Hosea 4:5). Hosea 4:7 draws a direct parallel between priests of Israel and the sin of the people—the more priests, the more sin.

So what was the role of the priests in the spiritual decline of Israel? In addition to caring for the sanctuary and serving as mediators between God and the people, Israel's priests were charged with teaching the people God's law. They were the preservers of knowledge—God's written words and ways—and the curators of God's sacred revelation.

Not only did the priests fail to keep God's Word fresh in the minds of the people, but they sinned, too, even reveling in the wickedness of the people. In short, the behavior of the priests looked no different from the lives of the people.

Yet worship continued as if none of this was true.

Playing church is perhaps the most insidious kind of sin. It feels religious. It feels right. Yet God says that apart from truth, religious activity has no power. It offers no wisdom, no strength, and certainly no transformation. Without truth as their north star, the people of Israel floundered for lack of guidance. They became faithless, unmerciful, and unloving. Yet they played the church game as if that alone could save them.

And God was left with a people he could not use.

Is it any wonder that Hosea issued his most chilling prophecy of all—that God's people would be destroyed for their lack of knowledge? *Destroyed.* Not simply because they disobeyed truth, but because they didn't *have* truth.

Truth was nowhere to be found in the land. And it showed.

For Israel, this lack of knowledge meant destruction. For today's church it could mean irrelevance. A violent oppressor such as Assyria may not conquer the modern church, but the modern church can still be rendered useless to God.

Peter warns against this exact pitfall in the New Testament, urging believers to grow in knowledge (among other godly attributes) lest they be rendered "ineffective and unproductive" (irrelevant) in their saving knowledge of Jesus Christ (2 Peter 1:5-8).

How does the church know when it's in danger of becoming ineffective and unproductive in its knowledge of Christ? We only need to look around us. Most communities are filled with church buildings seemingly on every block. But when it comes to their messages, how many people are listening?

Without a Net

Without knowledge, the church—including its student ministries—is in a dangerous position. You might say we're working without a net.

A 2003 Barna survey of teenagers who grew up in the church found that only half (53 percent) understood enough of the Bible to make every decision based on biblical principles.[17]

Let that sink in for a minute. This indicates that the other half (47 percent) of the teenagers in our ministries cannot access our faith document—the things "written in this book"—in a useful, practical way.

Perhaps these students view the Bible as an overwhelming reference book. (We all have those on our shelves yet to be opened.) Maybe as they've cruised through adolescence, we've spoon-fed them answers to their questions and given them a fragmented, underdeveloped picture of God's story.

Half of our students admit that they're making decisions without the guidance of the Bible. Yet one of the great purposes of Scripture is to be a light to our paths, providing guidance for life (Psalm 119:105). Granted, the Bible isn't a computer program into which teenagers can enter their college criteria and wait for the top three options to appear. But as students' hearts and minds are changed by what they discover in God's Word, their thoughts and desires begin to reflect the mind of Christ. This in turn will impact their daily decisions.

Soul Searching

Christian Smith's National Study of Youth and Religion, purported to be the largest and most detailed study of teenagers and religion ever undertaken, surveyed 3,370 in a nationally representative random sample. Of those surveyed 267 were selected for more in-depth interviews.

A striking observation Smith derived from these interviews (as revealed in his book *Soul Searching: The Religious and Spiritual Lives of American Teenagers*) is that the vast majority of teenagers are "incredibly inarticulate about their faith, their religious beliefs and practices, and its meaning or place in their lives."

For example Smith describes a 15-year-old girl in Michigan who attends two church services every Sunday, plus Sunday school, youth group, and Wednesday-night Bible study. Here's how she responded to a question about her religious beliefs:

Teen:	[pause] I don't really know how to answer that.
Interviewer:	Are there any beliefs at all that are important to you? Really generally?
Teen:	[pause] I don't know.
Interviewer:	Take your time if you want.
Teen:	I think that you should just, if you're gonna do something wrong then you should always ask for forgiveness, and

> he's gonna forgive you no matter what, 'cause he gave up his only son to take all the sins for you.[18]

Smith notes that this teenager and others like her are quite articulate and conversant on other life issues about which they've been educated—such as drug abuse and sexually transmitted diseases. Smith concludes that such teenagers cannot articulate matters of faith because they haven't been properly educated in the faith.[19] (In this regard, Christian students fared far worse than those of other faiths, such as Mormonism, Buddhism, and Judaism.)[20]

Smith speculates that if the majority of American teenagers were to take a short-answer test on the basics of the Christian faith, they'd fail miserably.

And in fact, he's right.

Down to Basics

Not long ago, instructors from the department of religion at Wheaton College—a competitive Christian school that attracts top students from around the world—surveyed their incoming freshman class on basic Bible knowledge. They were shocked at the lack of Bible literacy, especially considering the fact that these students represented the best and brightest products of modern youth ministry.

Curious to see what was happening in youth ministries across the nation, the Wheaton instructors next administered the survey to high school seniors from large evangelical churches. Here are some highlights of that survey:[21]

- 80 percent could not place in order Moses, Adam, David, Solomon, Abraham.
- 15 percent could place in order the major events of Paul's and Jesus' lives.
- 20 percent knew to look in Acts for Paul's travels.

- 60 percent could locate the exodus story in Exodus.

- 33 percent could find the Sermon on the Mount in the New Testament.

- 80 percent did not know how to find the Lord's Prayer.

To determine whether or not these figures still held, the survey was repeated in 2006. Four hundred teenagers (grades six through 12) in a large metropolitan area were surveyed in a variety of settings, including Sunday school, small-group discipleship, and large-group youth gatherings. These teenagers showed marginal improvement over those in the Wheaton College survey group. The most notable difference was the 2006 group's ability to locate the Lord's Prayer in Scripture. Half of the 2006 group knew how to find the Lord's Prayer—a 30 percent improvement over the Wheaton group.

But a few other highlights from the 2006 survey show that teenage Bible knowledge is still pretty bleak:

- 51 percent selected Hezekiah as a book of the Bible.

- 52 percent didn't know that Saul was the first king of Israel.

- 59 percent selected Moses' brother Aaron as a prophet.

- 66 percent could not order major events of the Old Testament, including Creation, the Fall, the Flood, and the Exodus.

- Only 13 percent could order the major events of Paul's and Jesus' lives.

- Only 35 percent knew to look in Exodus for the first Passover.

- Only 35 percent knew that the Sermon on the Mount was in the Gospels.

- 51 percent placed in Genesis the phrase "In the beginning was the Word." (It's found in John 1.)

Clearly we have some ground to make up. But lack of knowledge isn't just a teenage problem; it's a youth worker problem, too.

Remember from the preceding chapter our national pop quiz for youth workers? Take a second to check your answers against the correct historical order of these Bible people:

Noah

Abraham

Moses

Samson

King Saul

Daniel

Esther

Paul

How did you do? If you didn't ace the quiz, you have plenty of company. According to our national tally, only 12 percent of youth workers have been able to order these folks correctly.

Why is this important? For one thing, the people in this quiz are not obscure Bible people. Each person represents a key era in God's unfolding revelation.

Obviously, it's not a matter of memorizing facts; anyone can memorize such a list but never move an inch closer to God. Rather, it's a matter of increasing our knowledge of God's Word—paying attention to the things that are important to God—for the sole purpose of increasing our intimacy with God.

God gave us his Word so we could know him better. If these stats are any indication, we have a long way to go.

One Generation from Extinction

A major goal of student ministry is to equip teenagers for the many challenges adult life will throw their way: *How do I find God in the middle of pain and tragedy? How can I break this habit that's tearing me down? How can I beat this temptation? Why can't I find a job?*

How our students respond to these and other circumstances will be closely linked to their total picture of God and their ability to find him in the midst of challenges. The teenage years are ripe for quantum leaps in faith development. In fact, there's probably not a six-year stretch in all of life that generally produces more spiritual development than the adolescent years. Youth ministry presents us with a tremendous window of opportunity to impact this development and help students get the right knowledge. It appears, though, that we haven't taken full advantage of that window.

Proclamations from the likes of Josh McDowell and George Gallup, Jr. eerily sound like our man Hosea.

"The church is one generation from extinction," Gallup predicted in 1997.[22] McDowell came to the same conclusion, boldly titling his recent book about today's teenagers *The Last Christian Generation*. Reminiscent of Hosea's lament, "My people are destroyed for lack of knowledge," both men point to the church's loosening grip on truth as the impetus behind their dire predictions.

Learn This Inside and Out

How is it possible that God's people, specifically his teenage generation, could be destroyed by a lack of knowledge? Is it the literal *absence* of knowledge that destroys?

Probably not. They're destroyed by suicide, Internet porn, substance abuse, premarital sex, STDs. Later in life, they're destroyed by failed marriages or insidious consumerism and greed, which the Bible calls idolatry. They're destroyed by incapacitating guilt and regret over past mistakes, choices they made when the lines between right and wrong were blurred. They're destroyed by not knowing firsthand the God who has a better destiny in mind for them—the God who wants to call them, save them, and preserve them.

Hosea concluded his oracle with a final plea, one that applies not only to his prophecy but to the entire counsel of God's Word. "If you want to live well, make sure you understand all of this. If you know what's good for you, you'll learn this inside and out" (Hosea 14:9, *The Message*).

CHAPTER FOUR

Getting the Word in Edgewise

It is an immense irony that a generation that has access to the best in biblical exegesis is, even among the so-called "educated clergy," so largely indifferent to it.

EUGENE PETERSON • *EAT THIS BOOK*

What makes you uneasy about leading teenagers in Bible study?

All of us have something that makes us put on the brakes. Maybe it's that question from the thinking student that we fear will unravel the whole system of faith. Maybe it's a lack of confidence in our own skills. Or maybe it's the deer-hunter principle: You only get one shot to make an impact—and if you blow it (by boring them) they'll never open the Bible again. On some deeper level maybe we're not sure we believe everything that's in there ourselves.

Or maybe it's a little bit of all the above.

All it takes is one hesitation. And like a log across a river, it becomes a snag, causing other barriers to pile up. And when the risks seem to outweigh the benefits, we shy away from the task, easily busying ourselves with other youth ministry priorities such as relationship building, missions experiences, worship planning, and even the ubiquitous fund-raising. When we finally try to take the plunge into Bible study, it may be only with our big toe.

Deeper Teaching?

I recently interviewed volunteer and paid youth workers from 27 churches in a metro area about their Bible study efforts. Roughly 70

percent of these youth ministers told me they have a designated time when students voluntarily attend a deeper teaching experience such as a small-group Bible study, discipleship
group, or accountability group.

At first glance, 70 percent looks like an encouraging stat.
But then I asked the leaders to describe the content of their
time using the following options:

1. discussion of issues

2. devotional talk by a leader

3. Bible reading and discussion

4. in-depth Bible study

Of the 70 percent, *none* of the youth workers described
their deeper teaching time as in-depth Bible study. The most
popular format was discussion of issues, the most shallow of
the four options. When asked about their prep for the teaching time, the responses were sketchy, varying from "I wing
it" to "I cut and paste from many things" to "I tweak the curriculum."

Left to our default settings, our attempts at leading Bible
study often follow the path of least resistance. We find ourselves spending little to no time in preparation as tasks more
immediate and urgent overshadow the important.

I'm convinced that there's not a more conscientious group
of people on the planet than Christian youth workers—church
or parachurch, volunteer or paid. We want the best for the
teenagers entrusted to our care, and we'll go to great lengths
to achieve that. If there's a fault in our conscientiousness, it's
that we try to accomplish too many agenda items, letting the
good squeeze out the best.

The apparent non-urgency of Bible study can keep Scripture buried beneath the stacks of resources in our offices. And
let's face it: Sometimes the Bible just doesn't seem all that

practical. It doesn't sell itself as a short-term fix—and we're ready to see changes in our students *now*! (They want stuff to happen for them *now*, too.)

Listen closely to Jesus, however, and you'll hear him making a desperate pitch for the urgency of Bible study, talking up Scripture's ability to deliver both short- and long-term changes in the lives of our students.

Let's look at two prominent youth ministry goals, agenda items that occupy an enormous amount of time and resource: Helping teenagers beat temptation and encouraging them to share their faith. And let's see what Jesus had to say about how the Word of God can help with these two goals.

Beating Temptation

Remember the old Sunday school song about the wise man who built his house upon the rock? Do you know what that analogy referred to or what the rock represented? The song never gave us the answer, only the fact that the man was wise because he built his house upon rock, which sounds like old-fashioned common sense to me.

The obvious conclusion is that Jesus is the rock. But when Jesus gave the illustration, He was slightly more specific.

> "Why do you call me, 'Lord, Lord,' and do not do what I say? As for those who come to me and hear my words and put them into practice, I will show you what they are like. They are like a man building a house, who dug down deep and laid the foundation on rock. When a flood came, the torrent struck that house but could not shake it, because it was well built. But those who hear my words and do not put them into practice are like a man who built a house on the ground without a foundation. The moment the torrent struck that

house, it collapsed and its destruction was complete." (LUKE 6:46-49, TNIV)

According to Jesus, the wise person is the one who hears his words and puts them into practice. The construction project he spoke of wasn't just a matter of bolting a foundation to the nearest slab of rock (as I tended to picture it in my early Sunday school days). Jesus described building on the rock as digging down deep *to* the rock and *then* laying the foundation. That takes a little more work.

But look at the payoff Jesus described. The flood and the torrent wreaked havoc, smashing the poorly built homes, especially those on the sand. But the house on the rock stood firm because it was well built.

May that be the picture of our students as they navigate the torrents indigenous to adolescence. May faith win over every temptation because it is sturdy and well constructed. And how does it get that way? As we've seen, one of the most important ways is through hearing Jesus' words and putting them into practice.

In the next few chapters we'll discuss how in greater detail. But for now, take a quick mental stroll through your student ministry calendar. When in your busy schedule do students have an opportunity to hear the words of Jesus? Bear in mind that this type of hearing implies more than dissemination. You may provide regular opportunities for Jesus' words in talks, lessons, and the like—but are they really being *heard*? Is there a process in place for students to hear, dig deep, and metabolize the Word?

The apostle Peter shed some light on what this can look like in 2 Peter. Writing to folks who were already well grounded in the faith, he reminded them of several ways to stay spiritually productive and avoid stumbling (two more great goals for student ministry).

One of Peter's heartfelt reminders is in 2 Peter 1:19: "We also have the prophetic message as something completely reliable, and you will do well to pay attention to it, as to a light shining in a dark place, until the day dawns and the morning star rises in your hearts" (TNIV).

Whether the prophetic message Peter refers to is from the Old Testament prophets, the Messianic prophecies, or the entire Old Testament (all are possible), this most certainly is a reference to the written Word of God. And we're to pay attention to it "as to a light shining in a dark place" until something happens.

But what?

"Until the day dawns" sounds a lot like Jesus' return. But look again. The dawning in this passage actually happens *in our hearts*, which means it can happen *now*. And, of course, it doesn't take much digging to figure out whom Peter is calling the morning star (check out Revelation 22:16).

In short, Peter is telling us to pay attention to the written Word of God until something dawns on us like a light bulb coming on in a dark room—until Jesus himself rises up in our hearts.

You've probably felt that before: The *aha* moment, the *oh, wow* realization, the epiphany.

Wow moments are worthy goals for any Bible study, whether it's our personal time in Scripture or group study. But *wow* moments can be elusive. They stay just beneath the surface unless we dig down deep as Jesus described.

Then at those moments, hearing becomes *owning*.

And when we own it, we *do* it. In fact, we fulfill Jesus' second prerequisite for wise builders: We put his words into practice.

Putting into practice is what secures the building to bedrock in Jesus' analogy. The man who built the foundationless house heard Jesus' words, but he failed to put them to use.

So if we're hoping to help teenagers beat temptation, our approach might look something like this: Provide opportunities for students to pay attention to God's Word—to dig down deep until Jesus rises up in their hearts.

Can you see how a personal revelation of Jesus would give students the resolve to resist the traps and temptations of adolescence, the insight to see behind the deception of the Enemy, and the wisdom to refute the hollow philosophies that swirl around them? Can you see how it would help give them a well-built faith?

Perhaps you've seen the prayer acronym PUSH (Pray Until Something Happens). Maybe we should coin a Bible study spin-off: HUSH (*Hear* Until Something Happens).

Sharing Their Faith

Youth ministry is one of the most effective evangelistic arms of the church. With the wide majority of adult Christians becoming believers before age 18,[23] the church has rightly invested significant outreach resources in student ministry. Many student pastors and volunteer youth workers have the spiritual gift of evangelism and love to exercise it with teenagers. In addition, a large percentage of our youth ministry resources are geared toward helping teenagers share their faith.

But what if there were an even more effective, more mind-blowing way of reaping a harvest among the teenage generation? In fact, Jesus gives us a better way in the well-known parable of the soils.

You know the story. A farmer went about scattering seed. Some fell on rocky soil, some was devoured by birds, and some produced spindly plants that were scorched by the sun. But some fell on good soil—and that's where we see the amazing growth. "But the seed falling on good soil refers to people who hear the word and understand it. They produce a crop, yielding a hundred, sixty or thirty times what was sown" (Matthew 13:23, TNIV).

Jesus explained the parable saying that the good soil refers to people who hear the Word, understand it (Matthew), and retain it (Luke). "But the seed on good soil stands for those with a noble and good heart, who hear the word, retain it, and by persevering produce a crop" (Luke 8:15). These folks produce a crop that's exponentially greater than what was sown. Not simply *more* than what was sown, as in simple addition, but up to *a hundred times* what was sown, as in rampant multiplication!

That's growth. A group of 50 believers has the potential to grow to 5,000. And even if Jesus were referring to our spiritual insides—our hearts—as the objects of this exponential growth (a credible application), students experiencing such significant spiritual maturity would undoubtedly attract other students.

But think for a minute. Have you ever noticed that each of the four soil types *heard* the Word? In the case of the first three groups, the Word went in one ear and out the other—the very thing we often imagine when we picture teenagers and Bible study. It was only the seed on soft soil that *heard, understood, retained* the Word, and experienced the exponential growth.

I love the words Matthew and Luke used in this account. The word translated as *understand* (*suniemi*) in Matthew conveys the sense of organizing individual facts into a whole as collecting the pieces of a puzzle and putting them all together.[24] (If you've ever had the good fortune of hearing a student say, "It's all starting to fit together now!" that's *suniemi*.) The word also expresses participation on the part of the hearer in processing what's being heard.

Maybe you've heard the phrase "a job isn't done until it's done right"? Applying the same principle, God's Word isn't truly heard until it's understood.

In New Testament days to retain (Luke's word *katecho*) meant to cling to or hold fast.[25] Picture the grip you might have if you were riding on the *outside* of a train. The Greek historian Philo used this word to describe having a great passion for good and virtue, or being seized by an idea or truth and embracing it with zeal and enthusiasm.[26] If we hold to God's Word as if we're holding on for dear life or if we roll it around in our minds until we're seized by truth, then you can bet we're way more likely to experience a deeper faith.

How cool would it be to see a book entitled *Two Steps to Exponential Growth in Your Youth Ministry*—and the only thing printed on its pages would be the parable of the soils? Step one: Hear Jesus' words. Step two: Understand and retain them. In our efforts to evangelize students, why shouldn't we take Jesus' parable that seriously?

The probing question is, *What's happening in our student ministries that enables kids to understand Jesus' words? To roll Jesus' words around in their minds until they're seized by what Jesus is saying?*

Youth ministry is well-resourced for the task of helping teenagers share their faith. But Jesus gave a framework to use in evaluating these resources—and in creating our own approach. Are we frontloading our students with techniques and training to the neglect of helping them understand God's Word? Because understanding the Word is what leads to exponential growth. It's what enables lifestyle evangelism. It's what equips students to give an answer when asked about their hope (1 Peter 3:15). It's what gives them the boldness to engage the skeptic.

Making It Happen

At this point you may be wondering when this deep digging and understanding can happen in your breakneck ministry week. Considering our already packed schedules, how can we get the Word in edgewise?

It might help you to know that engaging with the Word may be precisely what your students are looking for. *Time* recently cited a study that asked 2,400 teenagers what they look for in a church.[27] The answer that garnered the most "very important" and "somewhat important" votes? "To understand better what I believe" (71 percent).

There's that word again: *understand*. Nearly three-fourths of our teenagers are lining up to experience the growth Jesus promised—letting us know that they're poised and ready to be "good soil."

In that same survey, 36 percent of students rated "participate in study of sacred Scripture" as "important" or "very important." Considering the teen-unfriendly wording of that response, 36 percent is impressive.

In my own research I recently surveyed 400 middle and high school teenagers from several thriving churches. In that survey, 32 percent indicated that they desire more depth in the Bible study aspect of their student ministry. Curiously, only 6 percent said that the Bible study offerings were too deep. With stats like that, there's surely room for us to confidently raise the bar in challenging students to hear Jesus' words, understand them, retain them, and put them into practice.

Researching *Soul Searching*, Christian Smith was surprised by Christian teenagers' lack of religious knowledge and inability to articulate the tenets of their faith. He concluded, "Many adults seem to us to be almost intimidated by teenagers, afraid to be seen as 'uncool.' And it seems many religious youth workers are under a lot of pressure to entertain teens. In fact, however, we believe that most teenagers are teachable, even if they themselves do not really know that or let on that they are interested. Parents, ministers, and adult mentors need, it seems to us, to develop more confidence in teaching youth about their faith traditions and expecting meaningful responses from them...Teenagers learn everything they know from someone, somewhere. Many youth actually consciously do want to be taught; they are open to being influenced by good word and example. Faith communities have no reason to apologize for or be insecure about teaching their youth."[28]

Research confirms what intuition has been telling us: That teenagers are up for spiritual challenge. They're eager to add diligence in their pursuit of God. Meanwhile, God is as ready as ever to reward the diligent pursuer.

At times I wonder if we're sitting on a powder keg for revolution and if youth workers' top priority should simply be to light the fuse. To connect students' readiness for challenge with God's potential payoff and then get out of the way.

Worldwide Impact

I've always been intrigued by the instruction my doctor gives when prescribing an antibiotic: "Take this medicine until it's finished, even if all your symptoms are gone." The reason, of course, is that if I don't finish the medication and still have the bacteria in my body, the bacteria may become immune to that particular drug.

What's also true—though I find it more difficult to fathom—is that by my failing to take the antibiotic as prescribed, *society* could eventually lose that medicine as a tool against the particular bacteria.

I'll admit it. Continuing to take a pill when the symptoms are gone is hard for me to do. And I can hardly see how I could carry the medical burden of society in the privacy of my own bathroom. It's an instruction that's easy to skip, but the consequences could have worldwide impact.

The same is true for Bible study on both counts. It's easy to skip, and the consequences are worldwide.

In the privacy of our offices and youth rooms, it's hard to think that our actions can affect the church globally—or that our student programming could have any impact on a generational level. But it does.

When discipling kids with the Word amid a busy youth ministry agenda, it's easy to grab a piece of curriculum off the shelf and show up ready to go—our deepest prep consisting of scanning the page for the bold print telling us to "say this now."

Granted, there are hectic weeks when this has to suffice—and good Bible study can be found in curriculum. But a steady diet of lessons out of a can won't bring the lasting change we desire in our students. It's not that working from a can is sinful or bad, but you'll never find that approach in Scripture. God's words changed the hearts of his leaders before the leaders got anywhere near the people.

It's tempting to take the path of least resistance. To schedule events that students enjoy. To prepare talks that will get a laugh—or maybe even a tear. To make good discussion the goal of Bible study.

But before long, hearing, understanding and applying Jesus' words become things we squeeze in rather than things we build our ministry around. Or worse, they become things we squeeze out entirely.

Meanwhile, stacks of resources intended to help us achieve all the goals and agendas of ministry pile up in our offices. While right under our noses—and under the stacks—is the single most untapped resource that promises the highest possible payoff in ministering to students: God's Word.

So go ahead. View it as a game of Jenga and carefully pull the Bible out from under the stacks. Then take a look. It's more practical than you think.

CHAPTER FIVE

Is the B-I-B-L-E a Book for Youth Ministry?

Some trust in chariots and some in horses, but we trust in the name of the LORD our God. PSALM 20:7

Parting the Sea

On paper, Bible study and student ministry don't mix. And that apparent incompatibility can play into our worst fears. Those of us who work with middle school students are scared to death of the famous middle-school attention span (or more accurately, the lack thereof). And here we are with a *big book* that's full of *words* that we're asking students to *read*—a surefire recipe for boredom!

Those who work with high school students are fearful to near incapacitation of being perceived as irrelevant or cheesy. (One youth ministry friend has an enviable "cheese-tector," an internal antenna that can smoke out the cheese factor in virtually any game or activity before it's tried. I find myself wanting to run everything I do past him to avoid the dreaded eye-roll from students.) Yet here we are with a book of ancient laws and stories that's reminiscent of a school textbook—a combination that seems destined for eye rolling and irrelevance.

But think about it. Isn't it *just like God* to call us to something that requires us to step through our deepest fears? Throughout the Bible, God called people to join him in endeavors in which if God didn't show up, they'd look pretty silly.

Picture the Red Sea *not* parting as Moses confidently thrust out his staff and stretched his hand over the sea. Picture 6 million-plus folks shrugging their shoulders, giving ol' Moses a patronizing wave, and shuffling back to Egypt. *What a goofball*, they'd mutter under their breath.

Imagine the walls of Jericho *not* coming down as Joshua and the people marched around the city. Talk about a collective eye rolling! Trumpets blast, people shout, and the walls... just...stand there. Of course Joshua wouldn't have had to endure the eye-rolling for long, since Jericho's armies would have been alerted by the blasting trumpets that an enemy was outside the city. What a failure.

But here's the point. The walls *did* fall. The Red Sea parted, God delivered, and Joshua and Moses were added to the roster of those who trusted God to come through—even at the risk of looking silly.

Radical Dependence

I'm wondering if God wants to add you to that roster. If I could be so bold as to ask, what's going on in your life that's radically dependent on God to come through? If you're involved in youth ministry, there's surely a thing or two. How about considering something else? Why not lead your teenagers on a journey through Scripture in a way that trusts God's Word to do what it says it can do?

What can the Word do? Frankly, it depends. On one hand, the implicit nature of God's Word is to transform—without us even lifting a finger. It's *alive*. It's *active*. Despite physical barriers, such as an overloaded agenda or an inadequate meeting space, and spiritual roadblocks, such as doubt or fear, it can find its way into our inner beings and deliver a well-placed pang of conviction (Hebrews 4:12).

On the other hand, if we *do* put the slightest bit of muscle into pursuing God through his Word, the impact of Scripture increases exponentially—with Richter-scale intensity!

Explaining to his disciples how to get along in the world after his physical departure, Jesus gave a nice, two-step action that would guarantee their continued fellowship with him. In John 14:21 Jesus said that whoever *has* and *obeys* his commands is showing the kind of love that he and the Father are looking for. The Greek word we translate as *has* connotes ownership—in this verse a sense of bringing Jesus' words and commands into our lives and *owning* them.

So what kind of connection with Jesus can we expect when we intensify our pursuit to *own* and *obey* his commands? Much greater; Jesus will show himself to us! The word *show* in John 14:21 expresses the idea of a physical manifestation. This isn't a showing that's reserved for Jesus' second coming; it's a showing that can happen *now*. We'll be warmed by God's love and experience the palpable presence of Jesus.

This isn't a proposition God reserves for work camps and missions trips. Instead, it's the attitude of trust God is looking for in every arena of our lives and ministries.

Picture a time when Jesus revealed himself to you. Maybe you were praying, walking, or studying Scripture. Now imagine a small group of students gathering to *have, own,* and *obey* what Jesus said. Picture them pressing in to know him—to the point at which they're overwhelmed by God's love and wowed by the personal presence of Christ. That type of encounter is promised straight from the mouth of Jesus.

Seeing It in Scripture

Scripture is packed with if-then propositions similar to what we see in John 14:21, commands that assure a great payoff when we put them into action. These aren't prosperity payoffs, but presence payoffs—promises that we will find God or experience spiritual rewards from him only if we fulfill certain conditions. (Check out Deuteronomy 4:29-31 and Jeremiah 29:11-13.)

One particular if-then proverb is worth mining out. Proverbs 2 is an introduction written by Solomon to his son, prepping him for the wisdom Solomon is about to dispense—wisdom that came from God. These words also serve as an awesome introduction for us, not only for the wisdom that follows in the book of Proverbs but in all of Scripture.

The passage is a classic if-then setup: The *ifs* come in the form of action phrases; the *thens* are the results of the actions. Take a minute to reflect on Solomon's words in Proverbs 2. As you do, list in the space provided all the action phrases (the ifs), as well as the results promised in the passage (the thens).

> My son, if you accept my words and store up my commands within you, turning your ear to wisdom and applying your heart to understanding—indeed, if you call out for insight and cry aloud for understanding, and if you look for it as for silver and search for it as for hidden treasure, then you will understand the fear of the LORD and find the knowledge of God. For the LORD gives wisdom; from his mouth come knowledge and understanding. He holds success in store for the upright, he is a shield to those whose walk is blameless, for he guards the course of the just and protects the way of his faithful ones. Then you will understand what is right and just and fair—every good path. For wisdom will enter your heart, and knowledge will be pleasant to your soul. Discretion will protect you, and understanding will guard you. Wisdom will save you from the ways of wicked men, from men whose words are perverse, who have left the straight paths to walk in dark ways, who delight in doing wrong and rejoice in the perverseness of evil, whose paths are crooked and who are devious in their ways.

(PROVERBS 2:1-15, TNIV)

Think for a minute about your approach to Bible study—both when and how you do it. Now look at the actions asked for in Proverbs 2 and compare your approach. When was the last time you asked God for insight? Are you still searching and digging—or living off past insights and the understanding of others?

Now think about your work with students and about all the programming elements in your youth ministry. Discipleship. Outreach events. Small groups. Sunday school. Is there a time in the mix that gives students the opportunity to do the actions described in Proverbs 2?

The Payoff

Now for the fun part. Think about the goals you have for your youth ministry. Consider what you hope will happen in the lives of your students and how you want to equip them for adulthood. (Go ahead. I'll wait.) Compare these hopes and goals with the results in Proverbs 2.

Perhaps it strikes you that the goals in Proverbs 2 sound strangely similar to a list of goals that might come from a roundtable discussion of youth workers. We talk about wanting teenagers to respect and obey God, to discover God's will, to choose the right paths, to make good decisions, and to see through Satan's deceptions.

Here's the good news: No matter which expert you ask about teenagers, he'll tell you that a common characteristic is the desire to be challenged. Students today are looking for authentic things to sell out to, to give their all to. Nothing in life promises greater payoff than a diligent quest for God. This is fruit so ripe in today's teenage culture that it practically picks itself.

Dan Kimball in *The Emerging Church* describes students and young adults of the postmodern age as desiring "vintage Christianity," Christianity in its rawest form, which unapologetically calls for our priorities to focus on God's Kingdom. With regard to worship these folks are looking for a "full display of spirituality" in order to experience and be transformed by the message of Jesus.[29]

What Kimball cites with regard to worship can also be said for Bible study.

Trust Like You Mean It

Proverbs 2 shows an approach to Scripture that displays trust in God's Word to do what it says it can do. It also reveals precise results of this trust. If you've been in youth ministry longer than a couple of years, you know what trust in other approaches can look like.

An hour of great discussion displays trust in our own ability to be culturally relevant. An hour of active learning displays trust in learning styles. An hour of hot media displays trust in opinions about what teenagers will pay attention to.

None of these approaches is bad. In fact, each is quite needed. But if today's youth offerings are any indication of what we trust, a case could be made that we trust everything *but* the Word of God.

If you believe Scripture is a capable tool, then believe that it also can address teenagers' various learning styles. It can cater to the idiosyncrasies of any culture. And it can deliver God's unchanging message throughout the changing eras of history, including the postmodern era.

So we're back to our original question: What's going on in your life and ministry that radically depends on God to come through? Like Moses and Joshua, are you ready to take your students on a journey—a journey in God's Word on which you might feel silly or inadequate if God *doesn't* come through? It may not be as risky as it sounds.

The Trust Fall

Try this quick exercise: Think of five or 10 students, and list below the activities they're intensely involved in, such as academics, athletics, music or games.

Picture the steps they've taken to improve in those areas—skills they've honed, lessons they've taken, time they've spent, initiative they've shown. Got a picture? What you've tapped into are the two things historians, sociologists, and theologians agree on regarding postmodern teenagers: *They'll sell out to something they believe is worth selling out to. And they're up for a challenge.*

On a hot August afternoon, I drove past our local high school's football practice field. I saw a lone player running 40-yard dashes while his friend timed him with a stopwatch. No coaches. No observers. All the other players had gone home after practice. Despite the summer heat, this player was dedicated to improving his skills. That's a vivid portrayal of the sellout factor that's in our favor.

Review the *ifs* you found in Proverbs 2. Is there a parallel between this characteristic inherent to today's students and the kind of intensity God asks for when we open up his Word? With a little encouragement students will gladly increase their intensity with Scripture.

Remember the well-used trust fall? In that team-building exercise, someone is asked to fall backward and trust that the team will catch them? Asking students to ramp up their intensity with Scripture feels to many youth workers like taking a trust fall. As you take the blind step and begin to fall, you wonder, *Who's going to catch me?* You may wonder the same thing about the Bible when you ask students to engage with a passage of Scripture. *Will it catch me? Or will I look stupid?*

The Word on the Word

Here are some things God says about Scripture. As you read these words, jot in the margins what God claims the Word can do. These are the very reasons you can trust it.

> The law of the LORD is perfect, refreshing the soul. The statutes of the LORD are trustworthy, making wise the simple. The precepts of the LORD are right, giving joy to the heart. The commands of the LORD are radiant, giving light to the eyes. The fear of the LORD is pure, enduring forever. The ordinances of the LORD are sure, and all of them are righteous. They are more precious than gold, than much pure gold; they are sweeter than honey, than honey from the honeycomb. By them your servant is warned; in keeping them there is great reward. (PSALM 19:7-11, TNIV)

"Is not my word like fire," declares the LORD, "and like a hammer that breaks a rock in pieces?" (JEREMIAH 23:29)

But as for you, continue in what you have learned and have become convinced of, because you know those from whom you learned it, and how from infancy you have known the Holy Scriptures, which are able to make you wise for salvation through faith in Christ Jesus. All Scripture is God-breathed and is useful for teaching, rebuking, correcting and training in righteousness, so that all God's people may be thoroughly equipped for every good work. (2 TIMOTHY 3:14-17, TNIV)

For the word of God is living and active. Sharper than any double-edged sword, it penetrates even to dividing soul and spirit, joints and marrow; it judges the thoughts and attitudes of the heart.

(HEBREWS 4:12)

When students raise their intensity with Scripture—even slightly—they experience a taste of the promises God talks about in these passages and Proverbs 2. And when teenagers experience these things, game on! It's like that trust fall...with a thousand mighty arms waiting to catch you.

Beyond the Shortcuts

David wrote, "Some trust in chariots and some in horses, but we trust in the name of the LORD our God" (Psalm 20:7). It's not difficult to assess whether you trust in horses and chariots or in God. Just glance around your office or take a hard look at your youth ministry calendar. There's nothing wrong with *using* horses and chariots—or even *maximizing* horses and chariots if you're fortunate enough to have some. But in a world that thrives on shortcuts, it's easy for Christians to make a slow, almost imperceptible slide toward man-made tools and methods—and away from God.

Students today are ready to be involved. They're gearing up for short-term missions in record numbers. They're volunteering for community projects. They're signing on to *anything* that has *deeper* in the title. That alone should give you the confidence that God's Word can do what it says it can.

Still nervous? Don't sweat it. That only means God has you in a place where you *have* to trust him. And that's exactly where God wants you.

PART TWO

OUR QUEST FOR GOD

CHAPTER SIX

Love Letter

The Bible feeds not only the hungry heart but the hunger it-self, constantly increasing our appetite to know more of God and hence our passion to dig more deeply into His Word.

J.I. PACKER• *TRUTH & POWER: THE PLACE OF SCRIPTURE IN THE CHRISTIAN LIFE*

Have you ever received a love letter? One from someone you really liked?

Think about how you felt when you read that letter, how eagerly you tore into it. Chances are you read each line a dozen times or more. You read between the lines, through the lines, and over the lines. If you're female, you may have shared it with your friends. If you're a guy, probably not. You kept it close, maybe in your pocket where you could take it out and read it again.

And chances are, you responded.

Now think about how it feels to *send* a love letter. That's a whole different ballgame. You put yourself out there, anxiously hoping that the special someone on the other end will read it just the way you intended—between the lines, through the lines, and over the lines.

And you hope they'll respond.

Two Love Letters

I've sent two major love letters in my life. Donna was the cutest girl in third grade, and her desk sat right behind mine. After enduring an unbearable crush for a few days, I decided to take the risk. One morning I drafted the classic yes-no love letter and worked up the courage to thrust it her way at the start of school.

Her response to me in the lunch line was impossible for my third-grade brain to decipher: "I may tear it up, or I may put it under my pillow."

What?

But it must have worked. Donna and I "went steady" the rest of the school year and even made the jump to fourth grade—the toughest move in grade school.

Donna's initial response must have scarred me though, because the next love letter I sent wasn't until well after college. Well after the point when I should have known better.

On the first day of class my sophomore year in college, I met a girl I liked instantly. We shared the same major and studied together a lot. Most of all we laughed a lot. In short this girl took me to new heights of interaction. And it felt great. For some strange reason, there was no romantic pressure on the relationship from either of us. (Not that it hadn't crossed my mind. You know us guys in relationships—first in, last out.)

We went out a few times, but mostly we were friends. In fact, this girl made me aware of my status in no uncertain terms. I was her "most special friend in the world"—like the brother she'd never had.

That status, of course, is the kiss of death.

Fast-forward a couple of years. After college she and I went our separate ways. And after several dating relationships, I came to realize that no one seemed to measure up. No other girl brought me to the heights of interaction I remembered in college. So, acting on a friend's advice, I decided to take the plunge. I put all my feelings in a letter. A love letter.

Actually, a love manifesto.

Recalling my grade school experience, I branched out from the standard yes-no format to something more complex—four legal-sized pages covered front and back with my thoughts, emotions, and all the reasons I thought we'd make a great pair. And I stuck it in the mailbox.

Not wanting to seem too eager, I waited a week before even thinking about a response. But by the following week, I'd become an obsessive mail checker—a near mailman stalker. Still, no response. After several months I gave up the search, humiliated. I never got a response.

Years later, I met up with her. We talked about the ups and downs we'd each experienced over the years, and how we missed the almost magic relationship we'd shared in college. At some point I casually threw it out there—that I once had put all this in a letter to her.

She replied, "Really? What letter?"

If you happened to hear a cosmic wail piercing that night in October 1990, it was mine. Why hadn't I sprung for more postage? It was a *big* letter. But as we talked, it all came back to her. She'd gotten the letter, but it had come at a rough time in her life. Not knowing how to respond without hurting her like-a-brother friend, she'd said nothing.

We still don't know where that letter ended up, but we'd give anything to find it. Fast-forward another couple of years, and Dana became my wife.

(Side note. If any of you have been relegated to that special friend black hole of relationships, let me know. Maybe I can help you out.)

Love-Letter Intensity

Have you ever thought about what a magnificent love letter God's Word is to you? I thought four legal pages was pretty intense—but picture how much God poured into his letter just to tell you how much he loves you, how often he thinks about you, what a great relationship he thinks the two of you could have. And God told you all about his favorite person, his Son.

What if we learned to read God's Word with love-letter intensity? Between the lines, through the lines, and over the lines. And what would it look like for us to give God the response he's desperately looking for?

So what is love-letter intensity? Is it memorizing? Reading and rereading? God never gave us a step-by-step method for how to best experience his Word. But God dropped a few strong hints.

Consider all the times in Scripture when God encouraged people to experience his Word, and you'll find that he never just instructed us to read it. Reading is almost a given with God. Instead, he uses words that convey some kind of action—words that represent levels deeper than reading the text, such as *walk in, fully obey, meditate on,* and *heed.* In the previous chapter we looked at Proverbs 2, mining out phrases such as "store up," "cry aloud," "look for it as for silver," and "search for it as for hidden treasure." In Revelation we're told to read the book aloud, to hear it, and to take it to heart (Revelation 1:3).

Active and Alive

Is this bad news or good for those who don't like to read? It's good news! Because experiencing Scripture is more like eating ice cream than reading a book. And who doesn't like to eat ice cream?

When our eyes take in the words of Scripture, we see beauty and majesty unfolding before us. God's Word is living and active, never stagnant or frozen in time. Gaze at the same passage every day, and like a sunset it will look different every time.

The difference between *reading* Scripture and *experiencing* Scripture is like the difference between *carrying* a baby and *holding* a baby. Between *hearing* your spouse and really *listening to* your spouse. Between *speaking* and *communicating*. Just reading the text won't get you to all the gems God has hidden there. And without the gems, the Bible can be tedious and dry. The Bible becomes difficult for those who don't like to read when it's viewed as only another book to be read rather than a living text to be observed, explored, mined, and lived out—in essence, metabolized.

How do we harness those great activities of *walking in, fully obeying, meditating on* and *heeding*? How do we create a practical approach to experiencing God's Word? Thankfully, we don't have to start from scratch. Scholars, reformers, pastors, and Bible students of all stripes have been searching the Scriptures for centuries. Think millions of people over hundreds of years studying the very same book. From all of those centuries and all of those seekers, three steps have emerged that are common to any thorough method of Bible study: Observe. Interpret. Apply.

Three Requests

The three steps of *observing, interpreting,* and *applying* Scripture fall under the umbrella of inductive study, a technique that's been around a while but that has only casually been applied to youth ministry. You may have bumped into inductive study through InterVarsity, Precept Ministries, or a Thompson Chain-Reference Bible. Some curriculum houses have used the approach. If you've ever taken Bible 101 in college or 501 in seminary, you may know it as *exegesis*—a lofty word that may have seemed to have no practical relationship to youth ministry.

But here's why inductive study *does* apply to youth ministry: The greatest barrier to personal and small-group Bible study is not having a plan. Inductive study gives us a plan. It was an inductive approach that enabled our students to experience the incredible uptake of Colossians during that watershed summer study I described in Chapter 1.

What's more, inductive study provides a way to infuse the Word of God into both of the elements that *are* youth ministry: Youth workers and students.

And inductive study offers the very approach God's Word seems to call for. Eugene Peterson, author of *The Message,* writes, "There is only one way of reading that is congruent with our Holy Scriptures, writing that trusts in the power of words to penetrate our lives and create truth and beauty and goodness, writing that requires a reader who, in the words of Rainer Maria Rilke, 'does not always remain bent over his pages; he often leans back and closes his eyes over a line he has been reading again, and its meaning spreads through his blood.' This is the kind of reading named by our ancestors as *lectio divina,* often translated 'spiritual reading,' reading that enters our souls as food enters our stomachs, spreads through our blood, and becomes holiness and love and wisdom."[30]

Now that's *metabolism.*

I believe, as does Peterson, that there is something deep inside us designed to connect with God's Word—something in our spiritual DNA. When the connection is made, transformation becomes an inside job. Applied to youth workers, this internal transformation is something students can see happening in us, creating a natural attraction to the things of God. Applied to students, the transformation occurs as an internal, supernatural work of the Holy Spirit, rather than out of external pressure from us. (External pressure, I might add, seldom brings authentic, built-to-last transformation).

Distilled for youth ministry, *observe, interpret,* and *apply* (the inductive triple play) become three simple requests of God: God, show me! God, teach me! God, change me!

These are requests we can make as we examine any verse, any chapter, or any book of the Bible. And whenever we direct those requests to God, we're guaranteed to see, to learn, and to change. (That's God's guarantee, not mine.) We'll look at each request in detail in the next three chapters.

Message over Method

Jesus said, "You study the Scriptures diligently because you think that in them you possess eternal life. These are the very Scriptures that testify about me, yet you refuse to come to me to have life" (John 5:39-40, TNIV).

If you've learned anything about the Pharisees of Jesus' day, you know it's important never to let a system or a method supersede the message. If you're task-oriented like the Pharisees (or, in fact, like me), you can reduce the beauty of a sunset to a personal checklist in a matter of seconds. The same can happen to Bible study. *Observed?* Check. *Interpreted?* Check. *Applied?* Check. Not bad for 10 minutes. At this rate I can knock out Ephesians in 15 days.

Jesus had a special warning regarding this type of Bible study. In John 5 he warned the Jews that Scripture study alone—even the most diligent study—wouldn't lead them to eternal life. Finding *him* would.

The reason to apply an intentional process when we study the Scriptures is not to embrace a method. It's simply to slow ourselves down, to give ourselves ample opportunity to connect with Jesus and his words, and to observe and apply all that he wants us to know and see.

Many good methods of Bible study exist to slow us down and get us to Jesus. There are even several ways to do inductive study. The method itself isn't sacred. Spending time with God and his Word is. What we need is a time-tested plan that helps us go after God's Word the way he has asked us to. Without that plan, our default method (and the default of many of our students) comes down to point and shoot. Our students deserve better—and so do we.

Hmmm...Inductive?

The word *inductive* can mean different things to different people. Dictionaries define the inductive method as inferring conclusions or principles based only on the facts collected. The objective is to approach those facts without presupposition—from a blank slate if possible.

Picture a detective gathering clues at a crime scene or interrogating a witness to a crime. The detective's mantra? "Just the facts, ma'am."

Like the best detective work, inductive Bible study helps us form conclusions and make application based solely on the facts we observe in Scripture. It forces us to see what God said in the Bible—not what we think the Bible says, what our church believes, or what tradition has taught us. It helps us experience God's message firsthand, thereby experiencing God firsthand. It gives us a front-row seat to God's revelation.

This difference can be a refreshing change for those who've grown up in the church as I have or who are old hands at the Bible. Some of us have had the Bible interpreted *for* us so many times in books and sermons and songs and talks that we *think* we know what it says. This, I suspect, is the reason why many of us would secretly confess to being bored with the Bible—or why we fear boring students with the Bible. Haven't we heard and read it all before?

But imagine approaching God with no presuppositions. Imagine asking him what he has to say on a particular subject—and discovering that his Word says something richer than we've supposed. The experience can be blissfully exhilarating or downright scary, but never ho-hum.

Personal Discovery

One of the great payoffs of inductive study is the treasure of personal discovery. A truth or an *Oh, wow!* moment you've personally mined has greater transformative power than something you've read in a book. It also stands a better chance of being remembered, even years down the road. What's more, there's not a better moment in youth ministry than when you see light bulbs click on over students' heads and you know they've discovered something vital on their own—a discovery straight from God's heart to theirs.

It's often the opposite scenario in youth ministry: We back into Bible study by explaining the discovery we hope students will make. Then we build our talks and discussions around the intended discovery.

It goes something like this: We decide on a pertinent topic for a series, such as sex, or a great story for a talk, such as the funny thing that happened at the grocery store. Then we scramble to find Scriptures that reinforce or parallel the subject or story. This is called deductive study, and its effect is to attach Scripture to a preset conclusion as a Band-Aid.

Deductive study puts application *before* observation and interpretation. The result can be the misuse—and thus the misinterpretation and misapplication—of Scripture. Rarely does it lead to personal discovery and change.

On the flip side, the inductive approach might look like this: We look at Ephesians 1 and see where it leads us. It only takes doing this with a few Bible chapters to hit on most of the issues we might have built a series around—and we'll probably find a place to use that great grocery store story, too.

The point is that God will make an appearance, speaking personally to you and your students through his Word. And he knows better than you do what issues and topics to address.

Where It Fits in Student Ministry

God is the source of all thirst for his Word. Our job as youth workers is to identify that thirst and keep the path to the riverbank open.

Student ministry provides several natural opportunities to keep that path to the river clear and accessible. While every youth ministry is different, the following pathways can be duplicated in any ministry, whether in a small church, a megachurch, or a parachurch ministry such as Young Life or Youth for Christ.

Leaders' Personal Study

Leaders who inductively study the Bible soon find themselves armed with more ideas for talks and devotionals than they can use. They also find they're able to chart out multiple discipleship series after mining just one Bible book or theme or character.

As your own light bulbs begin to turn on, you'll soon be saying, "I can't wait for my students to get that!" Your personal study will start to seamlessly spill into your ministry and discipleship. In fact, this is one area of ministry where you can and should feel free to double dip—letting your personal study and your preparation for teaching and discipleship be one and the same.

Find yourself wrestling with that last point? If so, you're not alone. Senior pastors and youth ministry types alike often believe that it's better to let your personal discoveries in the Bible season *within* you before teaching them to others.

But I propose that there's nothing quite like leaders and students discovering and living out their discoveries in Scripture *together*, even if it means leaders must give the occasional "I don't know" in answer to a question. When you're studying inductively, there's nothing to fear from "I don't know"—especially when it's followed by "Let's dig that out next week."

Think about that one. Your greatest obstacle to teaching the Bible—not knowing everything in it—can become your greatest asset, a launch pad to another wave of discovery and the best incentive to keep students coming back for more.

Student Discipleship/Small Groups

As leaders hone their personal inductive skills, they'll find these skills easy to duplicate in a one-on-one or small-group discipleship setting. Students who seek small groups are typically the thirsty ones in whom God is creating an appetite for more. Small-group inductive studies ensure that these students spend quality "face time" with the one who can satisfy that thirst. They also may be the area of ministry where students can best metabolize God's Word as they process it together.

Small-group inductive studies are also great places to invite the skeptics, doubters, and truth-seeking nonbelievers in your group. Instead of encouraging them to read the book of John on their own, ask them to process it with you at the local coffee shop.

Whether you're an avid curriculum user, one who writes your own discipleship material, or a combination of both, you'll soon see how to infuse inductive tools into your approach. This will bring the vitality of personal discovery into your discipleship.

Student Devotions

A top priority of student ministry should be to make teenagers self-feeders on God's Word. After all, no matter how powerful your influence on them—or that of your church—they'll be on their own in one to six years, in a dorm room or student lounge with nothing but a Bible and how you taught them to access it.

Teaching students to search the Scriptures on their own is one of the beautiful features of inductive study—and it happens naturally. As you study with your students in the one-on-one or group setting, you're also training them, intentionally or unintentionally, to study the Bible with purpose.

Eventually they'll want to tackle the process on their own. And they'll know how to do it.

Large-Group Teaching

1. Sunday School: The great challenge facing Sunday school teachers is that every level of spiritual maturity and initiative is represented in this setting. You have students who saunter in out of habit, students who come by parental edict, those who show up for the doughnuts, and those who are genuinely engaged.

   Quite obviously, many students in this setting may not be ready for depth. But that doesn't mean we abandon Scripture. Teachers who prepare their lessons inductively out of an authentic quest for God and his Word, as opposed to an 11th-hour cram session with the curriculum, are better prepared to authentically teach in the Sunday school setting.

   It's like the difference between real coffee and decaf. Which would you and your students prefer on an early Sunday morning?

2. Outreach/Worship (Come One, Come All Gatherings): Teaching in this setting usually occurs in the context of a talk or a sermon accompanied by youth-driven worship and music. The best use of inductive study for this setting is the personal preparation of the leader who spends time with a passage, experiences a personal *Oh, wow!* moment, and lets the passage itself reveal how it can best be applied.

   Inductive speakers consider how to lead students to experience a similar *Oh, wow!* by focusing on the text but adding stories, illustrations, and analogies. The key is to keep God's words the point of the talk, rather than making them an illustration for our own point—or worse, forcing them to fit a story we want to tell just because we like it.

Waiting

God's instructions about how to metabolize his Word are full of intense action words. The reason Bible study often misses the transformational mark is because our efforts to *read* the Bible fall short of the intensity God desires. Inductive study forces us to make God's words—his thoughts, ideas, and desires—the subject of our pursuit instead of our own issues and stories. It gives us a framework from which to approach Scripture with love-letter intensity. And like any good love letter, it calls us to respond.

Imagine God going daily to that mailbox—just hoping for a response to his great love letter. He's waiting for a response from you.

CHAPTER SEVEN

God, Show Me!

Open my eyes that I may see wonderful things in your law.

PSALM 119:18

So now I read the Bible in this way. I ask in every place: What is God saying to us here? I ask God to show us what God wants to say...Since I have learned to read the Bible in this way—and that is not so very long ago—it becomes more wonderful to me every day...And every day I take for myself a text that I will have for the entire week and attempt to immerse myself entirely in it, in order to be able to really listen to it. I know that without this I would no longer be able to live properly. Or, even before that, to believe in the right way.

DIETRICH BONHOEFFER • *A TESTAMENT TO FREEDOM*

I made a startling discovery about myself a few years ago.

We were having an animated discussion in our college Bible study. It was one of those nights when everybody had done a fair amount of thinking on the subject at hand and was eager to weigh in.

I noticed that as the speaking bounced around the room, I only half-listened to what was being said. Instead, I devoted most of my mental energies to formulating what I wanted to say next. I figure I missed 80 percent of the discussion that night—and a full 100 percent of the hearts of the people in that Bible study.

Absurd? Incredibly selfish? You bet it was.

It was also a gracious discovery.

I've since realized how easy it is to do the same thing in personal Bible study or in study preparation to lead a group. I often gloss over a passage because I've had it figured out and tied up with a bow for years. Or maybe I have a cool point I want to get across, and I'm looking for a passage to back my point.

Either way, I devote more of my time to what I want to say with complete disregard for what God wants to say.

The first request in inductive Bible study—God, show me—forces me to slow down and listen to what God is saying through his Word. It helps me break up the crust that has developed over the surface of familiar passages, and it keeps me from using the Bible as my go-to proof text to back up foregone conclusions.

Lectio Divina

The request *God, show me* is hugely beneficial in getting us to Proverbs 2 diligence with God's Word (see Chapter 5). It's also a step toward making our Bible study time less of an obligation and more of a *lectio divina* experience—the ancient practice of *reading* the Scriptures, *meditating* on the Scriptures, *praying* the Scriptures, and *contemplating* the Scriptures.[31]

Whenever we look at a verse, chapter, or book of the Bible, there's one fundamental principle to keep in mind: God is saying *something* through the passage. I don't know about you, but I don't want to miss the statement because what God is saying is infinitely more important than whatever I think about the passage.

Scholar Alert

Before we go too far with Bible study tools, there's something you should know. People get Ph.D.s in this stuff.

You may be one of those people. Or you may be on the opposite end of the spectrum with little knowledge or training in studying the Bible.

Effective Bible study with teenagers lies somewhere in the middle. Know that for the purposes of this book we're taking a treetop tour of a subject that can go to the deepest roots of the trees we're surveying. My intent is to help the Bible scholar pare down and the novice ramp up—and for all of us to find the range that works for the students entrusted to our care.

As you're reading, you should find two channels of application: your personal Bible study and your work discipling students. My intent is to help with both.

For the sake of simplicity, this chapter and the following two will be directed toward your personal Bible study. After all, it starts with us leaders. And don't forget that your personal study of God's Word will become your best preparation for discipling your students.

Genre

I love the satellite imagery on Web sites like MapQuest and Google Maps. It's a better at-your-desk break than a game of *Minesweeper* or *Solitaire*. Type in the name or address of your last vacation spot and zoom in. Or pull up Google Earth, type in your home address, and watch the satellite image zoom from the entire earth to your own driveway.

Effective Bible study works the same way. We start with the big picture and gradually zoom in on the detail. In Bible study parlance this is known as setting the context.

Dictionary.com defines context as "the parts of a written or spoken statement that precede or follow a specific word or passage, usually influencing its meaning or effect."[32]

Did you catch that last phrase? *Usually influencing its meaning or effect.* Everything surrounding a passage will influence its meaning. Without due diligence in setting the context, we can run a high risk of misunderstanding or misapplying the passage and consequently losing the meaning and impact God intended.

When our focus is completely zoomed out, all we see of the Bible is 66 seemingly disjointed books. The first click in, however, shows that each book can be connected to one of the following genres. (More on these in Chapter 17):

History: Genesis to Esther and Acts.

Poetry: Job to Song of Solomon.

Prophecy: Isaiah to Malachi and Revelation.

Biography/History: The Gospels—Matthew, Mark, Luke, and John.

Letters (Epistles): Romans to Jude.

Why bother knowing this? Because the genre of a book sets the stage for how we approach that book. It helps us know which questions to ask of the passage when asking the Five Ws and the H. (We'll jump on that in a minute).

If you've ever taken a beach vacation, you may have spent some time deciding which book you wanted to read at the beach—the right book for that particular setting. Not too heady, but relaxing and enjoyable. By thinking about the type of book you wanted, you were processing book genre.

In the same way, we need to process the type of each book of the Bible. Genesis requires a different approach than Psalms. A Gospel may call for a different take than a New Testament letter.

Five Ws and the H

Pursuing my undergraduate degree in mass communications and spending more than a year as a staff writer for a newspaper taught me the journalist's cardinal rule. You've got to ask the right questions to get to the fundamental facts of a story: Who? What? When? Where? Why? and How?

In a fit of creativity, journalism experts named these questions the Five *W's* and the *H*. (Hey, journalists are supposed to be objective, not creative.) These questions are intended to keep journalists on task, enabling them to tell their readers what happened with as little embellishment or opinion as possible.

The same questions work in Bible study. To get to the purest information and precise view of what God wants to show us, we can benefit tremendously from basic questions such as:

Who is in this passage?

What is going on in the scene?

When is it happening?

Where is it happening?

Why is this important according to evidence in the passage?

How is this going to happen?

The type of book that you're studying will help shape the questions you're asking. For example, the question of *When?* won't produce much information from a poetry book such as Psalms, but it will mine out truckloads from a prophetic book such as Isaiah or a history book such as Acts.

As you ask the five *Ws* and the *H* of any passage, the difference between *reading* the passage and *ingesting* it comes when you engage one more of your five senses than simple sight. Don't just mentally register an answer to one of the questions; do something to engage with it. It's repeatedly been proven that the more senses we incorporate into learning, the more likely we are to remember the information. And the more we remember God's Word, the more likely we are to be changed by it.

The most convenient senses to use while studying the Bible are touch and sight. An easy exercise that combines these two senses is simply to mark or draw symbols over the info you find. For example, if the obvious *whos* in a chapter are Jesus, the disciples, and the Jews, you might mark Jesus with a cross, the disciples with a large *D*, and the Jews with a Star of David.

After reading and marking the passage several times in this way, stop and mull over what you've discovered. Start taking some notes in the margins. Look at what you marked and jot down what you've observed about Jesus. List the questions of the disciples. Note any salient characteristics of the Jews. In other words, process your observations by organizing them into short lists. As you do so, remember the detective's mantra: "Just the facts, ma'am." Right now you're in the "God, show me" stage of study, simply observing what God's Word says.

Don't Fear the Method

You may be thinking, *You just went all method on me!* If so, the next paragraph is for you.

There are many things we can do to become more intentional and purposeful in Bible study, to move from *reading* God's Word to *engaging* God's Word. Marking the text with symbols is one of many approaches, and I believe it's one of the best.

By now you might be asking: *So should I mark in my Bible? Or on printouts of Scripture?* If so, the answer is: Whatever works for you. If you're studying a short Bible book such as Ephesians, you can copy the entire book from Bible software or a Web site such as www.biblegateway.com and paste it into a word-processing document. Then format the pages with wide margins and lots of space for marking and writing notes. Print these and put them in a notebook. When you've finished studying, you'll have your own personal commentary on Ephesians.

Or you can purchase a Bible specifically for this purpose. With a little searching you can find a Bible formatted for this type of study. *The International Inductive Study Bible* is one example.

Who?

Obviously, the text you're studying will tell you who the main players are and who to mark. But whatever the passage, we're always wise to be on the lookout for the Bible's three main players: God, Jesus, and the Holy Spirit. So why not adopt a standard symbol for each one? Here are some examples, but feel free to make up your own:

Try It Out

Read the Colossians passage below and draw the appropriate symbol over every mention of God, Jesus, or the Spirit. Be sure to include pronouns such as *he* and *him*. The challenge is to keep track of which pronouns refer to God and which refer to Jesus.

> ⁹For this reason, since the day we heard about you, we have not stopped praying for you and asking God to fill you with the knowledge of his will through all spiritual wisdom and understanding. ¹⁰And we pray this in order that you may live a life worthy of the Lord and may please him in every way: bearing fruit in every good work, growing

in the knowledge of God, [11]being strengthened with all power according to his glorious might so that you may have great endurance and patience, and joyfully [12]giving thanks to the Father, who has qualified you to share in the inheritance of the saints in the kingdom of light. [13]For he has rescued us from the dominion of darkness and brought us into the kingdom of the Son he loves, [14]in whom we have redemption, the forgiveness of sins.

[15]He is the image of the invisible God, the first-born over all creation. [16]For by him all things were created: things in heaven and on earth, visible and invisible, whether thrones or powers or rulers or authorities; all things were created by him and for him. [17]He is before all things, and in him all things hold together. [18]And he is the head of the body, the church; he is the beginning and the firstborn from among the dead, so that in everything he might have the supremacy. [19]For God was pleased to have all his fullness dwell in him, [20]and through him to reconcile to himself all things, whether things on earth or things in heaven, by making peace through his blood, shed on the cross. (COLOSSIANS 1:9-20)

Writers and Recipients

Much of the New Testament is comprised of letters written from someone to someone. When studying a letter (also called an epistle), we can learn a great deal about the purpose, setting, and context of the book by collecting details about the author and the letter's first readers. Were they believers? Was there trouble?

Try It Out

As you read the following verses from Jude, draw a circle around anything that refers to the first readers, the original recipients of this letter. Don't forget to key in on pronouns such as *who*.

> [1]Jude, a servant of Jesus Christ and a brother of James, To those who have been called, who are loved by God the Father and kept by Jesus Christ:
>
> [2]Mercy, peace and love be yours in abundance.
>
> [3]Dear friends, although I was very eager to write to you about the salvation we share, I felt I had to write and urge you to contend for the faith that was once for all entrusted to the saints. [4]For certain men whose condemnation was written about long ago have secretly slipped in among you. They are godless men, who change the grace of our God into a license for immorality and deny Jesus Christ our only Sovereign and Lord. (Jude 1:1-4)

Did you notice how Jude's readers are described? Did you see what they were facing? This information will set the tone for everything else in Jude.

What?

The question *What?* helps us notice the action taking place in a given passage. You'll find this question most helpful in studying history books such as Genesis or the Gospels. In other types of books, it will help you observe truth principles such as *what* God has done for you.

Try It Out

Look back at Colossians 1. This time draw a box around anything that describes *what* God has done for you.

When?

This question yields great fruit when you're studying events in historical books or prophecy. Look for references to time of day or the year or era when events have taken or will take place. With prophecy keep asking, *Is this already fulfilled or yet to be fulfilled? When?* is also a helpful question when studying theological concepts such as blessings in Christ that became available to us at the Cross.

Try It Out

Read the following passages and draw a clock over any reference to time. Notice how a mention of time such as a particular day in John 5 changes the nature of the entire scene.

> [1]Some time later, Jesus went up to Jerusalem for a feast of the Jews. [2]Now there is in Jerusalem near the Sheep Gate a pool, which in Aramaic is called Bethesda and which is surrounded by five covered colonnades. [3]Here a great number of disabled people used to lie—the blind, the lame, the paralyzed. [5]One who was there had been an invalid for thirty-eight years. [6]When Jesus saw him lying there and learned that he had been in this condition for a long time, he asked him, "Do you want to get well?"
>
> [7]"Sir," the invalid replied, "I have no one to help me into the pool when the water is stirred. While I am trying to get in, someone else goes down ahead of me."

⁸Then Jesus said to him, "Get up! Pick up your mat and walk." ⁹At once the man was cured; he picked up his mat and walked. The day on which this took place was a Sabbath, ¹⁰and so the Jews said to the man who had been healed, "It is the Sabbath; the law forbids you to carry your mat." (JOHN 5:1-10)

⁸But God demonstrates his own love for us in this: While we were still sinners, Christ died for us.

⁹Since we have now been justified by his blood, how much more shall we be saved from God's wrath through him! ¹⁰For if, when we were God's enemies, we were reconciled to him through the death of his Son, how much more, having been reconciled, shall we be saved through his life! ¹¹Not only is this so, but we also rejoice in God through our Lord Jesus Christ, through whom we have now received reconciliation. (ROMANS 5:8-11)

²⁷"The days are coming," declares the LORD, "when I will plant the house of Israel and the house of Judah with the offspring of men and of animals. ²⁸Just as I watched over them to up- root and tear down, and to overthrow, destroy and bring disaster, so I will watch over them to build and to plant," declares the LORD. ²⁹"In those days people will no longer say, 'The fathers have eaten sour grapes, and the children's teeth are set on edge.'

³⁰Instead, everyone will die for his own sin; who- ever eats sour grapes—his own teeth will be set on edge.

³¹"The time is coming," declares the LORD, "when I will make a new covenant with the house of Israel and with the house of Judah.

³²It will not be like the covenant I made with their forefathers when I took them by the hand to lead them out of Egypt, because they broke my covenant, though I was a husband to them," declares the LORD.

³³"This is the covenant I will make with the house of Israel after that time," declares the LORD. "I will put my law in their minds and write it on their hearts. I will be their God, and they will be my people. (JEREMIAH 31:27-33)

Where?

The question *Where?* is beneficial in studying Bible books that cover history, such as Genesis, Exodus, or Acts.

Try It Out

As you read the passages below, mark the city mentioned and *where* Paul went each time he entered a city.

¹At Iconium Paul and Barnabas went as usual into the Jewish synagogue. There they spoke so effectively that a great number of Jews and Gentiles believed. (ACTS 14:1)

¹⁹They arrived at Ephesus, where Paul left Priscilla and Aquila. He himself went into the synagogue and reasoned with the Jews. (ACTS 18:19)

⁸Paul entered the synagogue and spoke boldly there for three months, arguing persuasively about the kingdom of God. (ACTS 19:8)

Did you spot a trend? Because Paul is so famous for his call to the Gentiles, it's surprising to discover that he spent much of his time in synagogues. But while Paul diligently and effectively fulfilled his call to bring salvation to the Gentiles, he also had a heartfelt burden for his fellow Jews (Romans 10:1). (As a bonus exercise, read the preceding passages again and note *what* Paul did in the synagogues and *how* he did it.)

Don't reserve the question *Where?* for books of history and geography. There are great theological concepts to explore that relate to matters of location, such as where God is in relation to our physical world (Psalm 139), where Jesus currently sits (Hebrews 8, 10, 12), and where our eternal home is prepared (John 14).

Why?

Words such as *because* and *so that* can clue us in that *Why?* is about to be answered by the text. You may want to designate a unique color or symbol to use when marking *whys*.

Try It Out

In the following passage, look for why we're instructed do something or why God did something. Note any benefits connected to reasons why.

> [3]All of us also lived among them at one time, gratifying the cravings of our sinful nature and following its desires and thoughts. Like the rest, we were by nature objects of wrath. [4]But because of his great love for us, God, who is rich in mercy, [5]made us alive with Christ even when we were dead in transgressions—it is by grace you have been saved. (EPHESIANS 2:3-5)

How?

How does God do it? How are we to do it? A passage of Scripture often will tell us.

Try It Out

The following passage contains a reference to how or to what extent God accomplished something. Watch for these key words and phrases: *Through* and *according to.*

> [9]For this reason, since the day we heard about you, we have not stopped praying for you and asking God to fill you with the knowledge of his will through all spiritual wisdom and understanding. [10]And we pray this in order that you may live a life worthy of the Lord and may please him in every way: bearing fruit in every good work, growing in the knowledge of God, [11]being strengthened with all power according to his glorious might so that you may have great endurance and patience, and joyfully [12]giving thanks to the Father, who has qualified you to share in the inheritance of the saints in the kingdom of light. (COLOSSIANS 1:9-12)

Zooming In

Once you've asked the five *Ws* and the *H* and made notes, you've already zoomed in closer than you could with a cursory read. But as you might have guessed, there's more. In fact, the first layer of observation often raises more questions than answers.

The next set of exercises will take you a few clicks closer as you zoom in on Scripture.

Key Words and Phrases

If you want to emphasize something, re-peat it. If you want to emphasize some-thing, repeat it. (You probably saw that one coming.) Nowhere is this truer than in Scripture. Nowhere is this truer than in Scripture. (Maybe that one caught you!)

When I was studying the Gospel of John a few years ago, I started to notice the word *believe* sprinkled like confetti throughout the text. So I started mark-ing *believe* with a yellow sunburst, keep-ing track of every principle or event con-nected with that word. I later learned that John used a form of the word *believe* more than 75 times in his Gospel. The other three Gospels combined don't use the word that often.

John was obviously emphasizing a point. In fact, he ex-plicitly stated why he wrote his Gospel: "But these are written that you may believe that Jesus is the Christ, the Son of God, and that by believing you may have life in his name" (John 20:31).

The word *believe*, in essence, unlocks the meaning of the book of John. That's exactly what *key* words or phrases do; they unlock the meaning God is expressing in a verse, chap-ter, or an entire book.

As you run across repeated words in Scripture, such as *love, righteousness, mercy,* or repeated phrases, such as *God said, by faith,* or *in Christ,* mark them each with a unique color or symbol. Observe how these key words relate to one another, and be sure to note how they unlock the message of the text.

Contrasts

One of my favorite phrases in all of Scripture is the simple...
but God. You'll often find it in stories of situations that were
utterly hopeless...*but God* intervened.

When you find and mark contrasts in Scripture, be sure
to list in the margin all the details given on either side of the
contrast word, such as *but*. What often emerges is a stunning
picture of God's grace.

Try It Out

Before marking the contrasts in the following passage, you
can use your imagination to think of a symbol for a *but*. (I use
a lightning bolt to denote a contrast.)

> [5]For when we came into Macedonia, this body of
> ours had no rest, but we were harassed at every
> turn—conflicts on the outside, fears within. [6]But
> God, who comforts the downcast, comforted us
> by the coming of Titus, [7]and not only by his com-
> ing but also by the comfort you had given him.
> He told us about your longing for me, your deep
> sorrow, your ardent concern for me, so that my joy
> was greater than ever. (2 CORINTHIANS 7:5-7)

Words of Conclusion

One of the handiest rules of Bible study—say it with me if you
know it—is simply "When you see a therefore, you should go
back and see what it's *there for.*" Terms of conclusion, such
as *therefore, so that,* and *and so,* indicate that the information
about to be shared is strongly linked with the information
previously shared. Thus, the only way to understand and accurately apply what's about to be shared is to understand the
preceding information.

Try It Out

Here's a good way to mark words of conclusion: Simply circle the word, such as *therefore*, and draw an arrow to the pertinent information preceding it. The verse below is a classic example of why terms of conclusion are important. Grab your Bible, and find out what precedes the info below; it may be more than one verse.

> [1]Therefore, I urge you, brothers, in view of God's mercy, to offer your bodies as living sacrifices, holy and pleasing to God—this is your spiritual act of worship. (ROMANS 12:1)

Words of Comparison

Words such as *like, as,* and *just as* are tips that two or more things are being compared. These words are like flashing neon signs telling us to explore the comparison, which may shed additional light on a spiritual concept. Think about what you typically do when you're desperate to get a point across; you use analogies and comparisons. This technique occurs repeatedly in Scripture and supplies us with countless opportunities for deeper exploration.

Try It Out

Circle the two elements being compared and draw a line or an arc to connect them.

> [31]He told them another parable: "The kingdom of heaven is like a mustard seed, which a man took and planted in his field. (MATTHEW 13:31)

Jesus' comparison in Matthew 13:31 prompts us to explore the properties of a mustard seed, particularly its size, as that's the characteristic Jesus singled out. We can then use that information to better apply the principles of the kingdom of heaven.

These comparisons open up a whole world of object lessons and visual illustrations, teaching tools that dovetail with how teenagers like to learn.

Promises

The Bible is full of promises that have the potential to profoundly impact our daily living. If all we did each time we opened our Bibles was to mark and list the promises of God and then live in light of them, we'd be miles down the road toward living the abundant life Jesus spoke of.

Try It Out

Taking a cue from one of the biggest promises in Scripture, a rainbow is a great symbol to use when marking a promise. Look again at the passage under *How?* and draw a rainbow over any promises you see.

Commands/Instructions

In a fit of exasperation during one of our Bible studies, a high school student once declared, "I just wish God would write on a piece of paper what he wants me to do and hand it to me!" Actually, God did. In fact, God's given us thousands of pieces of paper (depending on the size of our Bibles) with explicit instructions on what we're to do.

Marking God's commands and instructions alone could be one of the most practical exercises any of us could undertake with Scripture.

Make a List

I'm a list person. More accurately, I'm a cross-it-off-the-list person. That's because lists serve a great function. In the grocery store they keep me focused. In daily life they help me prioritize. At Christmas they keep me from the dreaded mall-browse shopping.

In Bible study they keep all of us engaged.

As you've marked the many passages under the *Try It Outs* in this chapter, you've observed a myriad of things. Take a minute now to organize those things by listing some of your observations. Write in the margin of the book, grab a separate notebook, or type the information into a computer.

Here are a few examples to get you started. In processing the *whos* of Colossians 1:9-20, you might ask *What do I learn about God?* and *What details about Jesus do I see?* Your answer lists may look something like this:

God

has rescued me from the dominion of darkness

loves his Son

is invisible

dwells fully in Christ

Jesus

is loved by the Father

is the image of God

is the firstborn over all creation

created all things

is before all things

is the head of the body, the church

is the beginning and the firstborn from among the dead

manifests the fullness of God

reconciled all things to himself by making peace through his blood

By observing the information broken out and highlighted in a list, we begin to notice things in Scripture we may never have seen before. (Chapter 12 hits on some creative ideas for lists.) We've also raised a few questions, not the least of which may be, *So what?*

That sets us up for the second big request of inductive study: God, teach me.

Hands-On Study
God, Show Me—Acts 4:1-13

To give you a practical handle on how the three requests *(show me, teach me, change me)* can work in your daily Bible time, this chapter and the next two contain a hands-on study to allow us together to take apart a chunk of Scripture. In Chapter 12 you'll see how your time with this passage can translate into a small-group study.

Background

Read Acts 1-3 to set the context on the passage. Here's a summary if you're short on time:

- Acts 1: Jesus, just before he ascends to the Father, tells his disciples to go to Jerusalem and sit tight until the Holy Spirit shows up.

- Acts 2: The Holy Spirit shows up, and the church explodes.

- Acts 3: Newly empowered by the Holy Spirit, the apostles begin to do things Jesus did, including healing people such as a beggar who'd been lame since birth. This catches the attention of some Jewish leaders who thought they had properly disposed of the Jesus threat.

God, Show Me

Because Acts is a history book, we can reference people, places, actions, and times to give us a framework for understanding the passage. As you read the passage below, look for *who, what, when,* and *where*. Mark each of these things with a unique symbol. Consider using a Star of David to mark the Jewish leaders and an *Ichthus* (sign of the fish) to mark the apostles, two of the key *whos* in this passage.

Now ask God to show you what he wants you to see, and dig into the passage using the five *Ws* and the *H*.

> ¹The priests and the captain of the temple guard and the Sadducees came up to Peter and John while they were speaking to the people. ²They were greatly disturbed because the apostles were teaching the people and proclaiming in Jesus the resurrection of the dead. ³They seized Peter and John, and because it was evening, they put them in jail until the next day. ⁴But many who heard the message believed, and the number of men grew to about five thousand. ⁵The next day the rulers, elders and teachers of the law met in Jerusalem. ⁶Annas the high priest was there, and so were Caiaphas, John, Alexander and the other men of the high priest's family. ⁷They had Peter and John brought before them and began to question them: "By what power or what name did you do this?"
>
> ⁸Then Peter, filled with the Holy Spirit, said to them: "Rulers and elders of the people! ⁹If we are being called to account today for an act of kindness shown to a cripple and are asked how he was healed, ¹⁰then know this, you and all the

people of Israel: It is by the name of Jesus Christ of Nazareth, whom you crucified but whom God raised from the dead, that this man stands before you healed. [11]He is 'the stone you builders rejected, which has become the capstone.' [12]Salvation is found in no one else, for there is no other name under heaven given to men by which we must be saved."

[13]When they saw the courage of Peter and John and realized that they were unschooled, ordinary men, they were astonished and they took note that these men had been with Jesus. (ACTS 4:1-13)

After you've marked the passage, look back at your symbols and markings. These point to a wealth of facts about the two main parties in this passage. Take yourself to a deeper layer of understanding by grabbing a sheet of paper and listing every fact you find about the Jewish leaders and the apostles.

Because there's a time element in the passage, you may want to organize your lists around Day One and Day Two, noting who was around and what they did on each day. Be sure to note anything you learn about the *whos* most likely to show up in any Bible passage: God, Jesus, and the Holy Spirit.

Review your lists and linger with the facts for a few minutes. Keep asking God to show you what he wants you to see. Ask, "Why is this event recorded for me in Scripture?" Circle, star, or note anything that pops out to you.

And that's it for now. You've observed the fundamental facts of Acts 4:1-13. If you find yourself asking *so what?* you're ready for the next request: God, teach me.

CHAPTER EIGHT

God, Teach Me!

Your hands made me and formed me; give me understanding to learn your commands. PSALM 119:73

It speaks no less than God in every line.

JOHN DRYDEN ON THE BIBLE • "RELIGIO LAICI" (A LAYMAN'S FAITH),
FROM *THE POETICAL WORKS OF JOHN DRYDEN*

Have you hung out in Psalm 119 lately?

If not, you may want to revisit that incredible chapter. Not only is Psalm 119 the longest chapter in the Bible, but also each verse is about the words, precepts, and statutes of God. For added interest, the author wrote this psalm as an acrostic with each of its 22 sections corresponding to a letter of the Hebrew alphabet. And as if that's not enough, in the original Hebrew each verse begins with the Hebrew letter corresponding to that section. (Obviously this was lost in the English translation.)

This psalm's author was one detail-oriented person!

Obvious, too, is the fact that the writer of Psalm 119 loved the Word of God and was serious about helping others metabolize it into their lives. The acrostic format was undoubtedly a tool to encourage memorization.

The writer was passionate about God's decrees and had full knowledge of what they can do and what they require: Obedience. Yet once about every 12 verses, the writer makes a heartfelt request of God—something along the lines of "God, give me understanding!" or "Lord, please teach me about your decrees!"

Even this astute Bible writer, the one inspired by the Spirit to write *the* definitive chapter on God's Word, asked for God's help in understanding Scripture.

Interpretation

After you've spent time carefully observing Scripture in the *God, show me* stage, you'll understand much more of what God is saying in a passage than had you given it only a cursory read. But in most cases questions of meaning will remain. For example, after you've uncovered and observed the basic facts in Jesus' famous teaching on the signs of his second coming (Matthew 24), you may still wonder: *Is the fig tree he mentions in verse 32 a literal fig tree or is it symbolic of something else? In the original language of Jesus' day, how long was a generation? Are there other places in the Bible that talk about these weird future events and shed a little more light on what we can expect?*

Questions like these that cannot immediately be answered by observing the text will lead you to the second step of inductive study: *Interpretation.*

Don't let the word *interpretation* scare you or make you think *This step is for folks with a lot more time than I have.* It could be scarier. The official, academic name for this stage of Bible study is *hermeneutics.*

In essence, this stage of Bible study makes the simple request: "God, teach me." Or perhaps more accurately, "Help!" And we all know how to ask for help.

A Love-Hate Relationship

To be honest, I've always had a love-hate relationship with the interpretation aspect of Bible study. At one time I probably let the pendulum swing a little too far toward minimizing interpretation in a noble attempt to stay as close as possible to the purity of what God said as discovered through accurate observation. In other words, I was hesitant to add to or take away from Scripture by running it through my own interpretive grid.

Through maturity (read *aging*) I've realized that it's impossible to *not* interpret. So as long as we're bound to interpret Scripture in some way, we may as well make sure we're doing it in a way that honors God—that is, as accurately as possible.

Among the many reasons why it's important for us to be familiar with good tools of interpretation, one seems paramount for youth ministry. When working with students, it's all too easy to get a little too cute at this point in Bible study. It's fun to come up with clever insights and "hidden" spiritual meanings behind the events and teachings in Scripture. It's also a bit of an ego feeder.

But if we're not leading students to the insight and meaning that a passage calls for, then we're remaking the Bible— and perhaps the God of the Bible—in our own image. And that's serious business with God.

Rehydrating the Word

Eugene Peterson uses this analogy to illustrate what interpretation does for Bible study. When we look at the print on the thin pages of our Bibles, we are looking at dehydrated content—words stripped of the smells, sounds, and facial reactions present at the original writing. By being diligent in our observation and interpretation, we are rehydrating the words, bringing the content back to its full, rich meaning.[33]

Peterson underscores the need for accurate interpretation, which he refers to as exegesis. He writes, "These words given to us in our Scriptures are constantly getting overlaid with personal preferences, cultural assumptions, sin distortions, and ignorant guesses that pollute the text. The pollutants are always in the air, gathering dust on our Bibles, corroding our use of the language, especially the language of faith. Exegesis is a dust cloth, a scrub brush, or even a Q-tip for keeping the words clean."[34]

When to Make the Request

The *God, show me* (observation) stage of inductive Bible study helps us see what God is saying in a passage by giving prime attention to the facts. The *God, teach me* (interpretation) stage helps us understand what these facts mean. The goal of *God, teach me* is to help us hear what God is saying, *not* to hear what we want him to say.

So when in the process of searching the Word do we ask *God, teach me?*

When We Don't Understand

Whenever you take intentional steps to slow down and become more diligent with Scripture, it's inevitable that you'll run into more things that you don't understand. That doesn't sound like a great advertisement for thorough, intentional Bible study, but picture the typical alternative to intentional Bible study: the drive-by devotional. When you're doing a drive-by devotional, what happens when you come across something you just don't get? If you're like most of us, you keep cruising right along—moving to the next verse before your brain has a chance to register what should have sparked a question. Opportunity lost.

Funny thing, though. When we do notice something that sparks a question—especially one that makes us uncomfortable—our default response is usually to skip it anyway. We need to reprogram our thinking so that we see our questions as vivid *Xs* on a treasure map, indicating where to begin the dig.

When We Want to Know More

Faithfully observing a passage—marking it with symbols and filling the margins with information—doesn't necessarily mean we have it all figured out. Other Scriptures may shed another light on the passage. Word definitions may bring a different twist.

When preparing for Bible study with students, one of the best ways to know whether you've understood what God is saying in a passage is to ask, "What will my students have questions about?" That question alone can trigger the *God, teach me* request.

When We Want to Accurately Apply Scripture

Because application (read *life-change*) is a primary goal in Bible study, this is probably the most critical reason to ask God to teach us about a passage. It's virtually impossible to approach Scripture devoid of the many personal filters we possess: The era we live in, our denominational background, our upbringing, and personal spiritual history. The *God, teach me* step forces us to consider historical and cultural dynamics to make sure we're accurately applying a passage in our time period and culture.

The Three Asks

Any quest to interpret Scripture accurately will involve some combination of three sources: God, more Scripture, and other people. We'll call these The Three Asks.

Ask God

Asking God should be our immediate response whenever we hit something we don't understand. Unfortunately, this isn't always the case. The usual shortcut is to bail out with a commentary, ask the pastor, or skip the pursuit entirely. Meanwhile God is looking over our shoulder and quite possibly muttering under his breath, "I wrote the thing; ask *me*."

Jesus told his disciples they'd be better off with the Holy Spirit present than with him. One reason is that the Holy Spirit would guide them into all truth, speaking what he heard from God and telling what's to come. One of the Spirit's key functions is to teach us and illuminate truth in our hearts. Thus, the simple step of asking God to teach us opens us to one of the Spirit's primary functions in our lives.

This step can be as simple as leaning back in your chair and asking God why he included a particular passage in the Bible. Even the driest list of *begats* can come to life with that question.

Asking God to teach us about a passage automatically brings meditation and prayer into the mix. Simply repeating *God, teach me* piques our minds and hearts and leads us to explore many other things inside of us or somewhere else in Scripture.

Try It Out

Flip back now to some of the Scriptures you observed in Chapter 7. Choose a passage and ask a few questions of God, such as *What do you want me to learn from this?* or *Why is this in the Bible?*

Ask Scripture

Perhaps you've heard the cardinal rule of accurate interpretation: Let Scripture interpret Scripture. In other words, the Word of God is its own best commentary. Let 1, 2, and 3 John help interpret the Gospel of John. Let Ephesians 3 shed light on the "mystery" in Colossians 1 and vice versa.

At times, letting Scripture interpret Scripture will seem like intricate detective work, but unlike a detective, you'll rarely run out of leads. Usually help from more Scripture is right around the corner. Sometimes you'll find it in the very next verse.

One of my all-time favorite verses is John 7:38, in which Jesus says, "Whoever believes in me, as the Scripture has said, streams of living water will flow from within him."

What a great image. I've given many talks on that passage, making clever application with the living water analogy. And if we stopped right here, you could probably come up with a 20-minute talk on the spot to teach this passage. And it would be good.

But here's what's easy to miss. In the very next verse, John tells us what Jesus meant by "living water." The Holy Spirit. I've had a lot of fun with the water analogy, asking kids questions such as "Which describes your spiritual life? A kiddie pool? A stagnant pond? A small creek? Or a river of living water?" But if I don't bring the teaching around to God's Spirit and his work in their lives (which I didn't for a while), I've completely missed the correct interpretation of the passage. We gain even more insight when we compare what some of the Old Testament prophets had to say about water. (See Isaiah 43:18-21, 44:1-4, Ezekiel 47:5-9.)

So how do we let Scripture interpret Scripture? By using a few handy tools that practically do the work for us. Most of them are available in books and on computer. I'll explain the tools in book form, touching briefly on Bible software and online tools.

1. Concordance: The go-to tool for finding additional Scriptures where a particular word is used or subject explained. Most Bibles include an abridged concordance that contains popular words and passages, but the most helpful concordance is one with *exhaustive* in its title. In

this type every word is indexed and assigned a number that can be helpful in tracking the word in the original Hebrew or Greek.

The search function included in most Bible software or Web sites can also serve as great concordance tools. Just type your word or phrase into the appropriate search box, and you'll be given a list of all the verses where your word or phrase appears.

2. Cross-Reference Bible: Maybe you own a Bible with micro-type down the middle of each page or in the side margins. And maybe you've completely ignored that fine print. However, this feature—known as a cross-reference system—can be your best friend in the task of making Scripture interpret Scripture. To learn how to use the cross-reference feature in your Bible, simply refer to the instructions in the introduction.

(By the way, I'm not referring to the footnotes or study notes in a given Bible, but to a full-fledged cross-reference system in which nearly every verse is linked to related verses. Most English translations of the Bible come with footnotes giving insight into translation decisions on certain words, but it's the publisher's decision as to whether to include a cross-reference system.)

Some Bible computer programs include this feature, giving you an efficient method of checking out other verses that give further insight on the passage you're studying.

3. Bible Dictionary: There's probably not a quicker way to track a Bible theme or a more effective way to cut through study clutter than to consult a Bible dictionary. This tool will give you comprehensive info about the people, places, and events in or related to the Bible.

The benefit of a Bible dictionary lies in the fact that it provides fairly raw data, with little theology or interpretation. However, I would consult the Bible dictionary only after doing your own cross-referencing and concordance work, thus preserving a few opportunities for self-discovery.

For example, when studying the book of James, you could open a Bible dictionary to see which *James* (of the several mentioned in the New Testament) wrote the book. Or you could look up James in a concordance, check out the various references to people named James, and do your own investigation of who wrote the book. You'd be surprised and intrigued by what you'll find following the latter route. That's why I recommend doing your own investigation, drawing your own conclusions, and *then* comparing those conclusions with a Bible dictionary.

Some Bible Web sites include a Bible dictionary, but these are often public domain dictionaries that may not reflect the most current archeology and research. Many Bible publishers do, however, offer their current Bible dictionaries in a software version.

4. *Thompson Chain-Reference Bible:* Many consider this the premium tool for letting Scripture interpret Scripture. In this Bible nearly every verse is linked to a theme you can track throughout the entire Bible. It's fair to say that this tool gives you cross-referencing, concordance help, and dictionary work all rolled into one.

    The Kirkbride Bible Company, publishers of the *Thompson Chain-Reference Bible*, offers a software version.

Try It Out

If you have one handy, grab a Bible with a concordance or cross-reference system and "ask Scripture" about one of the passages you observed in Chapter 7. Journal any new insights you glean from linking that passage to other related Scriptures.

Ask Others

The final stop in the interpretation process involves others— other resources and the insights of other believers, such as colleagues, friends, and pastors.

1. Other Resources: Commentaries and Bible handbooks can be helpful tools for drilling deeper into a passage or clarifying something you don't understand. But here's a caution: Make these the last stop in your study process, rather than an immediate bailout. Interpretation from commentators runs the gamut from dead-on to give me a break.

   The most useful commentaries give insight into the biblical languages of Hebrew and Greek rather than devotional thoughts. Those that shed light on the Hebrew and Greek texts include *The New International Commentary of the New Testament* (NICNT) and *The New International Commentary of the Old Testament* (NICOT), published by Eerdmans. These tend to be less interpretive, while devotional commentaries carry more opinion and leave less room for you to form your own conclusions.

   Obviously not all of us have access to commentary sets, but you may have luck checking with your pastoral staff, a church library, public library, or nearby college or seminary library.

2. Other People: Youth ministry colleagues and fellow church staff can be invaluable contributors as they journey with us in the Word—or they can be the end of the line. We in ministry too often believe we need to have everything wrapped up and organized into neat, theological boxes. Yes, we need to be confident in what we believe, but boxes and bows don't leave us much wiggle

room for grappling with Scripture and arriving at fresh conclusions should God lead us there.

Healthy give-and-take allows us to compare insights with those of others who have wrestled with a passage— and it's a valuable gut check to ensure that the interpretation we've arrived at isn't contradictory to Scripture's intention.

On the flip side, we youth workers are in a position to be other people our students can turn to when they want to drill deeper into Scripture. Instead of spouting off an answer, we should encourage them in the discovery process and teach them to ask God and ask Scripture before they ask us.

Interpretation Considerations

Much is being written these days about how our environment impacts our health, our personality, even our outlook on life. The same is true of the environment surrounding any Scripture we might study—it impacts interpretation. Each passage is surrounded by key influencers that must be considered in order to accurately interpret and apply the passage.

Genre

Just as a Bible book's genre is important in the observation (God, show me) stage, genre is a key starting point for interpretation. Generally speaking, the content of a history book, such as Genesis or Exodus, should be interpreted literally. Poetic language, such as that of Psalms or Song of Solomon, often contains elements that can be interpreted figuratively.

Literary Form

Just when you thought you were finished for life with literary terms, there are two you should consider when studying Scripture. A simile is a comparison that uses *like* or *as*. "At that moment heaven was opened, and he saw the Spirit of God descending *like a* dove and "lighting on him" (Matthew 3:16b). A metaphor is an implied comparison. *"I am the gate*; whoever enters through me will be saved" (John 10:9a, italics added).

In the preceding examples, did the Holy Spirit physically change himself into a dove? (And should we take extra care in the way we treat doves in case they're the Holy Spirit in bird form?) Did Jesus become a physical gate? Obviously not. But you'd be surprised how many incorrect interpretations have been built on an erroneous understanding of a literary device.

Attention to literary form is especially necessary for interpreting Jesus' teachings. Was he giving an illustration? Speaking in a parable? Describing an actual event? Take the story of the Good Samaritan. Was this an actual event or a parable? Check out Luke 10:30, and make your determination.

Culture

There's no denying that the Bible writers' cultures are reflected in Scripture. In God's providence we can trust that the timing was intentional. And rather than dismiss a cultural difference, we can use it to help with interpretation.

Take slavery, for example. Slavery was common in New Testament times, but it was also a different "slavery" than the kind that makes people into property (e.g., Africans seized on their native soil and shipped to America and England). In most cases New Testament-era slaves were known as bond servants and were paid for their work and could eventually buy their freedom. (You can glean that information from a Bible dictionary.)

None of these cultural differences mean we should ignore Bible references to slaves or slavery. Instead, good interpretation asks us to bring the cultural context of the passage into our present cultural context.

Notice the instructions to slaves in Ephesians 6:5-8: "Slaves, obey your earthly masters with respect and fear, and with sincerity of heart, just as you would obey Christ. Obey them not only to win their favor when their eye is on you, but like slaves of Christ, doing the will of God from your heart. Serve wholeheartedly, as if you were serving the Lord, not men, because you know that the Lord will reward everyone for whatever good he does, whether he is slave or free."

The drive-by reaction to this passage might be to gloss over it, dismissing its instructions because most of us today are not slaves. But a simple question such as "What was slavery like in New Testament days?" can easily lead us to helpful background information that paints a different picture of slavery than what we might expect. It can also lead to discussion about why so many Americans—including Christians— erroneously believed it was acceptable to have slaves as property all the way up to 1865 (as well as the ongoing problem of slavery in other countries today).

Text

The text itself will often give clues on how to interpret a verse or passage. In Matthew 25 Jesus is teaching about the end of the age. He uses three illustrations to teach us about the nature of his kingdom at that time: The parable of the 10 virgins, the parable of the bags of gold, and the scene between the sheep and goats. Two of these, the virgins and the bags of gold, begin with the phrase *It will be like*, which indicates that a simile follows, perhaps in the form of an analogy or parable. The account of the sheep and goats has no comparative phrase. It appears to be an actual scene.

One of our high school Bible study groups used to have fun reading Acts 2 and picturing people with their hair on fire. We're told that "tongues of fire came to rest on each of them." And when we think about Acts 2, we naturally think wind and fire. But look closely at the text. "When the day of Pentecost came, they were all together in one place. Suddenly a sound like the blowing of a violent wind came from heaven and filled the whole house where they were sitting. They saw what seemed to be tongues of fire that separated and came to rest on each of them" (Acts 2:1-3).

The sound was *like* a violent wind and the visual *seemed* to be tongues of fire. Other versions, such as New King James, say "as of fire." While it was certainly a climactic event, it probably didn't include actual wind and fire, but something like them.

If you really want some fun with the words *like* and *as*, check out Revelation. The word *like* shows up 66 times, and *as* makes 44 appearances. These little words are absolutely essential in interpreting the incredible imagery in this book, helping us keep track of literal events and figurative descriptions. Here's an example. "Also before the throne there was what looked like a sea of glass, clear as crystal. In the center, around the throne, were four living creatures, and they were covered with eyes, in front and in back. The first living creature was like a lion, the second was like an ox, the third had a face like a man, the fourth was like a flying eagle" (Revelation 4:6-7).

Does It Point to Jesus?

The final test for interpretation: It should point us to Jesus. To the most biblically literate of Jesus' day, he said these biting words: "You diligently study the Scriptures because you think that by them you possess eternal life. These are the Scriptures that testify about me, yet you refuse to come to me to have life" (John 5:39-40).

All Scripture was given to point us to Jesus. Old Testament history and prophecy. The poetry of the psalms. The letters of the New Testament. And, of course, the Gospels. The question we should always ask ourselves in interpretation is simply: How does this testify to me about Jesus?

Pitfalls to Avoid

You could write an entire book on interpretation pitfalls, but I've included a few of my personal favorites, probably because they're ones I've tended toward.

Spiritual Cleverness

Some of us have an almost irresistible urge to be "The Bible Answer Person." We love to be the ones to find the deeper spiritual meaning behind a passage. Sometimes there actually *is* a deeper meaning. But in many cases we end up looking for something that isn't there—or worse, *coming up with* something that isn't there.

One Easter, while reading the Gospel accounts of Jesus' arrest and crucifixion, my wife noticed something she'd never noticed before or perhaps had forgotten. It's the rather obscure reference to a young man fleeing Jesus' arrest scene *naked*. I've got to admit, it surprised me, too. "A young man, wearing nothing but a linen garment, was following Jesus. When they seized him, he fled naked, leaving his garment behind" (Mark 14:51-52).

A few days later we mentioned the passage to our adult fellowship group and were not only surprised at how many people had noticed the passage, but also at how many possible meanings they had heard. Here are a few examples from the group and a few others we've heard since:

- The nakedness of the man represented the uncleanliness and shame of Israel.

- The young man may have been Mark himself, and he was giving his testimony about Jesus without giving his name.

- The nakedness represents fear, pride, and apathy. Fear is a powerful motivator to leave a scene running. Other times we run out of pride, apathy, disappointment, or greed. But each time we figuratively run, we shed our faith in God's sovereignty like a garment left behind.

- The man's nakedness represents a sifting or refining of God's church.

At face value this verse in Mark is simply describing what happened when Jesus was arrested. Oddly enough, a young man fled the scene naked. Any deeper meaning ascribed to that information would have to be pure conjecture.

Granted, it's a worthy exercise to dig for possible answers. And when we ask God to teach us about this passage, we may be forced to consider a variety of explanations. It might even be fun to ask students for their possible explanations.

But here's the caution: When we conjure up a deeper meaning behind this scene, we run the risk of inventing things that aren't there. What's worse, we put across an air of spiritual cleverness—of having special insights that other, "average" Bible readers may not have. The unintended consequence of our cleverness is that others, such as the teenagers around us, come away thinking that this kind of super-spiritual cleverness needs to be a part of Bible study—that the goal of study is to find the hidden meaning behind every Bible passage. Or they may think *I could never be that smart or that spiritual, so why try?*

When you think you have a handle on a deeper meaning in Scripture, keep a healthy perspective on the info you're presenting. When you're speculating, be up-front about the fact that you're speculating. And beware of super-spiritualization.

What Does This Mean to You?

For years the default method of Bible study in many student ministries has been to read a verse or passage to a group of students, then toss out a question such as "What does this mean?" or "What does this mean to you?"

By now the downside of this approach should be obvious. Without spending at least a few minutes digging into the passage—discovering the context, observing the details, and asking some basic questions using the five *Ws* and the *H*—we're barely equipped to know what a passage says, let alone what it *means*. At that point all we're doing is bouncing around one another's opinions.

And a roomful of opinions may not have much to do with the actual meaning of a passage.

Don't stop at the questions *What does this passage mean?* or *What does it mean to you?* Make sure you come around to asking what the passage means to God.

Hands-On Study

God, Teach Me—Acts 4:1-13

Look back over the information you observed in Acts 4:1-13 during your *God, Show Me* study in Chapter 7. Then use the following questions as prompts to help you interpret this passage:

- Why was this scene recorded for us? What's the point of the action?

- What questions do you have that you'd like to investigate further?

- What do we know about the relationship between the Jewish leaders and the apostles? Are there other Scriptures that can provide insight here?

- What conclusions can you draw from this scene based on the information you've gathered?

- What similar situations do we have today?

- What from this scene can we imitate today?

As you grapple with these questions, don't forget about The Three Asks: Ask God, Ask Scripture, Ask others. Use any Bible study tools you have handy—a concordance, Bible software, a Bible dictionary—to shed more light on the passage.

Finally, write a paragraph to sum up what you believe the passage is about and any conclusions you want to remember.

One Interpretation

Now that you've done your own observation and interpretation, you can compare your insights with others' interpretations. Here's what I take from the passage:

The crux of this scene is found in the reaction of the intimidating Jewish leaders to the humble, unschooled, and ordinary apostles. These threatening leaders (the "big dogs" of

Jerusalem) were astonished at the courage of the apostles, noting that these men had been with Jesus. This courage apparently came from two sources: The Holy Spirit (verse 8) and time spent with Jesus (verse 13). Strengthened by this courage, the apostles not only were able to *resist the impact* of the Jewish leaders who were threatening to undo them, but also the apostles were able to *impact the religious leaders.*

We know that the relationship between the Jewish leaders and the apostles was quite antagonistic. In fact, the Jewish leaders were doing everything in their considerable power to keep the apostles from living out their faith.

So the question is, *what similar situations do we have in our lives? What are the big dogs around us (people, circumstances, temptations) that make it difficult for us to powerfully live out our faith?*

How can we imitate the actions of the apostles so that our "Jewish leader situations" will have no impact on us and that instead we will impact those situations?

CHAPTER NINE

God, Change Me!

How can a young man keep his way pure? By living according to your word. PSALM 119:9

Only in the doing of it does the word of Jesus retain its honor, might, and power among us. Now the storm can rage over the house, but it cannot shatter that union with him which his word has created.

DIETRICH BONHOEFFER • *THE COST OF DISCIPLESHIP*

Every time I hear a small-group Bible study referred to as a holy huddle, I cringe.

It springs from the realization that some Bible study efforts, by increasing in knowledge while exhibiting little change in behavior, have proven that it's all about the huddle—not the larger game in play.

The fact is that believers need holy huddles. In football the huddle is a strategy center. The way I see it, far too many in the body of Christ are involved in a no-huddle offense. But it's those who get in the huddle and never get out—those who never *use* all that knowledge to engage those they're facing—who give holy huddling its bad name.

Getting the Point

If we study the Bible but miss applying it, I wouldn't say we've wasted our time, but I'd sure say we've missed the point.

God is on a mission to redeem a lost world. He accomplishes this one person at a time, conforming us to the likeness of his Son. This conformation happens as we adjust our thoughts, beliefs, and behaviors to the things God teaches us. Done correctly, this process causes the unbelieving world around us to see what's going on in our lives and become attracted to the things of God. In other words, they want what we're having.

In Chapter 2 we looked at this theme in Deuteronomy, and it's a thread that runs throughout the entirety of Scripture.

In Deuteronomy 4 Moses told the people that their obedience to God's decrees would cause the surrounding nations to be impressed by Israel's wisdom and drawn to their God—without a single outreach event or seeker service. "Man, what a great God those people must have," their pagan neighbors would say, "a God who must be very real and near to them."

In John 13 Jesus told the disciples that as they obeyed his command to love one another, all people would have proof that they truly were his disciples. In his John 17 prayer for unity, Jesus promised that our oneness in him would lead the world to know that the Father sent him, the Son.

In Titus 2 Paul gave instructions to those working under human masters, imploring them to obey the Word. He said doing so would make the teachings about God attractive to others (Titus 2:10). In other words our obedience to and application of the Word has a direct impact on how unbelievers view our God and his teachings. Good application makes his teachings appealing—not as a set of rules that hangs like a weight around our necks.

In each of these examples, it's God's people obeying God's Word that causes unbelievers to take a favorable glance toward God—and to give honest consideration to what God's offering.

If good application makes the teachings of God attractive to non-Christians, then the converse is also true: Bad application (or no application at all) can make the teachings of God unattractive.

At this point we could make a case that the problem in the body of Christ today isn't so much a biblical literacy problem as an obedience problem. And in fact, it may be both.

Think for a moment about how the world would look if believers instantaneously decided to be accountable and obedient to the truth we already know—even if it's just a small sliver of truth. Just that slight shift would change the world.

Now consider what could happen if that sliver of truth were to grow and encompass more and more of what's between the covers of the Book. The world-change would be exponential.

Spiritual Windfall

One of the most endearing visual images I have from my childhood is of walking past my parents' half-open bedroom door most evenings at bedtime and seeing my mom kneeling at the bedside and my dad kneeling at a chair, praying. And praying for a *long* time, especially when measured in kid minutes.

My parents gave me a great example of the power of prayer, but its effect in my life was actually much bigger than that. Their everyday obedience taught me that the gospel is *real*.

This motivated me as a teenager addicted to sleeping in to pull myself out of bed on Sunday mornings. It motivated me as a teenager in full, male hormone development to live a life of sexual abstinence. Their obedience to God's Word had a windfall effect on my overall perception of the gospel.

This should come as no surprise: God's been saying it all along. But somehow it *does* surprise us that obedient actions speak louder than words.

The students in our ministries are watching the adults around them (this means you), looking to see if the gospel is real. They gauge that reality by whether or not what we claim to believe is transforming our behavior.

If you and I aren't often caught in the act of living out the Word we profess, we've removed a critical and foundational stone in the fragile wall between our students and their temptations.

What Do I Need to Do Now?

The familiar passage of 2 Timothy 2:15 defines the kind of Bible student God approves of: One who correctly handles the Word. The phrase *correctly handles* comes from the Greek word *orthotomeo*—a word builders used to describe accurately cutting something, such as a path for a road. Applied to communication, *orthotomeo* expresses one's self with a similar level of exactness and precision.[35] The *tomeo* half of the word, which means "to cut," can be found in the word we translate "to circumcise"—an exercise that certainly calls for accurate cutting! Timothy, the first reader of Paul's words, would have been acutely attuned to this, having been circumcised as an adult (Acts 16:3).

Carpenters live by the familiar phrase "measure twice, cut once." In other words, if you double-check your measurement, you're less likely to cut the wrong length. (For those like me who didn't get the carpentry gene, it's more like "measure thrice, cut twice.")

In order to correctly handle God's Word, this same level of precision is to be applied to Bible study. Measure twice: God, show me. God, teach me. Cut once: God, change me.

After God has shown us what he wants us to see and taught us what he wants us to learn, there's only one question we need to ask: "What do I need to do now?" The answer will be abundantly clear.

Internal Adjustments

Sometimes the application God is looking for happens in the mind. Maybe it's a habitual way of thinking that needs to be addressed. Maybe it's an attitude that isn't pleasing to God. One thing's for certain: It won't be an easy adjustment. That's why it helps to commit to application *early*—to frontload our Bible time with a commitment to God that we plan to respond, whatever God may show us or teach us.

For example, suppose you're someone who's easily frustrated with your family or your students or your church staff. Studying Ephesians 4, God uses verse 26 ("In your anger do not sin: Do not let the sun go down while you are still angry.") to convict you about your anger.

The best way to apply that instruction is to take it literally. Set an alarm on your watch or PDA to sound 30 minutes before sunset. When the alarm sounds, use that moment to think through your day, replaying your conversations. If any anger comes to mind, you'll have 30 minutes to rectify it.

After a few days that alarm will start to sound in your mind or heart at the moment frustration begins to rise. And transformation—that word we love to throw around in student ministry—will have begun.

External Actions

Perhaps the application God wants involves going to someone you've hurt and asking for forgiveness—or seeking out a widow in distress and ministering to her need. These are the kinds of actions that are easiest to put in the *someday* category.

But obedience *someday* isn't obedience at all.

If God is gracious enough to invade your study time with an action you need to take, don't leave your Bible time until you've made a move in that direction. Take a minute to do something specific, such as tracking down a way to contact the person God put on your heart. Make the contact later in the day.

Putting the Cart after the Horse

Here's a good thing about youth ministry: Rarely does it suffer from a lack of application or opportunities for obedience. Student ministry may be the most application-driven ministry. Often it's the youth ministry that takes regular short-term missions trips, works with the local homeless shelter, or volunteers with the various social service agencies in a community. In fact, student ministry may be *over*-applied.

Not over-applied in terms of *doing* ministry, but rather in our approach to teaching. It's not uncommon for us youth-ministry types to put the cart before the horse; we begin with the application we want and then back our way into Scripture. Too often the focus of a small-group study is driven by an issue, such as breaking from the past, and our study time is spent batting around application questions, such as "What should we do when we've blown it?" or "What should we do with our feelings of regret?" Then we close the time, often in a rush, with a Bible verse that speaks to the issue.

Let's flip that sequence around.

Let's start with a study of Scripture and let it drive the application. Instead of the latter scenario, what if we started with a study of Psalm 51? And what if we compared David's words in that psalm with the event that compelled him to write it—a deeply sinful period in his past. Processing David's experience and the song he wrote about it, students would see firsthand (God, show me) that even the Bible greats sinned, and that God forgives and restores those who confess their sin and leave it behind them. They would learn (God, teach me) what real repentance looks like.

And the application they need to make? Well, that would come from the Holy Spirit. And it would be tailor-made to each student.

Occasionally I'll hear someone talk about making Scripture relevant. That's a noble goal, but think about that phrase for a second. What is it saying about Scripture?

Exactly. That it's *not* relevant to begin with.

That's a subtle but huge distinction. When we let the Scripture drive the application, we are showing that the Bible *is* relevant. We don't have to force its relevance.

Kinds of Application

Different kinds of Scripture call for different types of application.

Applying a Truth

John 1 paints an incredible picture of Jesus as light and life. But there's not a practical instruction for miles around. Still, truth to learn is truth to apply. When making application of a truth like that in John 1, ask yourself, *How does this truth alter or reinforce my current picture of Jesus? How does it affect my relationship with him? What do I need to adjust internally as a follower of Jesus?*

Applying an Instruction

Instructions in Scripture fall into the "just do it" category of application. In fact, if you were to compile all the instructions in Scripture into one giant to-do list, you'd probably never again have to wonder about God's will for your life. *Give a cup of cold water to a child. Take care of orphans and widows in distress. Feed the hungry. Clothe the naked. Keep a tight reign on your tongue. Wash one another's feet.* (Try that last one both figuratively and literally!) According to James, to not do these things is to deceive ourselves. And we can't blame the Enemy for this type of deception. It's self-inflicted—and from God's perspective it makes our religion worthless (James 1:22, 26).

Applying a Promise

Promises in Scripture may be the hardest truths to apply, chiefly because application requires that we remember them. Throughout the Bible, God emphasized the need for physical reminders that would jog our sluggish memories and keep us walking in light of his promises. God even made a built-in reminder of his promise never again to destroy the earth with a flood. Sometimes the best first step we can take in applying a promise is to create a physical reminder that can keep our hearts attuned to it long after our Bibles are closed.

Some promises are conditional, calling for action on our part. Consider 1 John 1:9: "If we confess our sins, he is faithful and just and will forgive us our sins and purify us from all unrighteousness." Or John 3:16, "For God so loved the world that he gave his one and only Son, that whoever believes in him shall not perish but have eternal life." Other promises are true for all believers without condition, such as God's promise to meet all our needs according to his glorious riches in Christ (Philippians 4:19).

PRAY THE PRAYERS

There's not a more direct application of Scripture than literally to *do* what Scripture does. For example, when a Bible author prays a prayer, we can pray that prayer, too. After all, it has to be a prayer God likes—God included it in Scripture.

Here's a prayer Paul prayed on behalf of his friends, people under his spiritual mentorship in Colossae. Pray this prayer for your students, substituting their names for the word *you*. "We have not stopped praying for you and asking God to fill you with the knowledge of his will through all spiritual wisdom and understanding. And we pray this in order that you may live a life worthy of the Lord and may please him in every way: bearing fruit in every good work, growing in the knowledge of God" (Colossians 1:9-10).

Want a few more? Search Bible software for phrases such as "I pray" or "pray that," and see where it takes you. Or check out Ephesians 1:18-21, Ephesians 3:16-21, and Colossians 4:12. These are also great prayers for students to pray for one another.

Applying an Example

Observing people in Scripture as they reacted to their circumstances gives us a vast array of examples to follow. Check in on Joseph's life at any point in Genesis, and things look pretty bleak. But Joseph is the one whose life first embodied the amazing principle we later find in Romans 8:28. Joseph said, "You intended to harm me, but God intended it for good to accomplish what is now being done, the saving of many lives" (Genesis 50:20). His words speak to anyone who can't quite see how God can make good on his promise to bring good things out of bad.

Paul wrote that he'd learned to be content in all things (Philippians 4:12)—and he penned those words while in chains. Peter and John said they couldn't help but speak of Jesus despite the threat of imprisonment if they did (Acts 4:20). It's easy to find parallels to these situations in our lives and to apply the principles their stories teach us.

Applying the Word with Students

No Bible study or discipleship session should end without a to-do, whether it's an internal adjustment or an external action. The simple act of considering the to-do forces us leaders to make sure we're heading somewhere with the study.

Four words that should describe any application of Scripture are *accurate, specific, timely,* and *accountable.*

Accurate

Evaluate your application activities to make sure that they accurately reflect what Scripture is teaching. This may sound like hairsplitting, but it shows God that we're paying attention to detail and that we're more interested in obedience than in our own creativity. It also guarantees a more powerful application. If you sense that an application activity or action is slightly different from what Scripture is teaching but it's still a great activity and something worth doing, just make your students aware.

Specific

Specificity helps students see what the application really looks like in real life. If the passage you've been studying talks about forgiveness, help students put a plan in motion to *forgive* someone. This beats ending on a general adjustment students need to make, such as "We need to be more forgiving." If the study has focused on a key promise from God, brainstorm ways the students can plaster reminders of the promise all over their day-to-day world, such as Post-it notes, screen savers, and text messages.

Timely

Always suggest a timeframe for application, such as before the session is over, within the next 24 hours, or by the time the group meets again.

Accountable

Regularly set up a system or plan to encourage students to hold one another accountable to their application commitments. Use all available technology to make this happen.

Hands-On Study

God, Change Me—Acts 4:1-13

Review your notes on interpreting this passage from the previous chapter. Pay particular attention to your answers to the questions about today's parallel situations and how we can imitate the apostles. Then answer this question: *What do I need to do?*

Application Direction

If we have any hope in imitating the courage and boldness of the apostles, it all comes down to spending time with Jesus and trusting the presence of the Holy Spirit.

Spending Time with Jesus

The best kind of application is specific application. So let's get down to brass tacks. Ask yourself a few questions: *What do I need to change in order to spend courage-generating time with Jesus?* Evaluate the kind of time you spend with Jesus. *Is it quality time? Quantity time? Is it the kind of time in which you gain courage and conviction to beat back those big dogs that are antagonistic to your faith?*

Ask yourself: *How can I improve that time with Jesus? Could I lengthen or intensify my time with him? Add more Bible study? Work in some meditation?*

Make some commitments, such as setting up a daily appointment for the next 10 days. On the 10th day, evaluate your efforts and make plans for the next 10 days.

Trusting the Holy Spirit

Ask yourself: *Do I count on the presence of God's Spirit in my life? Do I trust him to guide me in truth, to remind me of what to say when I'm under pressure, to comfort and reassure me? What*

changes do I need to make to enable the Spirit to be more power-
fully present in my life?

And there you have it. You've spent lingering time with 13 verses of God's Word. You've observed it. Interpreted it. Applied it.

My hope is that you've metabolized truth—and that you'll experience the payoff God guarantees when we diligently seek him in spirit and truth. By now it's also likely that you've gotten a few things out of Acts 4 that you'd love to see your students get. Think about how you might lead your students through the passage in a way that leads to the same "light bulb moments" you've experienced.

And stay tuned. The next few chapters will focus on how to take your students on a similar journey in the Word.

CHAPTER TEN

Teaching the Jesus Way

They asked each other, "Were not our hearts burning within us while he talked with us on the road and opened the Scriptures to us?" LUKE 24:32

"You call me 'Teacher' and 'Lord,' and rightly so, for that is what I am." JOHN 13:13

We've all been there. A gathering of ministry types. Maybe it's a denominational event, a convention, or an annual meeting where you see friends and colleagues you haven't caught up with in a while. You're talking about ministry, and like clockwork, the conversation comes around to the inevitable question.

"How many you running these days?" somebody asks.

Your gut sinks. It's been a flat year, and there's no good number you can enthusiastically share.

Or maybe it's the other way around. You've got kids coming out your ears. You couldn't wait for that question! Breadth is no problem in your student ministry.

But maybe depth is.

How do you think Jesus would have responded to ministry's number one question? Not the same way you or I would, I'll bet.

That's not to say Jesus wasn't concerned about numbers—he was. Jesus was out to save not a few, but *the entire world*. And somebody had to have done the counting the day he fed the 5,000.

But for the most part, Jesus poured his life, time, and resources into 12 people. And over time, after much patience and persistence on his part, that small but mighty group grew to the robust size of...well, 11.

Imagine for a moment how Jesus' ministry might have been different had he spent his time chasing after the goal so many of us are chasing—numeric growth. A Jesus concerned mostly with numbers would have been bent on getting his disciples to like him, hoping no one would want to miss his next teaching session.

We might have overheard the disciples leaving his teaching sessions saying things such as: "He's funny. I'm bringing my friends next time." "I hear we're talking about sex next week." "That was a really good discussion. I like how he let us all talk at once."

But that wasn't the case.

In fact, the disciples often left Jesus' teaching times perplexed and confused. Possibly a little frustrated. Yet somehow they learned enough to keep this strange new faith alive after Jesus' departure. They managed to write (or at least orally convey) the bulk of New Testament truth. And eventually, they succeeded in changing the world.

Through the years I've heard countless talks and read numerous books analyzing Jesus' approach to ministry. He used the latest technology (parables). He used familiar, everyday items for object lessons (bread). He didn't shy away from the extravagant (miracles). He built rapport and nurtured relationships.

I wouldn't argue with any of these points. But if pressed to name the one thing above all others that Jesus set out to accomplish with his disciples, I'd have to base my decision on what the disciples themselves said of him.

They called him Teacher.

Above all else, Jesus taught the disciples. And surprisingly, he wasn't terribly concerned with how they received his teaching. He wasn't out to win their approval. Of course, Jesus had a lot to accomplish with these unschooled, ordinary men—preparing them to launch the church age and all. And he only had three years to do it.

Of course, you and I only have six years at best. And we're *not* Jesus.

As youth workers, you and I aren't preparing disciples to launch the church age. But we *are* preparing teenagers to take the gospel into *their* age, a critically important task for the survival of the church. And while we don't have the advantage of *being* Jesus, we do have the opportunity to be like Jesus in this effort.

You may be thinking, *But I didn't get into youth ministry to teach!* Perhaps not, but don't close your mind to the idea. A wise person once said, "Those who know how to learn know enough to teach." The inductive steps you're learning to master—careful observation, accurate interpretation, and high-impact application—are tools that can turn you into a lifelong learner, one who quests after God. Teaching is nothing more than taking what God teaches *you* and passing it on to someone else.

Let's look at a few of Jesus' prime teaching situations and how they can help us launch and maintain a teaching ministry of our own—one that emulates Jesus' teaching style and keeps students coming back for more.

Jesus Launched with Challenge

"Follow me."

That's all Jesus said—and the disciples' responses were instantaneous.

Was there something especially compelling about Jesus' voice and appearance? Were they sick of the prospect of handling fish—or the "fishy" business of collecting tax money—for the rest of their lives?

Given their family histories and the culture of the day, they most likely were glad to have been picked to follow any teacher. The fact that they were Jewish men involved in their families' businesses means there's a good chance they'd already been passed over as candidates for discipleship. Disciple groups were numerous: Philosophers, sophists, rabbis, Pharisees, zealots, and the like all had disciples.

Disciples would follow the master teacher with the hope that one day they'd be master teachers themselves with disciples following them. It was a track that Jewish boys of their day followed until they were asked to drop out. The next best option was to return to the family business.

What these fishermen and tax collectors heard when Jesus said "Follow me" was "I think you're up for the challenge." And that was enough to make them bite.

You and I can deliver a similar challenge to our students. I believe we instead have been selling our students too short for far too long by appealing to the lowest common denominator in our "deeper teaching" situations.

Fuller Theological Seminary's Center for Youth and Family Ministry has been monitoring the transition of students from our youth ministries to college. Part of this project has involved surveying high school seniors to document their experiences in youth ministry. In a recent survey, 56 percent said they wanted "more" or "much more" Bible study in their youth ministries. That's huge! (Incidentally, only 28 percent said they wanted more games.)[36]

On a more general but equally encouraging note, Christian Smith found that 25 percent of teenagers say they would attend religious services more often if it were left up to them.[37]

Our students are hungrier than we think. What are we doing to take full advantage of that hunger?

The disciples left everything on a simple challenge to follow Jesus, and they changed the world! All we're asking our students for is an hour or two each week. But by creating a similar atmosphere and attitude of challenge, we can expect the same results.

Let's set the bar high. Let's invite students to be a part of something big. Something deep. Something revolutionary—with power to show them things they've never seen, teach them things they've never learned, and change them in ways they've never imagined.

How do you launch students through challenge? Here are some practical points to consider.

Make it voluntary. Avoid the come-one-come-all cattle call. Instead use sign-ups to attract those who are up for it. Invite the hungry, and be sure to communicate to parents that you're looking for kids who *want* to participate—not those who attend out of obligation or a push from parents.

Communicate the challenge. Give your students something to bite into. Don't be afraid of words such as *deep, intense,* and *no games.* Let them know that this may be the most spiritually challenging part of your student ministry—that it may even take them deeper than the adults in your church are going. And then be sure it does.

Keep it manageable. Schedule your Bible studies in set blocks of time, such as six, eight or 10 weeks. This gives your group a definite start and stop date and helps students know what to expect.

Don't be afraid to challenge the few. Let's say only two sign up—and you happen to be one of them. Game on! Lead and disciple the one just as you would 20. Remember the exponential growth from good soil that Jesus promised? (Revisit Chapter 4 and check out Matthew 13:23 and Luke 8:15.) Good soil grows good fruit.

Jesus Taught with Scripture

Soon after Jesus' crucifixion, two disciples were walking to a village called Emmaus, apparently from Jerusalem. Talking a mile a minute about all the events that had just happened, they debated some rumors that Jesus' tomb had been found empty.

While they were engrossed in conversation, a stranger sidled up beside the two. Unbeknownst to them, it was Jesus. He asked the men what they were talking about, which drew a response that was something like, "What cave have you been in? You're the only one in this city who doesn't know about all this!"

(Had Jesus wanted to be a wisecracking Messiah, he'd have had a great comeback for the cave question.) What he did next, though, is striking. Rather than going for the obvious, instant revelation, he taught them.

And it wasn't a cute, little object lesson; it was a full-throttle teaching experience. Jesus started at the beginning with Moses and went through the entire Old Testament, including the prophets—moving through the Scriptures in order to explain the events the disciples were talking about.

Impressed with what they were hearing, the two invited Jesus to eat supper with them. And when he broke the bread, their eyes were opened, and they recognized their new companion as Jesus. At that moment, Jesus was spirited away.

The disciples immediately looked at each other and said the most amazing thing: "Were not our hearts burning within us while he talked with us on the road and opened the Scriptures to us?" (Luke 24:32).

The two disciples could've been wowed by other things. But notice what both of the men lit on: Jesus' teaching and how their hearts had burned when he taught them. It even took precedence over Jesus' miraculous disappearance.

And that's the target we need to shoot for: Bible studies that let Jesus himself do the teaching in a way that causes our students' hearts to burn from within.

Here are some practical points to shape such a study.

Make your time an actual study *of Scripture.* Investigate a book of the Bible (maybe a one-chapter book for starters) or one of God's great themes such as mercy, redemption, grace, and love. Or choose a wild character such as Jacob, Samson, Paul, or Peter. Don't be afraid of teaching about the prophets; Jesus wasn't. Whatever you choose to teach, trust the Scripture to provide the impact. It's all good.

Count on Jesus to sidle up. Throughout the Gospels, we see Jesus explaining the Scriptures. But he didn't stop there. Jesus still comes alongside those whose hearts are tuned to seeking and knowing him. Let's create an atmosphere that proves we trust that he'll show up.

Keep students tuned in to the big picture. Jesus went from beginning to end as he explained the Scriptures to the two disciples. Even as you zero in on the details, look for opportunities to enlarge your students' vision of God's grand redemptive story.

Jesus Taught with Purpose

Teaching wasn't something Jesus did during downtime between miracles. It was one of his primary activities. And more kingdom momentum was generated by Jesus' teaching than by his miracles. His teaching is certainly what led to his crucifixion—and on several occasions the Gospel writers highlighted the fact that it wasn't only signs and wonders that caused people to believe. Jesus left the crowds and his disciples spellbound by the things he taught and the way in which he taught them (Matthew 7:28-29).

Look with me at three situations in which Jesus taught. Notice the details (the *who, what, when, where, why, how,* and even *how much*) in the following verses:

With many similar parables Jesus spoke the word to them, as much as they could understand. He did not say anything to them without using a parable. But when he was alone with his own disciples, he explained everything. (MARK 4:33-34)

When Jesus landed and saw a large crowd, he had compassion on them, because they were like sheep without a shepherd. So he began teaching them many things. (MARK 6:34)

They left that place and passed through Galilee. Jesus did not want anyone to know where they were, because he was teaching his disciples.

(MARK 9:30-31)

Do you see the amazing priority Jesus placed on teaching? In Mark 4 Jesus gave the people all the teaching they could take, speaking the Word until they were filled. Later, he elaborated further with his disciples, providing even more insight when he was alone with them.

I wonder what Jesus was seeing when he gazed out on a crowd described in Mark 6 as "sheep without a shepherd." Was it guilt and regret from past mistakes? Aimless wandering—lives without purpose or direction? People under pressure? Lives without hope for a better day?

In other words, as Jesus scanned the expressions of the crowd, did he pick up on many of the same things you and I see in the faces of students today? Whatever he saw, his solution was teaching. In fact, Jesus taught them *many things.*

The scene that particularly moves me is in Mark 9. Here was the Son of God, with the power to forgive sins on the spot, to heal every disease, to increase food supplies, even to increase party supplies (see John 2). At any moment he could have literally saved the world. Yet at *that* moment he didn't want anyone to know where he was. The reason? He was teaching his disciples. At that moment there was *nothing* more important than teaching. This is what teaching looks like when the learner's *life* depends on what's being taught.

Jesus explained the kingdom of God and what it meant to follow him. Jesus was all about conveying these truths both in public and in disciples-only settings, and he used every means available: Parables, stories, object lessons, spontaneous teachable moments, questions from the people, and at least one lengthy sermon.

But Jesus' method never outshone his message. Even the miraculous feeding of the 5,000 didn't overshadow the teaching that Jesus was the bread of life. In fact, that lesson led to a mass exodus of followers who shuffled off grumbling that his teachings were too difficult to accept. Even supernaturally unlimited food that set the stage for one of the greatest object lessons of all time couldn't keep those folks enticed. Content and learning ruled the day. And it was hard content to take.

Jesus even built teaching into the self-perpetuating cycle of the Great Commission—a fact us ministry-types should never miss. In Matthew 28, he tells his disciples that their job and ours is to make more disciples by *teaching* them to obey all that he has commanded (taught). The Greek word for disciple is *mathetes*, which means "learner." To be a disciple is to learn—and then to produce more learners.

Here are some pointers for making teaching with purpose a reality with your group.

Don't fear the busy schedule. Jesus didn't. Your students' lives depend on the content of God's Word. Your teaching should reflect this in planning, budgeting, and creating your calendar.

Don't fear learning. Learning leads to fascination, which tweaks the appetite for more learning and can cause hardened skeptics to soften to the heart of God.

Don't fear the obvious. Asking inductive questions (who? what? when? where? why? how?) may seem a bit routine when the answers are obvious in Scripture. But obvious questions need to be asked and answered to move your group to the next level of discovery—the deeper dig. (And you never know when a student is seeing this information for the first time.) Feel free to be clear about covering the basics in a passage by saying: "Okay, first some obvious questions." Sometimes God can use the tiniest, most obvious detail in Scripture to speak. Solomon's Porch, an entire movement and a large church in Minneapolis, was built around the obvious questions *Where?* and *What kind of ministry was happening?* in Acts 5.[38]

Don't fear the whiteboard. Seeing information organized in ways other than paragraphs on a Bible page can lead to light bulbs—the kind you figuratively see over a student's head when something finally clicks. The act of recording on a board the group's observations from Scripture places importance on the material. And it immediately involves more senses and utilizes more brain power to process the info, which increases the likelihood that they'll remember the info, which improves the odds of them being *changed* by the info.

Don't let method replace message. The good news is, today we have so much creative media to help us teach Scripture. The bad news is, today we have so much creative media to help us teach Scripture. Whatever methods we use, let's be sure we don't miss the point.

Jesus Taught with Application

As perplexed as the disciples often seem to have been when they listened to Jesus teach, they were surprisingly enthusiastic whenever Jesus asked them to do something. From running crowd control before the feeding of the 5,000 to healing diseases throughout the land, the disciples did whatever Jesus asked them to do. In fact, when asked to make arrangements for the Passover meal that became the Last Supper, they followed Jesus' specific instructions right down to the correct donkey.

Perhaps the most significant example came mid-ministry, when Jesus sent the disciples into the villages to preach God's Kingdom, heal the sick, and cast out demons—basic Messiah kind of stuff. And they did it with amazing effectiveness. So much so that even the ruler, Herod, took note. (Check out Matthew 10, Mark 6, and Luke 9.)

These to-do jaunts kept the disciples acutely aware that whatever Jesus taught them would be put to use. High-octane application (*doing* precisely what they were learning—often in high-stakes situations) became a framework on which to hook all of the truths Jesus was teaching them.

I used to work in admissions for a Christian university and helped hundreds of applicants through the enrollment process each year. By the time each autumn rolled around, I had pretty much locked in the names of all the incoming freshmen. I gained a reputation for being a whiz at remembering names, even long after the students came to campus.

But I'm not really a whiz at remembering anything—ask my wife—let alone a few hundred names. As an admissions rep, I simply operated with the knowledge that when I saw a name, I was probably going to meet this person down the line. I knew I'd need the information, so I made sure it stuck. Amazing what that little fact does for the ability to concentrate and remember.

Any Bible study we undertake must reflect an urgency that what we're learning will be needed and used—a real sense that our lives depend on it. One way to make sure this is accomplished is to give students to-do jaunts as Jesus did, ones that provide opportunities to practice the truths they're learning. This also keeps a challenge in front of our students and regular reminders that we know they're up to the task.

Here are some ways to flesh out this principle with your group.

Alternate between being and doing. Study a Bible chapter one week (the being) and do what it says the next (the doing).

Finish the study with a project. Line up a service project or missions experience that coincides with the theme of a study series. For example, to top off a study of the book of James, plan some visits to and establish a relationship with a local retirement center to allow your group to minister to "widows in their distress" (James 1:27).

Pre-missions prep. Make preparation for your next missions trip more than a "tools and towels" orientation. Commit to study a Bible book or theme that will awaken your students' hearts to people in need and prepare them for the physical and spiritual challenge of the experience.

Do the everyday. God will provide to-do jaunts every day for you and your students. Keep your eyes peeled, and you'll see plenty of opportunities to apply what you're teaching and learning with uncanny specificity.

Jesus Taught with Patience

On more than one biblical occasion we see Jesus exhibiting some very human exasperation at the disciples' inability to get it. I have to applaud the Gospel writers—especially two of the Twelve, Matthew and John—for including these self-incriminating scenes.

What they didn't show us and what we can easily imagine is Jesus walking to a solitary place to talk with his Father and praying, "God, surely there are some others I can work with!"

What each glimpse of Jesus' exasperation does show us is his unlimited patience. He willingly gave further explanation many times when the disciples asked for it. One of Jesus' most animated expressions of frustration came when Peter asked him to explain a parable he'd used to describe the Pharisees and what makes a person unclean (Matthew 15). You can almost hear Jesus saying, "Peter, are you *trying* to not understand?" But then he graciously explained the parable. We see such patience time after time in the Gospels.

I'd be misleading you if I didn't tell you that your patience will be tested with any group of teenagers you lead in a Bible study. At times you'll wonder if you're doing any good. At times your students will get frustrated or confused. Some may drop out. When this happens, go back to Jesus. Look again at his patience and reflect on how motivated he was to make sure his disciples got it. This same motivation can help you persevere through the trying moments.

Make room for your students' busyness. Students are busy, and they may not grasp the importance of Bible study as you do. Encourage them to make a priority of time in God's Word by showing them your own enthusiasm for the Bible—not by guilt-tripping them into it.

Give yourself and your students some space for "Are you so dull?" Students learn in different ways and at varying paces. Hang in there when some seem to get it and some don't.

Monitor for glaze-over. As we saw in Mark 4:33, Jesus taught the people "as much as they could understand." You may hit a similar point with your students. Stay sensitive to this possibility and feel free to slow down or take a break.

Jesus Taught for Payoff

After one of Jesus' harder teachings—the one about eating his flesh in John 6—his followers began rapidly dropping off. (Admit it: That lesson would be hard to take if you weren't expecting it.) A day that had begun with an energetic crowd of thousands hanging on Jesus' every word ended with him and only the Twelve.

Giving them an out, Jesus asked if those disciples wanted to leave, too. Speaking for the group, Peter said, in not so many words, "Nope. You had us at eternal life."

At that moment the disciples were in touch with the great personal payoff for sticking close to Jesus. It was worth not having a home, facing an uncertain future, and crossing the local religious authorities. These guys were *staying.*

Nobody said following Jesus would be easy. And nobody said getting steeped in the Word would be as much fun as, say, an all-you-can-eat pizza party. But the payoff is much greater. And hey, you can always have the pizza party, too.

Keep the idea of personal payoff front-and-center in their minds as you study the Bible with students. By infusing God's Word into their lives, your students will gain the ability to see through Satan's deception and acquire the ammunition they need to fight and win over temptation (Luke 4:1-13). They'll discover the knowledge of God and begin to discern his will for their lives (Proverbs 2). They'll be cultivating their hearts as familiar places for Jesus to dwell (John 15). They'll be continually reminded of their future rewards in heaven and of eternal life with Christ.

Adverse effects such as tiredness, busyness, and the sense of difficulty have the potential to knock your students out of the game—just as they did Jesus' followers in John 6. You can protect them from life-scarring mistakes and help position them to be powerfully used by God by reminding them of the rewards from pursuing Christ.

Here's how to do so practically.

Eternal payoff. Keep heaven in front of your students. Heaven doesn't get enough airtime in youth ministry today.

Temporal payoff. Keep a party in front of your students. Have one when you finish a study. Choose a theme around what the students have seen in the Bible. And don't forget the all-you-can-eat pizza.

One of the best ways we can emulate the ministry of Jesus is to teach. It's what Jesus spent the majority of his time doing. It's also relatively easy for us to duplicate (easier than, say, healing our students' diseases or multiplying what food they have on hand).

What if teaching and learning formed the hub of our student ministries, and everything else—worship, outreach, missions—emanated from that hub?

Take another look at the Gospels and see if this approach isn't Jesus' way of doing ministry.

CHAPTER ELEVEN

The Equipping Trifecta

The morning sun's a new husband

    leaping from his honeymoon bed,

The daybreaking sun an athlete

    racing to the tape.

That's how God's Word vaults across the skies

    from sunrise to sunset,

Melting ice, scorching deserts,

    warming hearts to faith.

PSALM 19:5-6 • *THE MESSAGE*

After wrestling with Greek for two years in seminary, I had to wonder: If God is a loving God, why did he send his Son at a time when the dominant world language was Greek? Why not wait until something easier came along such as, say, pig Latin?

But God knew what he was doing. (And for the record, he *is* a loving God.)

Many have made a case that the Greek language of Jesus' day contained unique words and word pictures found in no other language, before or since. This alone can cause us to wonder whether the language played a providential role in God's timing for bringing Jesus to earth when he did.

The fact that the ancient Greeks had several words for love, each providing a unique and vital nuance, seems far from coincidental.

Consider *agape*. This love is God's dominant trait and his great motivation for pursuing a relationship with us. Many Greek words have been popularized in Christian circles because their nuances are richer than their English counterparts.

When you read *agape* in the previous paragraph, you immediately understood that I was talking about a sacrificial, unconditional, Christlike form of love—something worlds apart from sexual love, brotherly love, or a love for chips and salsa.

And when you hear someone talk about *koinonia*, you most likely know the kind of fellowship they mean—not a potluck dinner, but an entering in and carrying of one another's burdens.

In each of these examples the Greek language helps us form a fuller, more complete picture of a key element in God's redemptive story.

Katartizo

Believe it or not, the Greeks also gave us a word that paints a richer, fuller picture of Bible study. But it's a lesser-known word that lacks the evocative linguistic flow of *koinonia*. In fact, it sounds pretty stodgy and abrupt.

The word is *katartizo* (pronounced kah-tar-TEED-zo), and it's typically translated *to equip*. I doubt you've ever heard a sermon or talk on *katartizo*. And my guess is that when you saw the word *equip*, your mind went to *training*: uploading tools into a student so she may share or defend her faith. Teaching our leaders to...well, teach and lead.

A well-used (even overused) word in the church, *equipping* has become a utilitarian, lifeless concept for most of us. But like so many of God's best words and concepts that through centuries have lost their zing, *katartizo*-equipping means something more than we might think. Something supernatural. Something powerful. Something with unparalleled rewards.

A Little Background

In the secular Greek world, *katartizo* was a practical word. How practical? Here's a list of the many disciplines to which the Greeks applied it:

- In architecture *katartizo* meant to *restore* the walls of a city or a sanctuary.

- In hospitality the master of a house might practice *katartizo* by preparing a comfortable room that was *perfectly suited* for an honored guest.

- In sewing *katartizo* described a garment being made *ready to wear* by assembling pieces of fabric.

- In cooking *katartizo* conveyed that a meal was deemed *ready to eat*.

- In pharmacology a potion was considered *perfect* (a form of, you guessed it, *katartizo*) once it had healed a sick person.

- In medicine *katartizo* referred to *setting a broken bone*—restoring it to function, making it ready for use.

- In naval usage sailors used *katartizo* to describe outfitting a boat or preparing a fleet to set sail into battle.

- In fishing *katartizo* was the word of choice when *mending* a broken net.

- In accounting *katartizo* referred to the *preparation* of a payment.

- In education *katartizo* referred to a teacher *preparing* a child for adult life.

- In politics the word meant to *restore* opposing factions, to bring them to unity.[39]

Did you spot a common thread? Each use of *katartizo* conveys the idea of thorough preparation. In fact, you'll sometimes see this word rendered in Scripture as *complete* or *perfect*—not in a theological sense (as with the Greek word *telios*, which refers to a completeness of moral character or spiritual maturity), but in the sense of being completely prepared. Thoroughly equipped. Ready to go.

When New Testament writers such as Paul were rummaging around for a word to convey complete preparation in a spiritual sense, they appear to have made an intentional reach for *katartizo*. Scholars claim that the New Testament contains the first writings to apply this word to spiritual matters, moving it out of the practical and into the supernatural realm.

Fifteen of the 19 New Testament uses of *katartizo* are spiritual in nature and apply this word to personal faith or the church. The other four are practical or secular in nature, including that in Mark 1:19: Jesus sees James and John *preparing* their nets for a successful day of fishing.

So what was God trying to get across to us when he flashed this word across the minds of the Spirit-inspired writers?

Rather than me explaining what I've discovered about *katartizo*, we'll discover it together in the spirit of inductive study.

And here's a heads-up: This exercise will give you good practice on a word study in Scripture. And the finished product will provide a model for equipping that can be implemented in any student ministry.

God, Show Me

The three instances in which *katartizo* is translated *equip* in most English versions of the New Testament are Hebrews 13:21, 2 Timothy 3:17, and Ephesians 4:12. Read these passages that follow and ask *God, show me*. Each time you see a form of the word *equip*, mark it with a word burst. Then look around the word and note who or what equips, who is equipped, and the results of the equipping.

Take a moment to write the info in the chart following each Scripture passage.

> [20]May the God of peace, who through the blood of the eternal covenant brought back from the dead our Lord Jesus, that great Shepherd of the sheep, [21]equip you with everything good for doing his will, and may he work in us what is pleasing to him, through Jesus Christ, to whom be glory for ever and ever. Amen. (HEBREWS 13:20-21)

WHO/WHAT EQUIPS?	WHO IS EQUIPPED?	WHAT'S THE RESULT?

> [14]But as for you, continue in what you have learned and have become convinced of, because you know those from whom you learned it, [15]and how from infancy you have known the holy Scriptures, which are able to make you wise for salvation through faith in Christ Jesus. [16]All Scripture is God-breathed and is useful for teaching, rebuking, correcting and training in righteousness, [17]so that the man of God may be thoroughly equipped for every good work. (2 TIMOTHY 3:14-17)

[7]But to each one of us grace has been given as Christ apportioned it. [8]This is why it says: "When he ascended on high, he took many captives and gave gifts to his people." [9](What does "he ascended" mean except that he also descended to the lower, earthly regions? [10]He who descended is the very one who ascended higher than all the heavens, in order to fill the whole universe.) [11]So Christ himself gave the apostles, the prophets, the evangelists, the pastors and teachers, [12]to equip his people for works of service, so that the body of Christ may be built up [13]until we all reach unity in the faith and in the knowledge of the Son of God and become mature, attaining to the whole measure of the fullness of Christ.

[14]Then we will no longer be infants, tossed back and forth by the waves, and blown here and there by every wind of teaching and by the cunning and craftiness of people in their deceitful scheming. [15]Instead, speaking the truth in love, we will in all things grow up into him who is the head, that is, Christ. [16]From him the whole body, joined and held together by every supporting ligament, grows and builds itself up in love, as each part does its work.

THE EQUIPPING TRIFECTA

155

WHO/WHAT EQUIPS?	WHO IS EQUIPPED?	WHAT'S THE RESULT?

God, Teach Me

Meditate on the info you jotted in the charts. Reread the passages if necessary to make sure you've noticed the details. Ask God to teach you about the passages and use the following questions as prompts. What do you notice about who or what is doing the equipping? Do you spot any significant trends? What do you notice about who is being equipped? What do you notice about the results? Journal your thoughts or reactions.

In each of these three Scripture passages, we see a divine agent equipping. In Hebrews 13 God through Jesus equips. In 2 Timothy 3 the Word of God equips. In Ephesians 4 it's gifted leaders using gifts given by Jesus to equip.

God Equips

This simple truth is as easy to lose as spare change in the couch cushions. It's unfortunate because this little truth could save a lot of believers an enormous amount of worry and wasted effort. God himself can equip us. And did you catch why? To do his will.

Had I not lost this truth in the couch cushions of my young adult years, I might have saved myself a lot of money by not buying books with *finding God's will for your life* in the title. God has been ready from the get-go to help me know and do his will.

But *when* and *how* does God equip us? If we can figure out the *when*—as in, when in our frenetic schedules we give God a chance—God will take care of the *how*.

One of my favorite personalities in Scripture is Asaph, a Levite musician and the author of several psalms. Asaph opens Psalm 73 lamenting the fact that he's kept himself pure for nothing. The wicked—lazy slackers who haven't kept themselves pure at all—have no worries or cares. And they're having an awful lot of fun. Asaph is jealous to the point of wanting to throw in the towel and walk away from God.

Until Asaph enters the sanctuary of God. And in a burst of spiritual epiphany, he sees through the deception that's about to destroy him. He begins his psalm poised to cross over to the dark side, wanting nothing more to do with God, but he closes the psalm wanting *everything* to do with God. What made the difference?

Time in the sanctuary.

What's that all about? As a Levite during the reign of King David charged with ministering before the Ark of the Covenant, Asaph was in and out of God's sanctuary all the time—possibly even daily. Yet his spiritual zeal had been whittled down to nothing. Asaph was on the verge of checking out.

I know the feeling. It's a lot like getting up early on Sunday morning, setting out for church, frantically reviewing all I need to do—and passing neighbors retrieving the morning paper while still in their fuzzy slippers. Or seeing golfers teeing up on the golf course.

Must be nice, I've often thought.

But something happened on one particular occasion when Asaph was in and out of the sanctuary. Something powerful and unexpected.

Asaph became unmistakably aware of God's presence. And it changed him. What's more, it equipped him to beat back the temptation that was about to do him in.

That's what happens when we let God to do the equipping. We experience God. And suddenly somehow we find that we're able to know and do God's will. Our job is to find the sanctuary time. God will take it from there.

In ministering to students our job is to *provide* the sanctuary time—and trust God to do the equipping.

God's Word Equips

The fact that God's Word equips is what stirred me to write this book, and it may be what led you to pick it up. I hope that it will be a good first step toward seeing *how*—and that it will encourage you to find the *when*.

Second Timothy 3:16-17 offers a great glimpse of what God's Word can do to equip us: Teach. Rebuke. Correct. Train in righteousness. Not coincidentally, these are the very things you and I hope to accomplish in youth ministry. But Scripture can do it so much better than we can. And Scripture does it without manipulation or guilt. Scripture cuts right down to the joints and marrow (Hebrews 4:12).

The result? Every youth worker's dream: Students are equipped for good works.

That sounds as if students are fulfilling God's call on their lives. And that sounds as if a student ministry is vibrant.

One of the first steps we can take toward experiencing the equipping that can come from God's Word is this: *Let the Scripture teach.* Trust the fact that God is far more interested in using his Word to transform our students than one of our riveting stories or poignant illustrations.

Scripture is powerful on its own. In fact, it's probably best this way.

Consider one of Israel's most decisive victories when they annihilated the city of Ai. The battle had all the elements of an action thriller: Cunning, ambush, split-second timing, a communication blackout, total soldier-to-soldier dependence, and absolute, utter victory.

After the dust settled (literally) Joshua pulled together all of Israel for a victory party. The scene was like a locker room after a critical, clutch win. There were high fives to slap, stories to tell, necks to hug. When Joshua stood to address the crowd, he could have sounded like a football coach at a press conference after a Super Bowl win—doling out props and giving shout-outs to the ambushers whose impeccable timing had won the day.

But that's not what he did. After everyone had assembled, Joshua read from the Book of the Law. Every word (Joshua 8:34-35).

At the height of all the revelry, Joshua let the Scripture teach. As the people heard the words of God—specifically the blessings and curses he'd laid out for their obedience and disobedience—they saw that their magnificent victory should come as no surprise. If they obeyed, God would always deliver them. While Israel was poised for an end-zone celebration, Joshua was saying, "Act like you've been there before. And by all means, live in obedience so you can be there again."

But he let the Scriptures say it.

Gifted Leaders Equip

Here's where you, the youth worker, enter the equipping trifecta.

I sometimes suspect that the best thing gifted leaders can do to ignite real *katartizo*-equipping is to get out of the way and let the other two elements—God and his Word—take over. But

God has a special role for the gifted leader. Ephesians 4:7-16 revealed a list of results that students can experience when Spirit-gifted leaders are maximizing their gifts. If that doesn't wow you, let the Word metabolize a little more. I guarantee it will.

You may be wondering, *Am I one of these gifted leaders? Do I qualify for one of the five spiritual gifts Paul clicked off in Ephesians 4?*

Here's what we know: Spiritual gifts are supernatural abilities given by the Holy Spirit to believers in Christ (1 Corinthians 12:7). Every believer has at least one spiritual gift—and I promise you're not the lone exception, no matter how *ungifted* you may feel on a particular day.

An inductive study of three major passages will give you a broad overview of the kaleidoscope of richly varied spiritual gifts mentioned in the New Testament: 1 Corinthians 12, Ephesians 4, and Romans 12. If you've never identified your God-given spiritual gift (or gifts)—or if you question whether spiritual gifts are valid in our era—I strongly recommend doing your own personal digging in these power-packed chapters. Few things in life (dare I say *nothing* in life) are more rewarding than discovering how God has uniquely called, gifted, and equipped *you* for the good works he prepared in advance for you and you alone to do (Ephesians 2:10).

In the meantime here are a few thoughts on the specific gifts you observed in Ephesians 4. The five gifts mentioned there—apostleship, prophecy, evangelism, pastoring, and teaching—share an important common denominator. They each involve communication—speaking, if you will. This is why such gifts are sometimes known as speaking gifts.[40]

If you're involved in leading youth, chances are you have a speaking gift—perhaps even one of the leadership gifts mentioned in Ephesians 4.[41] Communication is a key part of youth ministry, whether you're the out-front person giving talks and leading worship or a volunteer who mentors kids one-on-one.

Communicating is communicating, whether your audience is a hundred kids or a handful.

Let's break it down a little more. Evidence that the Spirit has gifted you to speak on his behalf has little to do with whether or not you like to hear yourself speak, whether you love or hate to be the front person, or whether crowds of teenagers believe you're good. Gifted communication can happen in phone conversations, on the sideline at a soccer game, or in a home Bible study. Don't limit the ways in which God may use your mouth to communicate his truth.

If, after you've searched Scripture and talked it out with God, you honestly don't think he has gifted you to lead teenagers in a Bible study, then consider this: Maybe, just maybe, you're not the one to champion this effort.

Perhaps there's a volunteer or staff person in or around your student ministry who has a heart for God's Word and a love for kids. He or she may be one of the Spirit-gifted teacher-disciplers who can help bring about Ephesians 4 results in your student ministry. Turn those people loose on the task.

God, Change Me

Back to our study of *katartizo*-style equipping. Based on what we've seen in Scripture, the final question to ask is, "What do I need to do now?"

Picture your student ministry calendar. (Really do it. I'll wait!)

As you scan your discipleship efforts, how do they compare with the many uses of *katartizo* noted earlier? (By the way, I strongly suggest that you journal your responses to application questions such as these. It works for me, and I'm willing to bet it'll work for you, too.)

As you envision your ministry calendar, do you see an opportunity for God to do the equipping?

As you evaluate the various teaching times you have going, are you trusting God's Word to do the teaching? Picture some techniques or illustrations you might typically use to get your point across. Where does God's Word rank compared to those tools?

Think about your gifted leaders, the people who are spearheading these efforts. Are they enthused about God's Word, and do they have a heart to see students get it? Are they the gifted leaders to whom God has entrusted this ministry?

A Model for Discipleship

Let's get hyper-practical for a moment. Picture spending an hour with your students, studying a Bible passage in this way: As the gifted leader, you've spent time studying the passage yourself, asking God to show you what he wants you to see and teach you what he wants you to learn. You've committed to change, and you've made several adjustments to what God has taught you. You've even had a few *Oh, wow!* moments along the way.

Now it's time to lead your students. But instead of *telling* them what God has taught you, you let them discover it for themselves. You allow them to experience the benefit of God showing them firsthand.

Because you've done some preparation, you have a good idea how to guide them and prompt them to look for a few keys to unlock the passage, much as it came unlocked for you.

Because God speaks softly and personally to each heart, you include a little solitude, some space for each student to get alone with God and the passage. This guarantees that they'll have at least a few minutes when they're not listening to you, their friends, or anything else that's happening at the moment. It also allows God and his Word to enter directly and powerfully into the equipping experience.

After a few minutes, you get the group back together to process in community what the students experienced individually.

As the gifted leader, you have a feel for how to guide the discussion. You know when to give latitude as students think out loud about the passage. And you know when to reel them in when the discussion goes off course so that no one misses out on God's intended application of his Word.

Fully Prepared and Ready to Roll

Don't lose track of what *katartizo*-equipping does: *Makes thoroughly prepared, with no deficiencies.*

My favorite use of this word in Greek literature is the image of preparing a ship for battle—not just making it seaworthy (read *unsinkable*), but equipping it with all the offensive and defensive weaponry needed.

Isn't that what you and I are seeking to do with our students?

It's more than training. It's more than a discipleship program. Hebrews, 2 Timothy, and Ephesians suggest that it happens in the realm of the supernatural—when students personally experience God and his Word under the guidance of Spirit-called and Spirit-gifted leaders.

Unleash this Equipping Trifecta in your student ministry, and you'll begin to see more of what God promised in those passages.

Honestly, what more do we want than what God guarantees?

Answer that question, and your students' lives will never be the same.

KATARTIZO SIGHTINGS IN SCRIPTURE

We've looked together at three instances of *katartizo* in Scripture. Want a more complete picture? *Katartizo* is rendered to *equip* in Hebrews 13:21, 2 Timothy 3:17, and Ephesians 4:12. In the following Bible passages, translators rendered *katartizo* several different ways as noted. (All are from the TNIV translation.)

As you read each verse from your Bible, look for who equips, who is equipped, and what the results are. Make special note of the spiritual agent involved in the process:

1 Corinthians 1:10 *(perfectly united)*

2 Corinthians 9:5 *(be ready)*

2 Corinthians 13:9 *(fully restored)*

2 Corinthians 13:11 *(restoration)*

Galatians 6:1 *(restore)*

1 Thessalonians 3:10 *(supply what is lacking)*

Hebrews 11:3 *(formed)*

CHAPTER TWELVE

Feeding Frenzy

Then he said to me, "Son of man, eat this scroll I am giving you and fill your stomach with it." So I ate it, and it tasted as sweet as honey in my mouth. EZEKIEL 3:3

When my mom was a teenager, she once was given the responsibility of feeding the family canary. I say *once* because under her care the canary went straight to canary heaven.

Mom was diligent to check the bird's food tray every day. And every time she checked, the tray was full. *This is easy*, she thought. The bird hardly ever needed a refill.

What she didn't know is that after birdseed is eaten, it leaves a shell that *looks* like seed. The canary died of starvation. It had a tray of shells, but no food.

Is It Food?

As youth leaders, we may have Bible study listed on the calendar. But is our study the food students need, or is it a shell? Maybe it keeps kids engaged for an hour or so, but is it providing the substance? And is the food we're putting on the table being metabolized?

Metabolism is a process necessary to sustain life. We can have all the nutritional food in the world in front of us, but if we don't open our mouths and eat, we won't live. And even eating the food isn't enough. It must be metabolized—broken down and absorbed on a molecular level.

Our students can rub shoulders with the things of God at church and at home. They can be deeply involved in Christian activities. They can have Bibles all around them. They may even actively participate in a Bible study.

But if there isn't an uptake of God's Word into their spiritual bloodstream, it's as if they're picking at a tray of empty shells.

In this chapter we'll get down to the molecular level of helping students metabolize God's Word—making sure we're giving them Bible experiences with a high probability of uptake, not Bible studies in name only.

We'll look at some practical ways to implement points from the previous chapters, and we'll address some broader issues related to launching and sustaining a feeding frenzy on God's Word. Finally, we'll use our work in Acts 4 (see Chapters 7-9) to create a sample small-group Bible study we can test with our students.

Choose the Setting

Every aspect of your student ministry can benefit from increased intentionality with God's Word. Worship can deepen. One-on-one discipleship can become more purposeful. Leader talks and sermons can become more incisive and effective.

But the most natural gateway for bringing Bible study into a student ministry is the small-group setting. The way I see it, there's not a better place for students to metabolize the Word. Small-group intimacy encourages sharing. The relaxed format invites more lingering with Scripture. And meeting with the ones who've chosen to be part of a small group communicates a sense of seriousness and challenge.

So as we address a few issues key to launching and sustaining an effective ministry of the Word, let's use the small-group setting as our launch pad. As you'll soon see, it won't be a huge leap to take this information into other settings, such as one-to-one discipleship, Sunday school, worship gatherings, missions-trip preparation, and other venues.

Enlist a Prayer Team

Before you take a step toward moving students and Bible study into the same sentence (let alone the same room), before you create a sign-up sheet, or make your first announcement—recruit a team to pray for this effort.

Ask your partners to pray that the hungry students will participate. Once your study has begun, ask them to pray for each student by name throughout the course of the study. (Be sure to send them a roster of names.) Some of your prayer partners may be available to pray at the same time your group meets.

As you saw in Chapter 11, the results you're looking for are supernatural. Prayer is the catalyst for inviting and releasing the Spirit of God to illuminate his Word.

Voluntary Sign-Ups, Location, and Time

The best way to attract students who are hungry is to offer your study at a place and time that encourages voluntary attendance. Doing so communicates to students (and to their parents) that this time is for those who are curious or wanting to deepen their faith—which then gives you permission to go deep.

Meeting at a home is ideal. But if that's not practical, use a church or other location that's comfortable and conducive to lingering with Scripture.

When a senior high group outgrew our living room, one of our best Bible study locations was the small chapel of our church. The youth room felt too lounge-y. The Sunday school rooms felt too much like school. But the chapel was ideal, with its intimate lighting and carpeted floor. The students spread out their stuff and got comfortable on the floor. And on the rare occasions when searching the Word morphed into worship, that little sanctuary became the kind of sanctuary Asaph described in Psalm 73—a place where students could experience the presence of God.

Opening the Session

Once your students have gathered, it's always good to ease into study with an exercise that coalesces the group and gets their minds and hearts ready to focus on God's Word. It can be something as simple as "What was your high point today?" (Or your low point?) Or you could lead with a question that will be answered in the study: "What does God think about anger? Is it a good or a bad thing?" If they say it's bad, you can follow up with "Is there ever a time when it's right to be angry?"

If the makeup of your group calls for an icebreaker activity or game, feel free to use one. It doesn't have to be tied into the subject of the study, just something quick to call your students together.

WALL-SIZED SCRIPTURE

If turning your kids loose to search the Word in solitude sounds like a recipe for disaster, have them work as a group to find and mark the info in Scripture.

Go to any quick-print shop and have your Scripture sheets turned into *gigantic* printouts that can be taped to the wall and marked with markers. Or you can make your own wall-sized Scriptures using a marker and newsprint or poster board.

Ask volunteers to draw symbols over words and phrases on the gigantic Scripture sheets. (This works great with middle school students, by the way.) If you're studying the same passage for several weeks, it's cool to reuse the same sheets from week to week.

A variation on this technique is to project the Scripture onto the wall. Students can highlight words from a computer keyboard or with a laser pointer. Or if you project the image onto a writable surface, such as a giant whiteboard or a bedsheet, students can mark directly on that.

Transitioning into Study

After a minute or two, you'll want to introduce the subject matter. You can use a short video from a Christian band, a clip from a movie that introduces the topic, or a quick brainstorm discussion with questions such as: *What do you know about the book of Acts? Who wrote it? What's it about? Put yourself in the shoes of the apostles soon after Jesus' resurrection. What do you think those days were like?*

The Scripture Experience

God, Show Me

Think of the Scripture experience as the backbone of your time together. Nothing is more important than giving your students ample time for firsthand interaction with the Bible.

In Chapter 7 we suggested several tools to help you and your students dig deeper—tools such as using symbols to mark the *who, what, when, where, why* and *how* in the passage (the five Ws and the *H*), marking repeated words and phrases, and finding any promises or commands.

You'll recall that the purpose of these tools is to help you and your students accurately observe what Scripture is saying. Without accurate observation (God, show me), you'll find that your discussion consists mostly of opinions ("I think..."), info the students have picked up from other sources ("I heard that..."), and even made-up stuff (the last thing you want to hear in a Bible study).

The time-tested tools of inductive study have had great impact with Bible students of all ages. But like most things in youth ministry, the tools can be tweaked for your particular group or setting.

1. Scripture Sheets: Each student will need a copy of the Bible book or chapter the group is studying. The best way to make sure everyone has the same translation (and to keep some parents from blowing a gasket when the kids come home with marked up Bibles) is to give each student a printout of Scripture.

   If your group is studying a short book such as Colossians, you can copy the entire book from Bible software or a Web site such as www.biblegateway.com and paste it into a word processing document. If you're working with a longer book, hand out one chapter a week. Format these Scripture sheets with wide margins and lots of space for marking and making notes. Give each student a three-ring notebook to keep these in. When they've finished the study, they'll have their own personal record of how God spoke to them in the study.

2. Finding and Marking: Buy a few sets of colored pencils, and keep them around for every study session. Each student will need two or three colors to mark whatever words or facts you tell them to look for.

   So what should you tell them to look for? Because you, the leader, have spent time with the passage, you'll have a few ideas. If the chapter focuses on Abraham, you could have them find and mark every mention of Abraham, tracking everything he said and did in the passage.

   If it deals mostly with a concept, such as how we should use our tongues (James 3), you could have them draw a set of lips on all the mouth-related words, such as *mouth, tongue, praise,* and *cursing.*

   If the passage is packed with if-then commands and promises, ask your students to find and mark first the commands (maybe with a megaphone), then the promises (perhaps with a rainbow).

   This isn't rocket science. Just have your students look for a few things that caught your attention and helped you unpack the passage. If your group consists of good readers or older students, you can give them several things to look for.

   Don't be afraid to make it challenging. And don't hesitate to ask students to read the passage more than once and look for what they might have missed. Remember love-letter intensity in Chapter 6? It's hard to go after God's Word with intensity in just one pass.

3. Solitude: Obviously, reading with love-letter intensity isn't a group activity. During the course of each session, give students a few minutes of quiet for a personal mini-

retreat with God. After you've told them what to look for, ask them to take their Scripture printouts and colored pencils and find a place alone with God.

If you're meeting at the church or in a home, this might mean going to a quiet corner, a hallway, an empty room, or even under a tree outside. If you're working in a small space, these options may not be practical; simply give the students some time to experience Scripture on their own while gathered with the group.

God, Teach Me

After the students have had a few minutes to experience a Bible passage on their own, call them back together to process it as a group.

As the discussion leader, your job is to let the Scripture do the teaching. How? By asking questions that prompt your students to look again at what they've marked and to keep observing the passage until they've pulled out most of the pertinent details. Your best allies in this process will be your old buddies the five Ws and the H.

As you guide your group through the passage, your questions should be similar to these:

Who did you see in the passage?

What was he doing?

Where was he doing it?

Why was he doing it?

How did the people respond?

What happened as a result?

Sometimes the answers will be obvious. Sometimes the group will be forced to take a second look and be surprised at what they see. Sometimes they'll see a thing or two that even you missed.

Here's an important tip: Encourage your students to pull their answers out of Scripture, not from off the tops of their heads. You can help by limiting the number of questions that can't be answered from the passage.

For example, *What does this mean to you?* will draw a lot of opinions. *What do you think Jesus did when he was a child?* will call for a made-up answer. A better *what* question might be *What do you see?* or *What action is taking place here?*

The purpose of the *God, show me* and *God, teach me* phases of study is to get to the heart of what God is saying—not at opinions or what we *think* God is saying. Scripture will teach if you, the leader, keep pointing the group back to what it says.

INTERACTIVE OPTIONS

If you think of a more creative way to help your students experience the key points in a passage, don't hesitate to use it. This can help break the routine from session to session.

Recently our students were studying Jesus as "the light" in the book of John. Because the verses were full of words such as *light* and *dark*, the leaders cut out squares of white paper to represent light, black paper to represent dark, and gray paper for in between.

As someone read the passage aloud, students grabbed a white square each time the word *light* was read, a black square each time *dark* or *darkness* was read, and a gray square each time something in between was read.

This gave us a great, hands-on way of emphasizing two key words in John—and the students immediately caught on to the stark contrast between darkness and light. They also noticed that there were no gray squares collected, a great illustration that there's no in between in following Christ.

A youth pastor friend of mine likes to do impromptu theater with Scripture. He assigns parts and has students mime the scene, or read the parts if there's dialogue, as a narrator reads the passage. This brings the action of a passage off the printed page and helps students hear and visualize what's important.

1. Writing It Down: I'm an admitted whiteboard junkie. Forget carving it in stone. For me, it's not a real point until it's been scrawled on a board (often illegibly) with a funky-smelling marker.

   You don't have to get that obsessed. But using a whiteboard to track the discussion and organize key points will help draw your group's attention to the right information—the info you want them to retain and apply.

Keep a whiteboard handy and use it liberally even if you meet in a home. (If writing on a board feels too much like school, see the sidebar "Creative Lists.") And here's a bonus: At the end of the session, let your students take a picture of the board with their camera phones and use it as a memory device by making it the wallpaper on their computers or cell phones.

2. Cross-Referencing: Remember the *Three Asks* of accurate interpretation? Ask God. Ask Scripture. Ask others. (If not, see Chapter 8.)

The *asks* come into play when the Bible passage your group is studying raises more questions than it answers. Prayer covers the first *ask*. Working in community to analyze and discuss the passage covers the third.

But let's park on that second *ask*: Ask Scripture. Having studied the passage beforehand, you'll have found a few key cross-references that explain or shed further light on the questions or principles raised in the passage. You could provide printouts of these verses for your students to mark—or you could have students look them up in their Bibles. You make the call.

I typically like to have kids use their own Bibles. Printouts are great, but every opportunity to get students actually *using* their Bibles is another step toward teaching them "how to work one of these things." I suggest including at least one hands-on, look-it-up exercise in almost every study session.

3. Tangents: Teenagers discussing the Bible remind me of the old Yogi Berra line, "When they see a fork in the road, they'll take it." Every time you and your students open the Word together, you'll come upon plenty of forks—weird, obscure, even fascinating tangents that can quickly unravel a discussion and take it miles from the main point. Scripture is loaded with interesting

stuff—and good Bible study stimulates the mind. It's no wonder students' wheels start turning on questions and truths that weren't in your lesson plan. Here's a good rule of thumb for dealing with a tangent: Acknowledge it. Even spend a minute or two discussing it. Just don't let discussing a tangent eat into your precious Bible time. Keep the main thing the main thing. For example, studying Genesis 1 might raise a loosely related question such as "Why didn't God mention dinosaurs in Genesis 1?" That might lead to "Were dinosaurs around at creation? If so, where did they go?" Questions like these can generate a lot of speculation, and you won't find the answers in Genesis 1. If a tangent is worthy of further discussion, suggest going to Starbucks afterward and kicking it around. If it's a question that requires more study in Scripture, add a session or two to your series to pursue it. Or simply collect your students' questions, especially the theological ones, as you go. (You could keep another whiteboard handy for this.) Watch how God provides answers to many of these questions as you keep searching the Word together.

Tangents can also be great indicators of what's going on in the minds of your students and how God is working in their lives. If the Spirit moves you to go with the tangent, feel free to shelve your plan temporarily. You can always come back to it next week.

God, Change Me

Spend the last few minutes of every session discussing ways to apply the main truths the students have uncovered. Application works both individually and as a group.

Give the students an opportunity to make their own personal commitments. Have them share their personal applications if there's a high level of trust in the group. Then as a group identify ways your students can work together to live out specific instructions and truths.

1. Accountability: In-depth Bible study is convicting. Your students (and you) will make many commitments over the course of a study. Help one another keep these commitments by devising an accountability plan.

   For example, at the close of each session you might create a text message students can send one another as a reminder to do what they've learned or schedule a midweek check-in, either at a fast-food restaurant or online.

2. Takeaways: At the end of each session, give students a chance to boil the entire session down to one or two points—the takeaway from that hour in God's Word. Use a few of the following questions to get them thinking:

   What from this Scripture do you never want to forget?

   What surprised you?

   What new truth about God did you learn today?

   What challenged or convicted you?

   What do you want to know more about?

Offer a way for students to keep track of their takeaways, such as providing a review sheet or doing a quick craft. Either of these will give them a visual overview of the study's highlights—and it will help them track their personal high points and "God sightings" from the experience.

When our middle school group studied the basics of the Christian faith, at the close of each session we provided a small trinket to represent each faith basic they had studied. Sin was represented by a fishing lure and sinker. The Holy Spirit was depicted by a plug adapter (as in, plug into the power). The students strung these trinkets together on a large, loose-leaf notebook ring. It served as a great memory tool and an effective device for review.

3. Personal Devotions: The long-term goal of any inductive Bible study with youth is to help them become lifelong self-feeders on God's Word.

As you and your students use the inductive tools in your group sessions, you can be assured that they're diving deep with God for at least a few minutes each week. But what happens *between* these sessions is the proving ground— the place where the theory becomes reality.

How much you ask students to do on their own between sessions depends on your group. (Asking students to study the Bible at home in preparation for the group session can get iffy. The line between challenging teenagers and setting them up for failure is a fine one.)

If your students ask for more—or wonder how to make their personal devotional times more interesting and meaningful—experiment by giving them a few mini-searches in the Word to do on their own. This encourages them to develop holy habits *and* provides a means for them to do so. But make these optional or available on request.

CREATIVE LISTS

Don't be afraid to think outside the whiteboard when recording insights from the group. If you're studying a passage that's heavy on promises, buy a big beach ball to represent a rainbow and use a permanent marker to list promises on the ball. Hang the ball somewhere in your ministry area. Or buy small beach balls that students can write on and take home.

A megaphone is a great symbol to use when marking instructions and commands in Scripture. And a real megaphone makes a great "whiteboard" on which to record God's commands. You can track down a megaphone online (search cheerleader supplies) or at a sporting goods store. Write the instructions and commands on one large megaphone to display or on small megaphones for students to keep.

Hands-On Study

Leading the Group—Acts 4:1-13

Once you've studied a passage inductively, you'll almost instinctively know how to lead your students on a similar journey.

How would I know that? you ask.

First, you'll have had some personal epiphanies—*Oh, wow!* moments, convictions, and challenges that have changed you in some way. Second, you'll know the path you took to get there, including what key words unlocked the passage for you, what background info you found especially relevant, what word definition brought added meaning, and what cross-reference really shed light.

In short, you'll know the things you don't want your students to miss. Although you can't expect to cover *everything* you've learned with your students (you may have to do a little simplifying), you'll have a pretty good feel for how the passage *wants* to be taught.

In Chapters 7 through 9 we did a hands-on study of Acts 4:1-13. Have you thought about how you might lead your students on a similar journey? What follows below is my take on a small-group session that parallels our hands-on study. We'll join the session in progress after the opener and transition into study time.

Setting: Small-group Bible study

Materials needed:

- Acts 4:1-13 printed double-spaced with wide margins (one copy per student)

- Colored pencils (two per student)

- Whiteboard

- Bibles—(Encourage students to bring their own.)

Distribute your printouts of Acts 4:1-13. Share the bullet points below as a run-up to the passage:

- Acts 1: Jesus, just before he ascended to the Father, told his disciples, "Go to Jerusalem and sit tight until the Holy Spirit shows up."

- Acts 2: The Holy Spirit showed up, and the church exploded.

- Acts 3: Newly empowered by the Holy Spirit, the apostles began to do the things Jesus did, including healing a beggar who'd been lame since birth. This caught the attention of some Jewish leaders who thought they had gotten rid of Jesus.

Tell the group that they're going to be looking for info about these Jewish leaders and the apostles. They're also going to be looking for any references to time.

Ask the students what symbols they could use to represent Jewish leaders, apostles, and references to time. Here are some suggestions:

God, Show Me

Give the students a few minutes of solitude to search the passage. Ask them to find a place where they can be alone with God to read and mark the verses using their colored pencils. If space is limited, have them stay where they are.

After most have finished, get the group back together. Ask them to tell you what action took place in the passage—who was there and what they did. List the info in chronological order on a whiteboard. To make sure they give you the info in chronological order, you might begin by asking, "How many days does the passage cover?" Then divide the board into two columns: Day 1 and Day 2.

Here are some questions you could use to prompt the discussion. Check out the sample "whiteboard" that follows:

What Jewish leaders were present on Day 1?

priests, Sadducees, captain of the temple guard (verse 1)

What apostles were present on Day 1?

Peter and John (verse 1)

What was the attitude of the Jewish leaders toward the apostles on Day 1?

greatly disturbed (verse 2)

What did the Jewish leaders do to the apostles that day?

threw them in jail (verse 3)

What Jewish leaders were present on Day 2?

Annas, Caiaphas, John, Alexander (verse 6)

Was there a difference between these leaders and those present on Day 1?

Yes, these were the big dogs.

What apostles were present on Day 2?

Peter and John (verse 7)

How were the apostles described?

unschooled and ordinary (verse 13)

How did the Jewish leaders respond to Peter's speech?

They were astonished (verse 13).

What was it that astonished them?

their courage (verse 13)

Where did the apostles get their courage? Does the passage give you any clues?

1. They'd been with Jesus (verse 13).

2. They'd been filled with the Holy Spirit (verse 8).

Sample Whiteboard

DAY 1

Jewish leaders:
priests, Sadducees, captain of the temple guard (v. 1)

    greatly disturbed

    threw apostles in jail

Apostles: Peter, John (v. 1)

DAY 2

Jewish leaders: Annas, Caiaphas (v. 6)

    the big dogs

    astonished at apostles' courage

Apostles: Peter, John (v. 7)

    unschooled and ordinary (v. 13)

    had great courage (v. 13)

    courage from:

    being with Jesus (v. 13)

    filled with the Holy Spirit (v. 8)

God, Teach Me

Now help your students process the information they've uncovered by asking a few questions:

What is the point of this scene? Why was it recorded in the Bible for us?

Possible responses: To show us what the Christian life was like in the early days; how to respond when we're antagonized because of our faith.

What do we know about the relationship between the Jewish leaders and the apostles?

It was very antagonistic. These Jewish leaders were after the apostles, trying to keep them from living out their faith.

What stands out about how the apostles dealt with this situation?

These unschooled, ordinary men weren't intimidated by the threatening Jewish leaders.

What stands out to you about the effect the apostles had on the Jewish leaders?

The big dogs didn't want to mess with the apostles.

Cross-Referencing

There are several routes you could take in letting Scripture interpret Scripture. If you'd like to add a cross-referencing exercise to your session, choose one of the three options below. Have the students get alone to read the Bible passages. Then discuss how these verses shed light on the action in Acts 4:

1. Familiar names at Jesus' trial and crucifixion. The last time Peter and John would have seen these Jewish leaders was at Jesus' trial and crucifixion, when these same men ruled that Jesus should be turned over to the Romans. Have the group look at Matthew 26:57-61, Luke 22:52-53, and John 18:19-24.

2. Peter's before and after makeover. Compare Peter's responses to people who were far less powerful and physically imposing than those he faced in Acts 4. Look at Matthew 26:69-75, Mark 14:66-72, Luke 22:56-62, and John 18:15-18, 25-28.

3. Characteristics of people God uses for his work. In these passages, note the traits of people God uses. How are these similar to the description of the apostles in Acts 4? Look at Matthew 11:25, 1 Corinthians 1:27, and Judges 6:11-16.

God, Change Me

Point out that not only did the Jewish leaders have no impact on the apostles, but that the apostles instead impacted the Jewish leaders! Then help the students move to specific application by asking a few questions.

What similar situations do you have in your life right now? What people or things are antagonistic toward your faith and make it hard for you to live the way you know Jesus wants you to live?

Possible responses: School, work, family, friends, temptations, busyness, school teachers who belittle Christianity or teach ideas contradictory to the Bible, etc.

What would your life look like if you were impacting others—rather than them impacting you?

Possible responses: I would have greater resolve when facing temptation; I would be more confident in sharing my faith; mine would be a better example of a Christlike lifestyle.

What changes could you make to have an impact similar to what the apostles had on the Jewish leaders?

Possible response: See "unschooled" and "ordinary" as strengths for God to use; pray for God's Spirit to give me a strength and confidence similar to Peter's.

What are some ways you could make sure that you're experiencing the power of God's Spirit more and more? What do you need to change so that you trust the Spirit will come through for you?

Possible responses: Be more aware of situations in my day when I can trust the Spirit; count on the fact that the Spirit is patiently waiting to come through for me; develop a prayer life that gives the Spirit a chance to get through to me.

Is spending time with Jesus a growing part of your life? Are you getting bolder and more courageous? What do you need to do to put more priority on the devotional part of your day?

Possible responses: Get more intentional about spending time with Jesus; improve my quality of time—listen to more of Jesus' words in Scripture, speak fewer of my words in prayer.

Encourage specific application in your students' answers. Rather than settling for "I need to spend more time with Jesus," encourage your students to make appointments with Jesus by really writing it on a calendar every day this week. Or encourage them to read one of the Gospels this month.

Closing

Use a few of the following questions to help your students identify a takeaway lesson from this session. Invite them to write down their responses:

What's something you never want to forget?

What surprised you?

What's something new about God that you didn't know before today?

What challenged or convicted you?

What do you want to know more about?

Ask for some suggested ways to keep one another accountable to make the changes they've discussed. Don't leave the session without a plan in place.

Finally, choose five questions from the *God, Show Me* exercise. Ask these questions rapid-fire, and have the students shout out answers from memory. They'll be surprised to find they're experts on Acts 4:1-13.

PART THREE

TOOLS FOR THE QUEST

CHAPTER THIRTEEN

Leveraging Teenagers' Desperation for Depth

"Isn't it cool to be a part of something where the Word of God is the star of the show?" TIC LONG, DCLA 2003

This generation of students has the ability to breathe new life into our sacred text.

TONY JONES • *POSTMODERN YOUTH MINISTRY*

The quest for authentic spiritual depth has been documented by student ministry's top authors, speakers, and researchers, as well as by leading-edge youth ministry networks. Even *Time* magazine, an unlikely prophetic voice, has noted the trend. Chances are, you've observed it, too.

Teenagers are asking—even begging and screaming for—depth.

Several vital components of student ministry have benefited greatly from this quest for depth—worship and missions, to name two. Or perhaps it's the other way around; maybe these were catalysts that spurred the hunger. Either way, we've seen tremendous revival in student worship in recent years. And youth missions experiences are flourishing like never before.

But one component of youth ministry hasn't kept pace with the quest for spiritual depth, and that's Bible study.

Why? After all, the Word of God has the power not only to feed the hunger, but to transform it into all-out revival with lasting results that will flow into future generations and ensure that they'll hunger for depth as well. With the proper infusion of God's Word at this moment in history, I believe we can blow that door wide open.

So let's look together at three components of modern youth ministry—worship, missions, and postmodernism—and see how they can be leveraged to give students what they're craving: A deeper experience in God's Word.

Lose the Candy

"Sugarcoated, MTV-style youth ministry is over."

So notes a two-page perspective on modern youth ministry by *Time* religion writer Sonja Steptoe documenting a growing disinterest among teenagers in the pop-culture packaging so prevalent in youth ministries of the 1980s and 1990s.[42]

Citing a well-known stat from Barna—that 61 percent of twentysomethings polled said that they used to participate in church as a teenager but no longer do so[43]—the article indicates that watered-down youth ministry is the reason why our students are tuning out.

Steptoe goes on to describe several prominent youth ministries that have seen a marked increase in conversions and spiritual growth after changing from an entertainment-driven approach to a more Bible-centered approach.

In a follow-up article, she cites Barna research, revealing the reasons why teenagers attend church.[44] Topping the list are "to worship or make a connection with God" and "to understand better what I believe."

These reasons represent a quantum leap forward from a 1996 survey by Search Institute, in which teenagers said that the number-one thing they wanted from their youth ministries was help with friendship-making skills.

Compare yourself with your youth ministry counterparts of one or two decades ago, and you'll find yourself in an enviable position. Kids today want what you have to offer.

Cut-and-Paste Spirituality?

Some observers have deduced that today's teenagers are seeking more of a New Age hodgepodge than genuine, biblical faith. But in *The New Faithful*, author Colleen Carroll Campbell argues that students may not be as cut-and-paste in their spirituality as some might think.

Over a year's time, Campbell interviewed hundreds of teenagers and twentysomethings, as well as leading sociologists, religious leaders, and youth ministers across the nation.[45] Here are four of her conclusions:

> [They] are not perpetual seekers. They are committed to a religious worldview that grounds their lives and shapes their morality. They are not lukewarm believers or passionate dissenters. When they are embracing a faith tradition or deepening their commitment to it, they want to do so wholeheartedly or not at all.
>
> They embrace challenging faith commitments that offer them firm guidelines on how to live their lives.
>
> Their adherence to traditional morality and religious devotion often comes at considerable personal cost, and the sacrificial nature of these commitments is often precisely what makes them attractive.
>
> They strive for personal holiness, authenticity, and integration in their spiritual lives and are attracted to people and congregations that do the same. Conversely, they are repelled by complacency, hypocrisy, and pandering.[46]

Based on Campbell's observations, the majority of today's teenagers are evaluating faith experiences based on their depths. These students aren't looking for the least they can do to get by. Our responsibility as youth workers is to take their cries for depth seriously, letting it impact our planning, our vision, our interaction with them, and ultimately, how we perceive their spirituality.

How do we take advantage of our students' desire for depth? Here are some ideas:

- Make it a personal goal to ensure that your graduating teenagers have no reason to say, "I wish we'd gone deeper"—or even "I wish I understood better what I believe." Maximize their desire for depth while you still have them.

- Don't fear asking for their time and commitment. These are parameters teenagers use to measure the sacrifice factor. Don't shrink back from letting them count the cost.

- If the Bible is black and white about a topic, don't grayscale it. Give your students clear measures of holiness and authenticity to strive for.

- Let students see the stark difference between a biblical worldview and a secular worldview. Let these differences stir their hearts and their passions.

Worship

Student worship has undergone a palpable change in recent years. It was a welcome relief a few years ago when I noticed that we were no longer singing "Little Bunny Foo Foo" at youth camps and conventions. (I'll wager the field mice were relieved, too.)

Group singing has moved to all worship, all the time— and it's not just music for music's sake. Now that student ministries of every shape and size have their own worship bands, students are entering *weekly* into authentic worship experiences. And they're *expecting* energizing worship at large events, such as regional retreats and national conventions.

Consider how this worship revival gives us an opportunity to live out Paul's instruction in Colossians 3:16: "Let the word of Christ dwell in you richly as you teach and admonish one another with all wisdom, and as you sing psalms, hymns and spiritual songs with gratitude in your hearts to God."

There is the ideal—a worship team's perfect mission statement. Use all available kinds of worship—psalms, hymns, spiritual songs—to create a warmly familiar spot in the heart of each worshiper where the Word of Christ can settle. Let Word and worship intertwine.

We can begin to achieve that ideal by becoming more intentional in letting worship and teaching become natural outgrowths, or supports, of one another. Colossians 3:16 implies that worship and teaching were never intended to be segregated. In fact, Paul was echoing what Jesus himself said about true worship—that it's done in spirit *and* in truth (John 4:24). Jesus said that this is the kind of worshiper God seeks.

Paul's and Jesus' statements about worship tell us that God is looking for worshipers who worship in spirit—singing psalms, hymns, and spiritual songs with genuine passion. He's looking for worshipers who worship in truth—letting the word of Christ dwell richly in them.

Many of us have seen a vivid example of this combination of word and worship at recent DC/LA conferences. The three-day student evangelism training conferences in Washington, D.C., and Los Angeles were built around the Gospel of John.

The teaching came out of John. The large corporate worship times were carefully planned so that the students had experienced the entire Gospel of John—every word!—by the time the event was over. Whether it was a dramatic reading, a hip-hop song, a comedy sketch, or a cartoon, the content was driven by John's message of Jesus Christ.

In other words, worship and teaching were seamlessly intertwined.

This intentionality with the Word and worship can happen on any scale, large or small. It can happen with a band or without one. Authentic worship has gripped our teenagers. With a little nurturing on our part, worship can spill into our Bible study efforts, and the Word can spill into worship. Both will be enhanced.

Here are some ideas to help us take advantage of our students' desire for authentic worship:

- Consider adding a brief time of worship to your small-group gatherings.

- Integrate Scripture teaching into your worship gatherings. When singing a psalm or a Bible passage, set the context for your group. Many students have no idea that the words came from the Bible or the circumstances in which they were written.

- Plan worship around key Bible truths or themes, such as mercy or grace. Then teach on the same truth or concept. Base your other teaching efforts on the same theme.

Missions

Short-term missions experiences—work camps, service projects, and the like—have increased exponentially over the past 20 years. Not only has the number of missions organizations increased, but existing organizations have greatly expanded their offerings to meet the growing demand. There's also been an across-the-board increase in volunteerism—adult and student, Christian and secular.

What is it that makes a missions trip such a mountaintop experience for many believers and a watershed moment in the lives of many students?

Jesus said, "Whoever has my commands and obeys them, he is the one who loves me. He who loves me will be loved by my Father, and I too will love him and show myself to him" (John 14:21).

A real and personal revelation of Jesus is quite a reward for *having* and *obeying*. My guess is that it'd keep you coming back for more.

Missions experiences are textbook opportunities for *having* and *obeying* Jesus' commands. In most cases the experience happens out of obedience to one or more of Jesus' commands: Serve others, visit those in prison, care for the sick, feed the hungry, wash others' feet, look after the poor, go out and make disciples.

And working shoulder-to-shoulder with a community of fellow believers provides the chance to obey another of Jesus' commands: Love one another.

While the *obey* factor is intensified on missions experiences, the *have* factor is typically kicked up a notch, too. Many students are involved in pre-trip preparation that includes Bible study, which helps them *have* or *own* Jesus' commands. And they're often encouraged to be more intentional with their quiet times while away from home.

Is it any wonder then that many work-campers have profound mountaintop experiences with Jesus while serving on missions trips? Jesus has delivered on his promise to those who *have* and *obey* his commands. He's shown himself personally to them. And it's enough to keep them coming back for more.

Of course, the word *mountaintop* implies a descent. But it doesn't have to be that way. The one-two punch of having and obeying Jesus' commands doesn't have to stop when the missions project is over. Instead, it can be a launching pad to a new way of living—a pursuit of God that invites regular "showings" from Jesus.

Here are a few ways to help take advantage of your students' desire to serve and do missions:

- In your prep meetings for any missions trip or project, talk about more than what-to-bring lists and logistics.

Show your students the biblical reasons for what they'll be doing. Let their participation be driven more by a calling from God through his Word than by anything else.

- In the course of *doing* Jesus' commands, provide ample time for students to *own* Jesus' commands. Set aside designated quiet time each day and offer inductive ideas and study materials that allow students to interact with God's Word. Do *not* miss this incredible opportunity to help students develop holy habits.

- When students arrive home, be ready with a weekly or semi-weekly Bible study. Funnel your students' fresh commitments and renewed enthusiasm about God into deeper experiences with him and his Word. Your students' hearts may never be softer. Don't pass up this chance to turn a one-week experience with God into a lasting, daily relationship with him.

The Postmodern Era

We student ministry-types spend a lot of time spinning our wheels on how to reach postmodern kids.

I've read postmodern authors who seem to suggest that if we don't adjust our methods of presenting the gospel to a postmodern mindset, we're going to lose a generation. While it's never a bad idea to reevaluate our methods, let's not lose sight of God's most common description of his Word...

It endures.

The Word of God is able to do its work in any age—Pre-Patriarch, Patriarch, Divided Kingdom, the Silent Years, Incarnation (it even picked up a little steam here), Apostolic, Dark, Enlightenment, Renaissance, Industrial, Modern, Boomer, Buster, Gen X, Gen Me, Postmodern.

All of us are arriving at the postmodern ministry party in our own time. Some got here early and have been eagerly engrossed in what's been called the emerging church movement for several years. Others, fashionably late, are just waking up to what it's all about.

Some critics see postmodernism as a reworked warm-fuzzy fad. (Light a candle and share your feelings.) Some proponents see it as the last hope before church extinction. (If we don't adapt to this era's way of thinking, the church will soon become irrelevant.)

Wherever you are in the process, you need to know that postmodern ministry isn't just for others anymore. *It's here.* Even if you don't see postmodern ministry as a legitimate concern, it's a subject so deeply resourced and thoroughly analyzed that it's become part of virtually any dialogue about youth ministry today. Plan to bump into it.

This is why we need to devote some space to the subject of postmodernism—simply because there has been significant discussion as to how youth ministry should adjust to postmodern characteristics. And because these very characteristics may be giving youth ministry golden opportunities to unleash a feeding frenzy on the Word of God—both the written *and* the living Word.

I offer these summaries of the postmodern landscape from Tony Jones' book *Postmodern Youth Ministry:*

> Narrative is becoming the primary means of communicating beliefs. Since propositional logic has fallen on hard times, stories carry more weight in conveying truths.
>
> Postmoderns have argued that pinning down definitive meaning to text is difficult since each reader imports meaning into the reading of text; even the author's meaning has been deconstructed.
>
> Objectivity is out; subjectivity is in. One person, or group of people, cannot claim an objective viewpoint.

Question everything. Nothing escapes deconstruction. There are no thoughts, theories, assumptions, or hypotheses that get a free pass, even if they seem to make perfect sense.

There is no Truth with a capital *T*. Truth is in the eye of the beholder—one person's truth is another person's theory.[47] (Incidentally, as I was typing this point, I took a call from a youth pastor asking if our ministry offered a Bible study that could help his teenagers answer their number-one question: "How do I know the Bible is true?")

Postmoderns are experiential, spiritual (as opposed to *religious*), pluralistic, and communal. This represents a shift from traditional, monotheistic, and isolated. For youth workers who have spanned this transition, it's a tough adjustment to make.

But it's doable.

As youth ministry has processed these characteristics in recent years, I've watched youth workers try to fit what they know about Bible study into their newfound perspectives on postmodern teenagers. This has led to questions such as How does Bible study—an exercise in text and Truth (with a capital *T*)—connect with today's experience-oriented, truth-is-relative teenager? Why study facts when postmoderns respond best to story and narrative? And how does subjectivity fit with a pursuit of objective Truth?

Suddenly it sounds like Bible study is up for grabs. And for some, it may be.

But I think that's a misreading of what's being taught and written about postmodern youth ministry. We may speculate that a postmodern approach could lighten the role of the Bible by giving us license to tell more story and teach less Scripture. Instead postmodernism may have heightened the role by placing even more responsibility on youth workers to know Scripture well enough to let it tell its own story.

Writers addressing the postmodern era, such as Brian McLaren, Rob Bell, and Tony Jones, certainly challenge our conventional approaches to Scripture. And that's a good thing. But to declare that these and other writers are advocating loosening our grip on the Bible misses the mark. In fact, a closer look reveals that these writers underscore our need to intensify our teaching of Scripture in order to take advantage of the postmodern mindset.

McLaren's writings in particular have generated some lively discussions within the church about absolute and propositional truth, causing some to rethink the Bible's role in ministry. Yet throughout his writings McLaren makes statements such as this (from *A Generous Orthodoxy*):

> I have spent my entire life learning, understanding, reappraising, wrestling with, trusting, applying, and obeying the Bible, and trying to help others do the same. I believe it is a gift from God, inspired by God, to benefit us in the most important way possible: equipping us so that we can benefit others, so that we can play our part in the ongoing mission of God. *My regard for the Bible is higher than ever.*[48] (Emphasis his.)

In *Velvet Elvis*, Rob Bell makes assertions that have generated spirited discussion regarding the Bible's use and authority. Yet Bell writes, "I understand the need to ground all that we do and say in the Bible, which is my life's work."[49]

True, Bell often challenges the modern paradigms and systems we bring to Bible study, strongly stating that it's impossible to read Scripture devoid of our personal backgrounds and agendas. Bell also notes that the notions of teaching "pure Bible" and of 21st-century believers becoming a "New Testament church" are simply unattainable.[50]

Yet Bell concludes that these are the very things that make God's Word so alive today. They force us to *know* the stories of the people who first read the Torah—or heard a prophecy or read a New Testament letter—so that we can better determine how those holy oracles apply to us in the postmodern era.

Postmodern Free-for-All?

The characteristics of the postmodern teenager that we read above may lead us to think we're given permission to let our small-group Bible study time be a free-for-all discussion—that sounds good because we don't really have time to prepare for anything else and Bible study isn't one of our favorite activities anyway, right? We're off the hook.

Not so fast. Jones provides helpful insight on how to adjust our ministry approaches to allow for the postmodern tenets just noted. And you'll see that we're not to adjust by turning Bible study into accountability and discussion time, but rather by approaching it as a deeper experience with truth.

In fact, Jones concludes that the postmodern era may give us our best opportunity yet for communicating God's faith document to our students. Jones writes of the consequences of today's biblical illiteracy, noting how it even robs students of spiritual allusions in cultural works ranging from *Moby Dick* to *The Matrix*. He writes:

> The Bible, with its stories of good and evil, its romance, its poetry, its death and destruction, and its science fiction, is not only rife with ideas for screenplays, it needs to be the basis of the moral imagination of our youth...Indeed, Scripture was long the common tongue of half the world. With its cultural demotion, our ability to communicate has been diminished. With its recovery, the students

with whom we work can revitalize and ennoble the currently banal level of cultural conversation.

That is to say, *this generation of students has the ability to breathe new life into our sacred text,* particularly because postmodernism has influenced many people to be more open to the biblical narrative.[51] (emphasis added)

Postmodernism and youth Bible study are not mutually exclusive. In fact, they enhance one another. Postmodern characteristics bring authenticity and depth to Scripture. The Bible is built for examination, struggle, and questioning. It delivers.

Yes, we should constantly and critically evaluate our methods and approaches. The caution, however, is that we don't turn our youth ministries—particularly the Bible study aspect—into nothing but a response to what we think students want. Here's the bottom line: God has given us a mandate to teach and disciple with his Word. If students aren't responding to our Bible study efforts, the proper response isn't to lop Bible study off the agenda or distill it down to an hour that's heavy on discussion, light on Bible.

If they're not being lit up by Bible study, it's not the Bible's fault.

Our students' characteristics and desires need to be melded with what God desires for his Word.

Earlier in these pages, Fuller Theological Seminary's Center for Youth and Family Ministry (CYFM) was mentioned, along with its endeavors. In particular it launched the College Transition Project—a three-year study designed to help us know what happens to students when they transition from youth-group life into college/young adult life and to identify components of student ministry associated with a healthy, or positive, transition into college.[52]

In this project, 70 percent of the seniors polled noted that they wanted "more" or "much more" time for deep conversation in their youth ministries (this ranked second behind service projects). This certainly supports the widely reported need among postmoderns for community, or "tribe," and caters to one of the key purposes of youth ministry: To create a safe place for honest exchange.

In our zeal to stay current, it may be tempting to wrap our small-group programs around deep conversations about deep issues. But consider the end result: Our students will head into young adulthood equipped with four years of others' opinions on deep issues. Rather, let's embrace this need and use it as a vehicle to help students interact with God's Word. What better combo is there than deep conversations driven by deep interaction with Scripture?

One trait of postmoderns that seems common to all definitions is that teenagers are looking for something real to sell out to. (It certainly holds true in my experience with students.) They're up for a challenge. And they're willing to commit seriously to what they perceive as authentic.

Scripture was built for the sellout search. God loaded his Word with a great payoff for those who will search the Scriptures as if searching for hidden treasure and for those who will devour his Word (Proverbs 2:1-15, Ezekiel 3:1-3, Revelation 10:9).

I've listened to youth workers deride postmodern youth ministry as touchy-feely. I've listened to youth workers who embrace postmodern approaches deride Bible study as archaic and out of touch. As with most things, the solution is in the middle.

Let me try to offer a bottom line: We live in an era that offers unparalleled potential for reclaiming lost ground regarding God's Word. Let's not miss the opportunity.

Here are a few ways to leverage the postmodern mindset:

Guide the postmodern desire for wholehearted sellout into an energetic study of Scripture.

Take advantage of the postmodern quest for mystery by helping students learn and experience the meditative disciplines of the faith.

Maximize Scripture's storytelling ability. See Bible study as the unearthing of God's macro-story line for humanity, as well as the discovery of many micro-stories that parallel our own journeys.

Value invigorating discussions that strike a balance. Respect how your students process information, but be bold with the fact that there are things you want them to learn.

Use all available art forms and media to help students understand biblical concepts and story lines.

Agents of Change

I'm convinced that the spiritual depth being sought by students today is more than a window of opportunity.

It's more than a tailwind.

It's more than momentum.

It's a shift that's occurred from the inside out. It's visible evidence of God's movement to revive his church and reach the world.

Youth ministry easily could be the agent God uses to ignite the flames of revival. The current landscape of teenage spirituality offers a fresh opportunity to plunge to depths we've never explored. To build foundations on a new strata of bedrock.

We've been given several gifts on a silver platter: a recognizable increase in teenagers' desire for things of God, a fresh quest for authentic worship, a consistent desire to serve through missions experiences.

What a heartbreak it would be to look back on this era and see depths left unexplored.

CHAPTER FOURTEEN

It's All Greek (or Hebrew) to Me

And the words of the LORD are flawless, like silver refined in a furnace of clay, purified seven times. PSALM 12:6

Greek and Hebrew are well worth learning, but if you haven't had the privilege, settle for English.

EUGENE PETERSON • *EAT THIS BOOK*

I've been a Green Bay Packers fan ever since the late '60s when I discovered my initials were the same as their famed quarterback, Bart Starr.

Having become aware of the NFL at a time when the Packers were dominating the football scene, it was easy to lock in on them as my favorite team. Little did I know I'd be heading into a long, dry spell of fanship. The Packers wouldn't get back to championship form until the era of another famed quarterback, Brett Favre, nearly 30 years later.

The Packers' great success of the 1960s came under the legendary coaching of Vince Lombardi (the namesake of today's Super Bowl trophy). After the team had won a few championships, they hit a lackluster stretch. And legend says that Lombardi called the team together and told them it was time to get back to the basics.

Holding up a football Lombardi said, "Gentlemen, this is a football."

To which one of his players replied, "Coach, could you take it a little slower?"

At the foundation of in-depth Bible study lie the major original languages of the Old and New Testaments—Hebrew and Greek. Looking at those languages is looking at the tongues of cultures that gave birth to God's revelations and give insight into his redemptive story. Looking at those languages is rooting around where the foundation attaches to bedrock.

Here's good news: You don't have to be an expert in Hebrew or Greek to take advantage of the richness they can add to our English Bibles. You don't even need to know the alphabets of these languages. You just have to know how to count. But more on that later.

Original Languages—Why Bother?

My goal here isn't to make us Greek or Hebrew scholars, but to add a layer of richness and accuracy to our observation and interpretation of Scripture. The more effort we build into these vital first steps of Bible study, the more powerful our application will be.

I mentioned earlier all the "fun" I had with two years of Greek in seminary. As much as I worked at the original languages, they never became a walk in the park. I remember speculating that the only reason I was forced to study Greek was because my instructors had been forced to study Greek. I thought it was all just a vicious, self-perpetuating cycle.

I've since realized that though I may never fall head over heels in love with language study, there is great reward in learning enough to have at least a casual friendship with it. Especially given that in today's culture many English words important to our understanding of God have become locked in cliché status. Or they've taken on a lofty "churchyness" never intended by their original users who were a ragtag bunch of renegades and outcasts from the religious establishment. Or they seem so complicated that they're dismissed out of hand.

But the Hebrew or Greek backgrounds of these words can give us fresh perspectives on these timeworn concepts simply by taking us down to the bare bones basics.

And there's another benefit of word study: This simple step forces us to slow down with the Word, to dig a little deeper, and to reflect a little longer on what we find. Whether we're looking at how an English word is used in other Bible passages or dipping our toes into the original Hebrew or Greek, this step can help keep our Bible time from becoming a rote checklist.

Word Pictures

How many times has it crossed your mind that teaching teenagers isn't much more than a search for The Great Analogy?

Analogy is one of the most powerful tools for helping adolescents grasp spiritual truth, especially as they begin to experiment with their newfound abstract thinking skills. Digging down to the original meaning of a word often opens up a whole new realm of analogy, yielding word pictures that are far better (and more accurate) than any youth worker could invent on the fly.

Our word study of *katartizo* ("to equip") in Chapter 11 unearthed several analogies we can use to paint a clearer picture of biblical equipping: Setting a broken bone, preparing a ship for battle, restoring the walls of a city. Each of these uses depicts the urgent necessity for thorough equipping and illustrates precisely what that equipping should look like. Observing how Bible words were used in everyday settings—outside of religious-speak—helps us do in our day what Jesus did best in his: Illustrate Kingdom concepts using objects and ideas that ordinary people, teenagers included, can understand.

Word Choice

Sometimes one word in our English Bibles is used to express multiple Greek or Hebrew words. Take the English word *word*, for example. The Greeks had two primary words that translated *word* in our Bibles—*logos*, which denotes a thought or concept, and *rhema*, which expresses a spoken word. So if we're kicking around John 1:1, in which we find the phrase "In the beginning was the Word," we're best served by tracking down the definition and cross-references related to the original Greek *logos* rather than the less specific English *word*.

On the flip side, sometimes more than one English word can be used to translate one Greek or Hebrew word. The Greek word *sozo* ("save; rescue") is used a variety of ways in the New Testament. When tracking this word in multiple passages, you'll see it used for *saved* from sin (Romans 5:10) and *healed* from sickness (Matthew 9:22). Its use in Matthew 8:25 gives an entirely different angle: Deliverance from danger. Each unique nuance helps inform the others—and the composite can lend new power to a word that's become stale and cliché for many believers.

Where to Start?

I could conclude this chapter in about 20 seconds with one quick tip: Google the phrase *Bible word study* (or something similar), and go at it.

You'd be off and running.

That's because the wealth of Bible software and online study tools now at our fingertips literally has revolutionized our ability to do word studies in the original languages.

But to maximize these tools, it helps to have a basic understanding of what they are and how they can help us. Let's do a few word studies together—first with a New Testament Greek word, then with an Old Testament Hebrew word—so that when you explore the online resources and helps available, you'll know what you're seeing.

Here are the tools we'll use. And by the way, none requires that you know Hebrew or Greek or even the alphabet of either language:

- Other English Bible translations (for parallel study)
- Concordance
- Interlinear Bible
- Word study dictionaries/lexicons (Vine's, Zodhiates)
- Text commentaries

New Testament Greek Word Study—*To Show*

Perhaps you've noticed that John 14:21 is a favorite verse of mine: "Whoever has my commands and keeps them is the one who loves me. Anyone who loves me will be loved by my Father, and I too will love them and show myself to them" (TNIV).

I'm awed that Jesus promises to show himself to us in a conspicuous manner, if only we'll demonstrate our love for him by having and obeying his commands.

But how do I know about this "conspicuous manner"? And how can you be sure I'm right about this, given my confession that I'm no Greek expert?

Let's use the following exercise to find out how.

Other English Versions (Parallel Study)

Comparing how a word is translated in several English versions of the Bible is a great first step in word study. This will help you see if there's more than one way a Greek word can be translated into English. It can also help you build a more complete picture of the word you're studying.

A good rule of thumb is to consult at least three Bible versions, each representing a different part of the translation spectrum. First, consult a more literal (and possibly more rigid-sounding) word-for-word translation, such as the New American Standard Bible or King James Version. Second, consult a less literal (and possibly more fluid-sounding) phrase-for-phrase translation, such as the New King James Version, New International Version, or Today's New International Version. And third, take a look at a modern paraphrase, such as *The Message.*

If you don't happen to have several Bible versions on-hand, check out a Web site such as www.biblegateway.com, which lets you compare several well-known translations at once.

When you're leading a group study with students who've brought their own Bibles, you can do a quick check on a word by asking the students how their different versions read. Here's what you'd find with John 14:21:

> He that hath my commandments, and keepeth them, he it is that loveth me: and he that loveth me shall be loved of my Father, and I will love him, and will *manifest* myself to him. (KJV, italics added)

> He who has My commandments and keeps them is the one who loves Me; and he who loves Me will be loved by My Father, and I will love him and will *disclose* Myself to him. (NASB, italics added)

> Whoever has my commands and obeys them, he is the one who loves me. He who loves me will be loved by my Father, and I too will love him and *show* myself to him. (NIV, italics added)

> The person who knows my commandments and keeps them, that's who loves me. And the person who loves me will be loved by my Father, and I will love him and *make* myself plain to him. (*The Message*, italics added)

By comparing these four English versions, you've already gained a more detailed picture of the type of showing Jesus promises. But this also raises a few questions: Which of these versions comes closest to conveying what Jesus actually said? Which more accurately conveys the word John, the writer, was inspired to use when he recorded Jesus' promise for us?

Concordance

The second step in our word study is to look in a Bible concordance.

An exhaustive Bible concordance is an index of every Greek or Hebrew word contained in the Bible. Mini-concordances are found in the backs of most Bibles; these contain many of the most frequently used Bible words in English. But, as noted previously, *exhaustive* is the word to look for in the Bible concordance you'll use for word study.

Handy exhaustive concordances have been around for some time helping seekers make sense of Scripture—and serving as pretty good infant booster seats in the days before telephone books were invented. The first concordance was Robert Young's *Analytical Concordance of the Bible*, released 268 years after the King James Version. It took 40 years of labor, including three years of typesetting, to create.

In 1894 James Strong produced Strong's *Exhaustive Concordance of the Bible*, also based on the King James Version. This hefty volume, still highly popular today, took nearly three decades to produce. Strong's concordance introduced the invaluable innovation of keying each Greek or Hebrew Bible word to a number, making it the go-to reference tool for generations of Bible students.[53] (This explains why you don't need to know Hebrew or Greek to use this incredible tool; you only need to be able to count.)

Using Strong's *Exhaustive Concordance* is easy:

1. Because Strong's is tied to the KJV, find the word you're looking for in the King James Version.

2. Look that word up in the main concordance section of Strong's. There you'll find a complete list of all the places where a specific word was used in Scripture. You can use this information to compare how the word was used from one verse to another or from one Bible writer to another (say, if you want to compare John's use of a word to Paul's use of the same word).

3. Look at the list of verse references where your word appears in Scripture and find the specific verse you're looking for. To the right of that verse, you'll find a number—the Strong's number for your word.

4. Flip to the back of your Strong's concordance to the Hebrew and Greek dictionaries. Now look up the number. (If it's an Old Testament word, use the Hebrew section. For a New Testament word, use the Greek section.) You'll find several things next to the Strong's number: Your word as it appears in Hebrew or Greek, the English transliteration of your word (the Greek or Hebrew word rendered in English letters), a guide for pronouncing the word, and a brief definition.

Back to our example from John 14:21. Let's say I want to know the Greek word John used for *show* in Jesus' promise.

Using my Strong's concordance, I look up the word manifest (remember, Strong's is keyed to the King James Version). The Strong's number for the word is 1718.

While I'm there, I see there are several other Bible verses that contain the word *manifest*. And I see that these verses offer some different numbers for the word *manifest*. This tips me off that more than one Greek word can be translated *manifest* or *show*.

Why does this matter? Because if I took the time to look up these words and their meanings, I'd learn about several Greek words John could have used for *show*—but didn't. These Greek words could add to my understanding of John 14:21 by telling me a little about what my word is not.

Armed with my trusty Strong's number, 1718, I head to the back of the concordance to locate my word in the Greek dictionary. Here I find the transliteration of my word: *Emphanizo*. I also find the definition: to exhibit (in person) or disclose (by words)—appear, declare (plainly), inform, (will) manifest, show, signify.

Voilà.

I'm no authority, but I now know the Greek word for *manifest*—and quite a bit about what it means. Before moving on to the next step, I'd want to record that info on my computer, or jot a few notes on paper or in my Bible.

Interlinear Bible

Interlinear Bibles help us delve more deeply into the grammar of the Hebrews and Greeks—again, without needing to know how to write or speak either language.

In an interlinear Bible the Hebrew or Greek text runs parallel to the English translation. *Interlinear* is scholar-speak for "between the lines"—which explains why you'd better grab your glasses before you use an interlinear Bible. The Greek or Hebrew text often runs in tiny type between the lines of the English translation.

Small print aside, interlinear Bibles provide a lot of extras that Bible questers love. Along with the Strong's number for each word, many interlinear Bibles tell what part of speech a word is (noun, verb, preposition, adjective). Verb tenses, moods, and voices are also provided, each of which can influence how the word is best translated and understood.

You'll also run across grammatical terms you've never seen in English—such as *nithpael*, the perfect tense in Hebrew, and the *aorist* tense in Greek. (Don't worry; these are described in the interlinear Bible you're referencing. Look for sections such as "grammatical notations" or "lexical aids.")

Let's see what happens when I consult an interlinear Bible—in this case *The Complete Word Study New Testament with Greek Parallel*[54]—about my word *emphanizo*. Turning to John 14:21, I see the word *manifest* with the following grammar code printed above it: ft1718.

The number 1718 is, of course, the Strong's reference number for *emphanizo*. The letters *ft* tell me the verb tense. The book's cheat sheet lets me know that ft indicates the future active tense.

The cheat sheet also points me to where in the book I can go to learn about the future active tense. There I learn that in ancient Greek, the future tense usually referred to punctiliar action, rather than linear action—which means absolutely nothing to most of us.

Thankfully, the book explains: *Punctiliar* indicates something that happens at a definite point in time, while linear describes something that continues to happen in a sequential fashion.

I'm also reminded that the writer of John 14:21 used the active voice, indicating that it's the subject who's doing the action in this verse.

To summarize the insights I've gleaned from using an interlinear Bible: According to John's use of *emphanizo*, Jesus will do the action when I have and obey his commands. He (the subject in the verse) will show himself to me at a definite point in time.

We could stop right there and know a good bit about what Jesus promised in John 14:21. But why quit when we're on a roll?

Word Study Dictionaries/Lexicons

These tell us how biblical words were used in the everyday speech of the ancient people and in extra-biblical literature. They also show us where else in Scripture words were used and provide more complete word definitions.[55]

These dictionaries are usually abridged, containing key words from the Old and New Testaments but not every word. They tend to be written on a popular level (as opposed to scholarly), and because the information is contained in one volume, they're not terribly expensive.

You need only the Strong's number to find the word you're looking for, so again, there's no need to know the Greek and Hebrew alphabets. Some are even alphabetized by the English words.

It may be tempting to simply pick the definition you like best, so make sure you're looking at the definition that's keyed to your passage. The immediate context of a word will govern its meaning, so don't assume that you can choose any of the possibilities based on which one will generate the strongest response from students.

Looking in *Vine's Expository Dictionary of Biblical Words*, I see that *manifest* (*emphanizo*) in John 14:21 is defined "to manifest, make manifest." That doesn't add much insight.

But then Vine's directs me to another form of the word, *emphaino*, which means "to show in, to exhibit," or "to cause to shine."

In Zodhiates' *Complete Word Study Dictionary* (New Testament), I look up Strong's number 1718 and find the main definition for *emphanizo*: "to make apparent, cause to be seen, to show." I also see a reference to John 14:21 with the more specific definition: "of a person, to manifest oneself, to let oneself be intimately known and understood."

Now John's use of *manifest* in John 14:21 is coming into focus. I'm intrigued that these definitions are lining up to convey a manifestation of Jesus that could only be described as obvious...a clear and present reality...something that can't be missed.

One more stop before I conclude my word study of *emphanizo*—at least for the time being.

Commentaries

When doing a word study, the most helpful commentaries are those that assist with the original Greek or Hebrew, rather than those that are more devotional in nature. Unfortunately, commentary sets are usually pricey. Your best bet is to find them in a pastor's or a church's library, at your local library, or at a nearby Christian college or seminary library.

In most cases, these types of commentaries assume some basic knowledge of the ancient languages—or at least familiarity with the alphabets. But you can still get good help from these tools even without that basic knowledge.[56]

You'll notice that I've saved commentaries for our last step. That's intentional. Why? Because it's easy to bail out to a commentary and miss the reward of personal discovery. Dependence on commentaries also teaches us (and sometimes tempts us) to rely more on someone else's opinion than on our own firsthand experience with God's Word. I recommend doing your own word study first, and then using commentaries to check your conclusions and perhaps put a little icing on the cake.

I'm fortunate to have on my office shelf the *New International Commentary on the New Testament*, published by Eerdmans. In the volume on John, I learn that the word *emphanizo* in John 14:21 carries the sense of a very clear and conspicuous showing.[57]

The Put-Together

So what does all this mean? Let's upload our new data on the word *emphanizo* into our original verse: "Whoever has my commands and keeps them is the one who loves me. Anyone who loves me will be loved by my Father, and I too will love them and *show* myself to them" (John 14:21, TNIV, italics added).

John's specific use of *emphanizo* indicates that this will be a noticeable appearance from Jesus—not some kind of mysterious sign. The verb tense tells us that this will happen at a definite point in time. And the use of the word in classical Greek literature tells us that it will be a conspicuous appearance, one we can't miss.

This doesn't sound like something that will happen "in theory"—or far away at the end of time. It sounds as if when we have and obey Jesus' commands, we will experience the noticeable, palpable presence of Jesus. Jesus will make an appearance. He will shine. We will gain a more intimate understanding of him.

Now that we better understand the word *manifest,* Jesus' promise is much more vivid, real, and difficult to meander past in Scripture. This gives us a new goal to shoot for in our interaction with Jesus' words. Our personal devotions may never be the same.

Imagine your students getting to have this kind of experience with Jesus. Consider how much spiritual resolve and faith fortitude they could gain from experiencing the tangible presence of Jesus on a regular basis.

Old Testament Hebrew Word Study—*Atonement*

Let's do one more word study, this time with the Old Testament word for atonement. We first see the word applied to the offerings made by Aaron and his sons in Exodus 29:33: "They are to eat these offerings by which atonement was made for their ordination and consecration. But no one else may eat them, because they are sacred."

Other English Versions (Parallel Study)

First let's check out how other English translations have rendered the word *atonement*:

And they shall eat those things wherewith the atonement was made, to consecrate and to sanctify them: but a stranger shall not eat thereof, because they are holy. (KJV)

Thus they shall eat those things by which atonement was made at their ordination and consecration; but a layman shall not eat them, because they are holy. (NASB)

Take the ordination ram and boil the meat in the Holy Place. At the entrance to the Tent of Meeting, Aaron and his sons will eat the boiled ram and the bread that is in the basket. Atoned by these offerings, ordained and consecrated by them, they are the only ones who are to eat them. No outsiders are to eat them; they're holy. Anything from the ordination ram or from the bread that is left over until morning you are to burn up. Don't eat it; it's holy. *(The Message)*

Looks like there's no doubt about how to translate the word *atonement*. Every English version we checked uses the same word, although *The Message* changed the form of the word to a passive verb, *atoned*.

Let's dig a little deeper.

Concordance

Using *Strong's Exhaustive Concordance*, I see that the word *atonement* used in Exodus 29:33 is assigned number 3722. I also come across many uses of the English word in other passages, including Romans 5:11 where I see that atonement is now achieved through Jesus Christ.

With the number 3722 in hand, I head for the Hebrew dictionary in the back of *Strong's*. Here I find this definition for *kaphar*: "a prim. root; to cover (spec. with bitumen); fig. to expiate or condone, to placate or cancel:—appease, make (an) atonement, cleanse, disannul, forgive, be merciful, pacify, pardon, to pitch, purge (away), put off, (make) reconcile (-liation)."

In this definition I see some words that can help me understand atonement: to cover, cleanse, annul. I also see a nonspiritual application: to cover with bitumen, which Webster's tells me is a tar-like pitch. I put this in the "things that make you go *hmmm*" category.

Interlinear Bible

My next stop is Zodhiates' *Complete Word Study Old Testament,* which contains an interlinear translation and dictionary aids. Again using *Strong's* number 3722, I go to the dictionary, where I find this entry: "The verb probably is derived from the noun *kippurim* 3725. *Kaphar* is one of the most important words in the Bible. Its first usage appears in Genesis 6:14 where Noah is given instructions to cover the ark inside and outside with pitch (bitumen). Most of the time the verb is used with reference to 'covering' (hiding) sin with the blood of a sacrifice. Leviticus 4:13-21 gives detailed instructions to the priests. When Isaiah received God's call in a vision, his lips were touched with a fiery coal from God's altar. Therefore, his sin was purged (kaphar; see Isaiah 6:7). The New English Bible sometimes translates this term as 'wiped away.'"[58]

Several things in this definition support what I learned from Strong's concordance, as well as add insight.

I see where the "cover with pitch" definition was applied in Scripture with Noah and the ark. That's a cool tie-in, and it gives me a great mental image of the kind of protection or covering atonement provides.

I also see a derivative form of *kaphar*, the noun *kippur* or *kippurim* (Strong's number 3725). Zodhiates tells me that this word means "expiation or atonement." It's here that I learn that the English word *atonement* has its roots in Middle English and means "to be *at one*." (Aha. This points to the origination of the familiar definition, "*at-one*-ment.")

In the interlinear translation I see this code over the phrase "atonement was made": pupf3722. This tells me that the phrase is in the verb tense of "pual perfect," defined as follows: "The Pual Perfect indicates achievement of a perfective result or state, viewed as a whole, in the passive voice."

The Put-Together

Through the process of word study, I've learned that the root word for *atonement* is the same root used when God instructed Noah to cover the ark with pitch, inside and out, thus making it waterproof and buoyant. While the use of the word in Exodus doesn't directly refer to the building of Noah's ark in Genesis, it does give me a picture I can use to understand atonement.

It was pitch that covered the ark to make it seaworthy. It was the blood of animals that covered the sins of Israel to make them God-worthy. Romans 5:11 (the New Testament use of *atonement* in the KJV) tells me that it's the blood of Christ that covers our sins and reconciles us to God.[59]

The root word of atonement describes the action of covering or wiping away. When we are covered with the blood of Christ, it's the blood that God sees, not the sin. This is how we are able to be "at one" with God. Further, the pual perfect verb tense conveys a "perfective result; viewed as a whole." This isn't to suggest that we've achieved perfection, but it describes how God sees us. Our sins are perfectly covered.

God sees nothing but the blood. And as they say down South, "That'll preach."

Our students desperately need the message of atonement. If the word itself sounds too churchy or lofty, the background of the Hebrew word may provide some handles they can grab. Through word study we now have several handles we can use in explaining this word to students. We have the example of the tar-like covering on the ark. We also have the mental image of Jesus' blood serving as a coating—a layer between God and us, which enables us to be God-worthy, no matter what sins the blood is covering.

Word Study with Students

You may have an advanced student or two who would be intrigued by doing a word study and who might even like to add a few word studies to their personal Bible study plan. In rare instances you may even find that you're working with a group that enjoys looking up a few Greek or Hebrew words now and then.

But the most likely use of word studies with your students will come in your personal leader prep. Understanding the meanings of certain Greek and Hebrew words and how they were used in Scripture will strengthen your teaching and prepare you to answer questions that come up as you work through a passage with students.

Online Tools

Many Bible versions are available online, as well as several of the best-known Bible study tools. The upside to online study tools, such as concordances and dictionaries, is that they're usually free.

But there's also a downside. Often they're free because they're in the public domain, which can mean they're outdated. They can still be useful, but know that you're not benefiting from the latest scholarship available.

Here's a short list of some Web sites offering helpful resources at the time of this writing:

Biblegateway.com

Blueletterbible.org

Crosswalk.com

Greekbible.com

Lightsource.com

Onlinebible.net

Sacrednamebible.com (scroll down to King James Bible with Strong's Concordance Bible)

Scripture4all.org (includes a free interlinear software package)

Zhubert.com

Bible Software

Good Bible software isn't cheap, but it's worth the investment. You'll be amazed at how much work is done for you with just the hover of your cursor. Logos, Bibleworks, QuickVerse, and Zondervan Bible Study Library include the newest (and oldest) translations—and gobs of them. You can also choose between standard and deluxe packages, the deluxe packages containing the better word study tools.

Purified Seven Times

In Psalm 12 David quotes God saying that he will protect those who are weak and needy. David then locks in that promise by confirming that the words of the Lord are flawless—like silver refined in a furnace, purified seven times.

In ancient times a refiner would heat silver to a liquid form, forcing the impurities in the lustrous metal to rise to the top. Then the refiner would scrape off the impurities, leaving the silver purer than before.

This heating and scraping process would continue until the liquid was so pure that it reflected the face of the refiner as a mirror would. When the refiner could see his own face reflected, this was evidence that the silver had been fully refined and was ready for its intended use.

The words of Scripture have been refined in a furnace, "purified seven times." In other words, God chose his words carefully. In them, God sees his reflection.

Understanding a word in its original language gets us closer to that mirror-like reflection—the moment when God scraped off the final layer of impurity and said, "Ah, that's it! There's the word that best reflects me."

CHAPTER FIFTEEN

Tracking a Character

These things happened to them as examples and were written down as warnings for us, on whom the fulfillment of the ages has come. 1 CORINTHIANS 10:11

I saw [the Bible] instead as a great, tattered compendium of writings, the underlying and unifying purpose of all of which is to show how God works through the Jacobs and Jabboks of history to make himself known to the world and to draw the world back to himself.

FREDERICK BUECHNER • *NOW AND THEN*

Shortly after Hurricanes Rita and Katrina ravaged the Gulf South, I found myself on a flight to Sacramento that made a stop in Houston. There I picked up a seat neighbor decked out in full Louisiana State University attire—shorts, T-shirt, even the dangly earrings.

There was no question where she was from. Yet as soon as she took her seat, she informed me (really, the entire plane), "I've survived Rita *and* Katrina, and I'm getting outta there!"

My new seatmate was on her way to live with her parents in California. As we talked I learned that Katrina had dealt her only a glancing blow. But the previous hurricane, Rita, had swamped her business, a liquor distributorship.

When she learned about my line of work, Christian ministry, she did some fast backpedaling, saying, "We sell liquor, but we don't drink."

"However," she added, "if they have Corona Light on this flight, I'm getting one." I guess she figured a beer or two was the least she deserved after surviving two hurricanes.

We continued to chat off and on as I tried to read my book, which happened to be Mike Yaconelli's *Messy Spirituality: God's Annoying Love for Imperfect People.*

After a while, the beverage cart came by. And while there was no Corona Light to be had, there *was* a Bloody Mary—which she promptly ordered, saying to me, "We don't drink, but I think one is okay."

I kept reading my book. She kept ordering Bloody Marys. And with each glass she ordered, she reminded me, "We don't drink, but..."

Between paragraphs (mine) and swigs (hers), she periodically engaged me on the subject of drinking alcohol as it relates to Christianity and eternity—seeking my advice, but perhaps even more, seeking absolution.

Meanwhile, I was engrossed in a chapter in which Mike describes Noah and his post-flood activities. (Remember what Noah did *after* the ark landed safely on dry land? No? Well, neither had I. It seems Noah's post-flood activities don't get much pulpit time these days.)

As my new friend kept pressing the alcohol question—and ordering Bloody Marys hand over fist—I started wondering whether my role was to be a voice of conscience in this woman's life. Typically not one to interfere, I soon convinced myself that it was by divine providence that I happened to be seated beside this now-drunk double-hurricane survivor. Maybe I should suggest a drink limit!

I even formulated the words in my mind, something light-hearted but with a suggested limit: *No, I don't think one Bloody Mary could send a person to hell, but 10 might.* They were on the tip of my tongue when my eyes landed on an observation in Mike's book about Noah—one of the greatest men of faith in all of history.

After surviving the flood, Noah got drunk and naked.[60]

It was timing worthy of Comedy Central.

And in a split second I realized that my seat neighbor—like Noah still handling the fresh horror of having survived the flood—was doing just fine. (Thankfully, she was only a little drunk and not naked.)

As I and other passengers (some of whom were headed to the same Youth Specialties convention I was headed to) helped our flood survivor off the plane, I realized once again that the people in the Bible and the events of their lives didn't tumble into Scripture by accident.

Every point of interaction we see between God and man in Scripture teaches us about the interaction between God and us. Paul even said, speaking of our forefathers in the faith, that the things written about them in Scripture were "written down as warnings for us" (1 Corinthians 10:11).

In another letter he noted that everything written in the past "was written to teach us, so that through endurance and the encouragement of the Scriptures we might have hope" (Romans 15:4).

James tells us that Elijah was a man just like us (James 5:17). *Just like us!* Not a spiritual giant or otherworldly wonder, but an ordinary guy with the same problems and shortcomings we have.

What's more, James's description of Elijah goes for everyone else in the Bible, including James. In their lives we see disappointments, victories, failed faith, mighty faith, mistakes, sinful moments, and complete restoration.

We see people just like us being used by God. I call that *hope.*

People Who Like People

Name someone who *doesn't* like the thought of taking a sneak peek into the private life of someone he admires. Most of us love a glimpse behind the scenes, "Behind the Music," or behind the closed doors of the rich and famous. It's what put cable TV on the map.

People magazine is another great case in point. The spin-off of a single-page feature in *Time* magazine (entitled "People"), as of 2006 *People* magazine has a circulation of 3.73 million with revenues expected to exceed $1.5 billion.[61]

So why not use this fascination with people—their passions and interests and weaknesses and quirks—as a gateway into Bible study? Delving into the life of someone in Bible history is called doing a character study. And believe me, they're a bunch of *characters*.

Yet the primary purpose of doing a character study in Scripture is not to learn about characters themselves, but about *God's* character. God is the main character in the Bible; the others are supporting actors who make the protagonist shine.

To put it more emphatically, if all you've gotten out of a study of Mary the mother of Jesus—or Daniel, Paul, Joseph, or David—is principles about the person, then you've missed the point of a character study.

The point is observing *God's* character, his traits and ways, which are best seen through God's interaction with people.

Connecting the Dots

A few years back I had a theory I wanted to test.

I was pretty sure my students knew quite a bit about the people in the Bible. But I guessed that they knew little about God through the stories of those people.

So I put together a little survey in which I listed the names of seven Bible people with three empty columns to the right. In the first empty column, I asked students to put the seven people in historical order. In the second column, I asked them to jot down what they knew about these people. And in the third column, I asked them to write what they knew for sure about God through the stories of these people in Scripture.

Over the course of a few weeks, I gave this survey to around 300 Christian students at various conferences. And my little theory proved dead-on correct.

Fewer than 10 percent of the students could put the Bible people in order. In the second columns the students wrote a fair amount about the characters themselves. But the third columns they left mostly blank—where they were to have listed info about God.

My students could wax eloquent about the people and stories in the Bible, but they were hard-pressed to come up with anything about God—the main person I'd wanted them to meet in Scripture. And their inability to put the people in some semblance of chronological order revealed just how jumbled God's revelation was to them.

Each character's story reveals a trait or an aspect of God's character that may not be addressed in the same way anyplace else in Scripture. As we put the lives of the people together as in a children's connect-the-dot game, a giant picture of God emerges. Each character and story contributes to the big picture. Even in a book such as Esther, where God isn't mentioned by name, we see God's providential hand and his character at work.

How to Do a Character Study

Most of your students who have grown up in church will have two-dimensional, cartoon, superhero images of many of the Bible greats from their Sunday school days.

So how do you take caricatures of men such as Abraham, Moses, Peter, and Paul and present them as the multidimensional, flesh-and-blood people they were?

Here's where inductive study can help.

By observing people firsthand in Scripture—unairbrushed and unedited—students will see just how real and raw these people truly were. That's when they become the kind of people your students can learn from and relate to.

Four Steps

1. Decide who you want to study.

   Begin your character study by finding where in Scripture this person is mentioned, using an exhaustive concordance or Bible software or online search tool. Be sure to record the primary passages that talk about the person (such as Abel's story in Genesis 4) and any pertinent cross-references (such as the important mention of Abel in Hebrews 11:4).

2. Collect the basic data.

   Read these passages from your Bible and note what you learn, or copy the verses into a word processing document.

3. Mine the information.

   Move through the basic steps of observation and interpretation, asking *God, show me* and *God, teach me*. Think about the following questions as well:

   - Is there a scene in which God calls this person to a special task? If so, what do you learn about how God calls people to do his work?

   - Why was this person's story included in the Bible? What timeless truths are communicated?

- What was the historical setting of this person's life? Where in God's big story does he or she fit?

- What does this person's interaction with God teach you about how to follow God?

- What does this person's past or present teach you about the kind of person God chooses and uses?

- If you're studying an Old Testament person, is he or she referred to in the New Testament? What insight about this person does the New Testament offer? How did Jesus and/or the New Testament writer interpret this person's story?

- Did the person write anything that's included in the Bible? What insight do these writings give you into his or her story or understanding of God?

4. Apply the truth.

After you've asked God to show you what he wants you to see and teach you what he wants you to learn, make the simple request *God, change me*. And add the following questions to help you apply what you've learned:

- What do I need to do to emulate the God-honoring traits of this person?

- What in my life parallels the circumstances of this person?

- How does this person's story give me hope?

- What can I imitate in my interaction with God?

- What do I learn about God from seeing him interact with this person? How can this knowledge help me in my circumstances?

As you follow these four steps in your personal study, you'll begin to see important truths that you'll also want your students to see. Because you've prepared, you'll have a good idea of how best to introduce this character to your students and prompt them to find and mark words that will unfold truth for them, much as it unfolded for you. The more prominent Bible people may take several study sessions to cover; other characters can be covered in one session.

Ideas for Group Study

People Magazine: Create a *People* magazine-style scrapbook that each student can use to collect information about Bible people from each session. Use your creativity here.

Personal Dossiers: Create an album of "personal dossiers" on the Bible people your group will be studying. On each page include an empty frame for an artist's rendering and a list of facts and questions. Students can draw a facial reaction based on a highlight from the person's life. Generic questions could include:

Name:

Age:

Tribe (of Israel):

Parents (if mentioned):

Spiritual background:

What task was this person recruited for?

What (if any) special qualities did this person exhibit, making them right for the task?

Was the person successful in his or her task?

sHow or why were they successful?

What was a highlight of this person's career?

What was the lasting impact of the person's career?

What does this person teach us about God?

In what ways would you like to imitate this person?

How can you learn from this person's mistakes?

Test Drive a Character Study

Ideas for character studies in Scripture are practically end-less. The following two sample studies will give you a test drive as you examine Elijah and Philip. Each sample lists pertinent Bible passages, suggested observations, and questions to explore.

Elijah

1. Spiritual Atmosphere: 1 Kings 16:29-33

   • What was the spiritual condition of God's people?

2. First Appearance: 1 Kings 17:1

   • What detail do you learn about Elijah from this verse?

3. The Challenge: 1 Kings 18

   • Tally the odds against Elijah.

   • Notice the details regarding Elijah's repair of the altar (a great indicator of Israel's spiritual condition).

   • Notice what Elijah prayed about himself, God, and the people.

4. New Testament Assessment: Romans 11:1-6 and James 5:17

   • What does the New Testament highlight about Elijah?

5. Application

   • How many of your students feel like they're the only one around (at school, at home, or on a sports team) trying to follow Christ? What can they learn from Elijah?

   • Taking a cue from Elijah's story, what can they count on from God when they feel like they're the only ones living for Him?

Philip

1. Spiritual Background: Acts 6:1-7

- What do these verses teach us about being in a state of readiness to be chosen by God for a task?

2. His Impact: Acts 8

- How did Philip respond to enormous spiritual persecution?

- What impact did he have around Samaria?

- What steps led to the Ethiopian's salvation?

3. Application

- What needs to change in order for you and your students to be described as Philip was described in Acts 6?

- How does Philip's impact in Samaria encourage you and your students?

- What can you learn from Philip's experience with the Ethiopian? How can it help you and your students share the faith?

- What does Philip's story teach us about how God uses people?

For Further Study

Listed below are Bible folks whose personality profiles and life circumstances lend themselves to teen Bible study. The short blurbs are intended to give a glimpse and pique your interest in further study. Using your electronic Bible tools, type their names into a search box—or crack open an exhaustive concordance—and you'll be off and running.

Enoch

This guy is mentioned primarily in the begats, but his unusual life and death (or lack thereof) garner special mention in the

New Testament. In one of the begats, his life is summed up in a tombstone-worthy phrase that's enviable still today.

Noah

When the world around him was evil, Noah found favor with God. Noah's story reveals one of the first situations in history in which God asked for obedience that was both counter-cultural *and* counter-intuitive. Noah's special mentions in the New Testament help us interpret his story today.

Abraham

With one man God launched His redemptive story—a story that eventually included you and me. Out of the blue, Abram was asked to leave his country, his household, and his father's family. And amazingly, he went. Some incredible things were asked of him along the way—to sacrifice his only son and circumcise the adult males in his family, to name a few. Abraham had a short stretch of weak faith, taking things into his own hands and fathering Ishmael, but later he was inducted into Hebrews' Hall of Fame of Faith.

Isaac

The "middle child" of the three great patriarchs of Israel, Isaac began his faith journey with the rather trepid observation, "The fire and wood are here, but where is the lamb for the burnt offering?" (Genesis 22:7)—and then found himself on top of an altar. Isaac gets less ink in Scripture than Abraham or Jacob, but he may have displayed greater faith than either of them in not overpowering his aged father and fleeing from that stack of firewood.

Jacob

The *tour de force* of character studies, Jacob's story has it all. Compliance. Rebellion. Patience. Impulsiveness. Obedience. Wrestling with God. Walking with God. Jacob's journey isn't just a character study; it's a character *mosaic* in which each tile gives us a unique view into the ways of God.

Joseph

You can check in at about any point in Joseph's story, and things look really bleak. But it was Joseph who gave us the phrase, "You intended to harm me, but God intended it for good" (Genesis 50:20). Joseph's story gives us a great handle on why bad things happen to good people.

Moses

Moses wrote the book on leadership. Literally. We can learn something new about God in every era of Moses' life: His fortunate childhood, his tumultuous young adulthood, his reluctant yes to leadership, his dealings with Pharaoh during the plagues, his unprecedented face time with God, and his leadership of God's obstinate and complaining people on a journey toward the Promised Land.

Caleb

You won't find a better example of finishing strong than Caleb. But Caleb also started strong, trusting God to deliver the Promised Land despite the gloomy report from his fellow spies. Caleb's feat of faith earned him an inheritance in the Promised Land (along with Joshua, the only other survivor from that faithless generation). But he didn't choose the relaxing retirement village when it came time to settle in the land.

Joshua

Joshua's life is a shining example of the victories we can expect when we follow God's instruction to have courage and stick close to his Word.

Rahab

Rahab gives us a good glimpse at an outsider looking in on the people of God. Her background offers all of us hope of being used by God, and her mentions in the New Testament indicate she was a popular character study, even then.

Deborah

The era of the judges is a lesson in God's patience and deliverance. Deborah's life gives us a picture of what resolute faith can look like, especially when the odds aren't so favorable. Much can be learned about Deborah and her reign from the song she wrote in Judges 5.

Gideon

Gideon's calling is a textbook example of how God calls and uses ordinary, imperfect people. His story gives great hope to those who feel inadequate for the task or who are experiencing a dry spell with God. It's also through Gideon that we learn one of God's most endearing traits: He's a dog lover!

Samson

Samson is a great example of how *not* to do it—a picture of what leadership looks like when the leader can't keep flesh under control. Samson's story gives us a birds-eye view as God uses someone despite obvious weaknesses and failings.

Samuel

Samuel was a one-stop shop in terms of leadership: Part judge, part prophet, part priest. You've known Samuel since your Sunday school days from his famous "Here am I" scene. But Samuel has much more to teach us about leadership and about God.

King Saul

God told the Israelites they'd regret succumbing to peer pressure and asking for a king. Sure enough, it happened on the very first try. But they weren't the only regretful ones. Saul's actions give us a glimpse into God's heart and character that's rarely seen in Scripture.

King David

David may be the most popular character to study of all time. And for good reason—he showed us how to succeed at

following God, how to fail at following God, and how to succeed when we fail, as noted in his Psalm 51 *mea culpa*. And
since the final word on David is that he was a man after God's
own heart (Acts 13:22), it's a worthy pursuit to find out why.

Solomon
Wow! We can we learn a lot from this guy. Not only from his
actions, but also from his writings about his actions (see Proverbs, Song of Solomon, and especially Ecclesiastes). Further-
more, Solomon implemented a plan that ultimately led to the
division of Israel.

The Kings
After the nation of Israel split into two nations (the Northern
Kingdom of Israel and the Southern Kingdom of Judah), Israel
never had a single king who could be characterized as God-
honoring, and Judah had only a handful. But this handful of
kings offers terrific insight into what God looks for in bringing
spiritual revival to his people.

The Prophets
Obviously we can learn a lot about these guys from their writings. But many of them are also written about in history books,
such as 1 and 2 Kings and 1 and 2 Chronicles. It's striking how
similar the spiritual atmosphere around these prophets is to
the spiritual atmosphere surrounding teenagers today. And
there's probably not a better window into God's heart than
through the messages of the prophets.

Ezra and Nehemiah
You know those times after a youth retreat or missions trip
when hearts are soft and repentant? That's the atmosphere
you'll find surrounding Ezra and Nehemiah. Their actions offer
a precedent on how to keep the spiritual momentum rolling.

Esther

Esther's courageous moves on behalf of her people can give your students a handle on how to engage their secular culture and surroundings. While God isn't mentioned by name in the book of Esther, his impact on the actions and attitudes of his people is obvious. May it always be.

John the Baptist

A favorite among character studies. Maybe it's the strange diet or the weird wardrobe, but John is the poster child for everything radical and extreme. Moreover, the interaction between John and Jesus provides a great model for our interaction with Jesus.

The Apostles

All the apostles can be tracked and profiled throughout the New Testament, though some are more prominent than others. Remember the old adage, "You are who your friends are"? By getting to know these guys, we get to know Jesus and see a side of him we otherwise might miss. As you pull together information on each apostle and see the personality characteristics of each, choose the apostle with whom your students will most readily identify. Contrast the apostles' actions before the resurrection with their actions after.

Paul

We probably have more personal spiritual information on Paul than on any other person in the Bible—not only from his writings, but also from the book of Acts. Find the places where Paul's background is described and compile a composite of his spiritual journey. You may find he's more like us than you've ever before considered.

Paul's Friends

You may have noticed that Paul never worked alone. In fact, Romans 16 contains greetings identifying 34 individuals and five groups. Each greeting includes a description that can teach us something about Kingdom work. Some names in this chapter show up in other places in the New Testament and give us a glimpse into the spiritual struggles of these first-century believers.

The Inside Track

I don't know what became of my hurricane-surviving seat-mate from that flight to Sacramento. I only know that Noah's story helped me understand her.

And in the long run she helped me understand Noah. As she described the nightmare of riding out the storm and climbing out from its devastation, I could picture the nervous anxiety that must have wracked poor Noah as he heard the cries of those outside the ark—the fear that must have gripped him as he wondered how things could ever turn out okay.

I could envision the muddy mess he had to endure when the ramp dropped open after the waters receded. I could imagine his thoughts: *Well, we made it, but what a mess. What an absolute mess. Now what?*

Noah and the other individuals described in the Bible were people just like us. They had setbacks. They made mistakes. Sometimes they soared with faith. Sometimes they fell flat on their faces.

These things were written down to warn us and give us hope. But best of all, they were written so that we could see the enduring traits of God, who works in and through people to display who he is.

The *characters* are an inside track to God's *character*.

CHAPTER SIXTEEN

Grab Bag

Nobody ever outgrows Scripture; the book widens and deepens with our years.

C.H. SPURGEON

So many ways, so little time.

One of the gifts of Scripture is the vast range of ways we can study it. There's something for every personality type and every learning style.

There's text for the reader. Images for the visual. Maps for the analytical. Timelines for the linear. Even gross stuff for the middle schooler.

You'd almost think the Bible was designed that way. And as a matter of fact, it probably was. It makes sense that the Designer of *how* we learn would embed in his Word a variety of vehicles to cater to the many *ways* we learn.

If you've ever made a major purchase of a car or a house, or even an intermediate purchase such as a set of golf clubs, you know it's easy to be overwhelmed by the options. When I bought my first (and so far only) set of golf clubs, I was overwhelmed to near incapacitation by the options and variables involved. Luckily I connected with an instructor who watched my swing and put three different types of clubs in my hand, narrowing my options to something I could manage.

The same can be true of ways we study the Bible. Decide to do a character study and you might be overwhelmed to find that the Bible names more than 3,000 characters.[62]

The purpose of this chapter is to help pare down the options to a manageable size as you learn to approach Scripture with love-letter intensity. You may want to experiment with one of these ideas in your personal study before breaking it out with your students.

Own a Bible Book

At first glance, how many squares do you see in the image below?

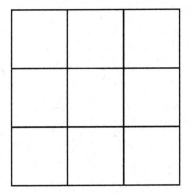

If your answer was in the single digits, look again.

Just glancing at the image, most of us would guess nine—maybe 10. Gaze another minute or two, and we might see a few more. Given time to really study the image, we'd land on a total of 14.[63]

Now superimpose that exercise over your knowledge of each book of the Bible. All of us have at least a thumbnail picture of what each Bible book is all about. But even in the books we're more familiar with, there's far more we could mine.

We just need to gaze a little longer...dig a little deeper.

God can use any book in the Bible to unfold his redemptive story. Just choose a book you and your students would enjoy exploring, and watch God bring it together. (Of course, if it's up to your students, they'll choose Revelation. Not a bad book for inductive study. But you might do better to get your feet wet with a smaller book and work your way up. When you *do* delve into Revelation, you can count on it to unfold God's redemptive story in an off-the-chart amazing way.)

After you've selected a book, dive into it using the Three Requests: *God, show me; God, teach me; God, change me.* As the leader, you'll want to study far enough ahead in order to have an overview of the entire book, as well as a feel for how the material in each chapter relates to the book's overall theme and purpose. This will help you know when and where to drill deep.

For example, with Colossians—a letter—you might want to focus on the *who?* in the first chapter. (*Whos* would include the writer and recipient of the letter, God, and Jesus). In chapter 2, you could hone in on the warnings; there are many. In chapter 3, you might park on the instructions. And in chapter 4, you might head back to the *whos*. Let the text itself drive which questions to ask to get to the right information.

Here are some rules of thumb to help the process.

Start small.

Begin with a one-chapter book such as Jude, Philemon, 2 John, or 3 John. Progress to an intermediate-sized book such as Colossians or Philippians.

Find the purpose statement.

Many New Testament writers stated explicitly why they wrote their particular books. If the book you're studying gives a purpose statement, encourage your group to find it—then keep it in front of your students from one session to the next.

Purpose statements are hugely important in setting the context for a book and in interpreting it correctly. Here are a few examples (all from the TNIV):

With this in mind, since I myself have carefully investigated everything from the beginning, I
too decided to write an orderly account for you,
most excellent Theophilus, so that you may know
the certainty of the things you have been taught.
(LUKE 1:3-4)

But these are written that you may believe that
Jesus is the Messiah, the Son of God, and that
by believing you may have life in his name.
(JOHN 20:31)

Dear friends, although I was very eager to write
to you about the salvation we share, I felt compelled to write and urge you to contend for the
faith that the Lord has once for all entrusted to
us, his people. (JUDE 1:3)

Think layer-by-layer.

Rather than drilling deep verse by verse, go deep by taking
a section of Scripture and peeling back the layers—much as
you'd remove the layers of an onion. For example, in the first
study session explore the *who* and *why* of a chapter; in the
next session go a layer deeper by examining the promises and
instructions of the same chapter.

Consider a combo.

Some books of the Bible seem to go hand in hand with each
other. How about studying...Deuteronomy alongside Romans/
Galatians? Leviticus with Hebrews? Luke and Acts together?
(Both almost unanimously believed to have been written by
Luke.) Colossians with Ephesians?

Don't be afraid to linger.

Think about how well your students will know the book of Jude—or Genesis or Philippians—if you really focus on it for a while. A few years back, my wife, Dana, was exploring James with a group of students. They started in September, and by Christmas they were halfway through. Given the normal 12-week church/school cycle, Dana figured it was time to move on to something else. To which the students replied, "No! This is great!"

Banish the study notes.

Most Bibles contain vast amounts of commentary in the form of study notes and introductory material on each book. Discipline yourself and your students to steer clear of this material—at least for a while. Why? Because it's a built-in discovery killer.

Let your students discover for themselves who wrote a book and why it was written. Let the text itself tell them what the book's first readers were experiencing. Leave the purpose statement (if there is one) buried as a gem for them to discover.

Draw a Picture

Remember the first time you went to see a movie of a book you liked, and the actor playing your favorite character was nothing you expected? "He was totally miscast," you might have said as you exited the theater. "In my mind he was taller—and his voice was completely different."

Whenever text from a page is unleashed in living color, it requires an expectation adjustment. Rarely does a live person look or sound or move like what we've imagined in our minds.

When it comes to unleashing the events of the Bible in living color, it helps to find ways to adjust our expectations and lose our stereotypes. Most of us carry around vague mental images of the main happenings and people in Scripture. Where the details are sketchy, our minds fill in the gaps with images from our childhood Bibles and Sunday school classes. (Remember the portrait of a mild-mannered Jesus? Or the compliant cartoon animals boarding the ark?)

Look closely at Scripture, and we'll find some entirely different visuals than what we've carried all these years.

One way to observe the details we've missed along the way is to draw what the Bible describes. (Stick figures will do just fine if you're not artistic.) For example, when you draw the ark using the dimensions of Noah's blueprint given in Genesis 6, you'll be surprised by its monolithic look—nothing like the arks you see in children's toys and coloring books.

Also consider drawing the Old Testament tabernacle, Isaiah's vision of God at his commissioning (Isaiah 6), Daniel's and King Nebuchadnezzar's dreams and their interpretations, Jesus' parables, and John's visions in Revelation. Don't be afraid to use graph paper to help you draw to scale objects that are given specific measurements in Scripture. And for a twist, consider making a clay model.

Map a Journey

My wife and I have totally different map philosophies. I love maps. Whenever we travel I'm in constant contact with at least one. For some strange reason (strange to Dana, that is) I like to know where I am in relation to where I'm going.

Dana loathes maps. She says they take the fun out of getting where you're going. They suck the adventure right out of the trip.

Depending on where you fall on the spectrum, you may love or loathe this next exercise.

The Bible is full of geographic references. In fact, apologists often point to the Bible's inclusion of these references as a stamp of its authenticity. Why, if you were creating a story out of thin air, would you include a lot of places and names that could easily be checked?

Obviously you could look in the back of your Bible for many of the map ideas that follow. But mapping a passage yourself provides yet another portal through which God can show you what he wants you to see. For visual learners, that's a bonus.

I suggest finding a map (or making your own) that shows the pertinent locations, but not the route the people took. As you study, draw the movement from one point to another in a connect-the-dots fashion—and list beside each key location any major events that occurred there. For a twist, draw the map on a floor-sized tarp. Good passages to map include the sojourns of Abraham, Isaac, or Jacob (Genesis); Israel's journey from Egypt to the Promised Land (Exodus, Numbers); Jesus' ministry (choose one of the Gospel accounts); and Paul's travels (Acts).

Create a Time Line

Your safest bet in understanding a historical but futuristic book such as Daniel is to make a time line. Then use it to plot each happening. Occasionally you'll bump into a date reference that will connect events to a past or future point on the calendar. But the primary benefit of a time line is to help you organize and understand events that occur chronologically in Scripture. For a twist, draw your time line on a sheet of newsprint the length of your longest wall. Begin with Israel's 40 years in the wilderness (Exodus, Numbers); Daniel's and Nebuchadnezzar's dreams and visions (Daniel); Jesus' final week in Jerusalem (choose one of the Gospel accounts); or what John saw in Revelation.

Tracking Themes

Bible theme ideas are practically endless. Pick up a topical Bible (such as *Nave's Topical Bible*), a Thompson Chain-Reference Bible, or a concordance. After you've chosen a theme you'd like to explore, collect the passages related to it. Then use the Three Requests (*God, show me; God, teach me; God, change me*) to explore your theme.

As you embark on a theme study, find where the theme is first introduced and follow it all the way through the Bible. Ask if there's an Old Testament event that serves as an object lesson for a New Testament theme or concept. Called "types" (from the Greek word *tupos*), these real-life happenings in Israel's history shed light on spiritual principles that came later with Christ. For example, Israel was physically redeemed from slavery in Egypt; believers in Jesus are redeemed from slavery to sin.

Consider how a theme begun in the Old Testament takes on a new or richer meaning when we encounter it in Jesus' teachings. And ask what issues in students' lives are addressed by the theme.

Some good topics for theme-related study include the following:

- Covenant
- Holiness and sanctification
- Adoption and the firstborn
- Inheritance
- Atonement and justification
- Redemption and the redeemed
- Blood and sacrifice
- Jesus' "I am" statements in John and God's "I am" statement in Exodus

- The names of God
- The names and titles of Jesus
- Jesus' parables that begin "The kingdom of heaven is like..."
- Calls to follow or be part of God's mission
- Places where God abides

Tracking Threads

Similar to theme studies are what you might call thread studies—passages from different parts of the Bible that are linked by a common thread. Here are a few examples.

Body Fluids

A youth pastor friend and his group had a blast studying the various body fluids mentioned in the Bible, using each fluid to tackle a life issue. Examples include a dog returning to its vomit (breaking free from the past), blood (salvation and redemption), and God blowing his nostrils (the sovereignty of God).

Benedictions and Goodbyes

The Old and the New Testaments are full of prayers, benedictions, and goodbye scenes, each giving an awesome picture of God—and in some cases, some great promises to claim. Some examples include Joshua's farewell in Joshua 23-24; Jesus' farewell in John 14-17; Paul's in Ephesians 3:20-21; and Jude's in Jude 1:24-25.

God's Playlist

Sometimes after a mighty act of God or a special revelation from him, God's people would be so overwhelmed with gratitude that they'd sing a song right on the spot. God made sure that a few of these made it into the Bible.

Like knowing a friend better by the songs she likes, studying God's playlist—along with the events that inspired each song—helps us better understand the attributes of God. Check out Moses' and the Israelites' song (Exodus 15:1-19), Deborah's song (Judges 5), Song of Solomon, and Mary's song (Luke 1:46-55)

Pray the Prayers

We saw in Chapter 9 that there's not a more direct application of Scripture than literally *doing* what Scripture does—such as when a Bible writer prays a prayer and we begin praying that prayer, too.

Use your Bible software or concordance to find a few prayers recorded in Scripture. Here are some examples to get you started: Matthew 6:9-13; Acts 4:24-31; Ephesians 3:16-19; Colossians 1:9-12. (Don't forget that many of the psalms are prayers.) Study these prayers using your inductive tools, being careful to note what happened when they were prayed.

Keep a running list of the important principles you and your group uncover about prayer. Encourage your students to record their favorite prayers from the Bible in a journal and then pray them on their own. When you run out of words to pray about a particular problem in life, let the words of some of the great pray-ers in history take over.

Judah's Revivals

Need a kick-start out of a spiritual rut? Study the spiritual revivals experienced by the nation of Judah under its few godly kings. Asa's revival (2 Chronicles 14-16), Jehoshaphat's revival (2 Chronicles 17-20), and Hezekiah's revival (2 Chronicles 29-32) will help you see God's pattern in bringing revival to his people today.

Read the Red

What if Jesus' words were the only Bible we had? What if we hung on every word from Jesus as the first disciples must have done—as if it really were our daily food?

One of the simplest and best ideas for transformational Bible study is to grab a red-letter edition of the New Testament and explore the words of Jesus. As you soak in his words, organize what you find into broad categories such as commands/instructions, teachings, and promises. As you progress, you may want to create a few subcategories, such as teachings on the end of the age or teachings on the kingdom of heaven.

Acts 2-4-2 Party

Church life doesn't get any purer than what's described in Acts 2:42—a great snapshot of the early church right after the Holy Spirit got it rolling. Study the spiritual atmosphere of the early church as recorded in Acts and the New Testament letters. Then plan a party that incorporates the activities of the early believers recorded in Acts 2:42. They devoted themselves to the apostles' teaching, fellowship, the breaking of bread, and prayer.

It Doesn't Stop Here

Can you see why a lifetime isn't long enough to explore all the possibilities between the pages of your Bible? Take advantage of the Bible's design and the myriad of ways it wants to be explored. Find a medium that caters to the students in your ministry, and use it as a gateway into the riches of God's Word.

CHAPTER SEVENTEEN

Where in the Word Are You?

The question of the proper feeding of our own devotional life must of course include the rightful use of spiritual reading. And with spiritual reading we may include formal or informal meditation upon Scripture or religious truth: the brooding consideration, the savouring—as it were the chewing of the cud—in which we digest that which we have absorbed, and apply it to our own needs.

EVELYN UNDERHILL • *CONCERNING THE INNER LIFE*

Remember the day when Saddam Hussein was pulled out of his now-famous spider hole and taken captive? What you may not know is the unlikely story of the intelligence work that led to his capture.

It started when a U.S. Army major handed two junior intelligence officers a list of four names that were part of a much larger web—and somehow connected to Hussein. The junior officers, who had only done a few small intelligence projects, thought it was a joke.

It wasn't.

They barely knew where to start. But given the orders, the two jumped in. And after some preliminary work, the four names grew to a list of 9,000.

Now what?

They began poring over the data. And after several months, the 9,000 were whittled down to 300. Those 300 names were plotted on a 46-by-42-inch color-coded chart that resembled a family tree, with

Saddam at the center. Blood ties and tribal relationships connected the massive web of names. The two officers mined huge databases and reams of reports to add detail to each name, including addresses, spouses, ages, and physical descriptions.

As information was added, the pair began to see some key patterns, layers, and trends—such as those who had tribal and family loyalties to Hussein and those who were apparently in the mix for the money. As they lived with the data, the officers were confident that a major puzzle piece would emerge.

And it did.

Over time, a single name on the chart emerged as out of the ordinary—someone with deep ties to Hussein and to others on the list. After a few failed attempts, this man was finally captured in a house raid in Baghdad. Saddam Hussein was taken captive the very next day.[64]

Sometimes the Bible can look like that massive list of 9,000 names. Where in the world do we start?

Sleuthing in the Word

The Bible wasn't built to be read like a novel from start to finish— though that's certainly a rewarding exercise, especially with a version that reads more like a novel, such as *The Message*.

Its best rewards come from a diligent approach that lets God's great truths and themes emerge from the labyrinth. The amazing traits of God become giant hooks on which to hang our insights. God's grand mission to redeem a lost world provides a solid framework on which to hang the stories of those who joined (or resisted) his plan.

Before long, the Old Testament is more than a jumbled collection of talking donkeys, floating arks, glorious victories, resounding defeats, mighty leaders, weird prophets, and evil kings. And the New Testament becomes more than a random collection of letters and tales of a startling new faith.

The character and ways of God begin to emerge—and then, as with the army and its 9,000 names, one Name begins to emerge.

This chapter is here to help you and your students find a place to start. It's organized so that familiar people, scenes, and stories are seen within the context of God's unfolding revelation. (By the way, the Old Testament instantly shrinks when you discover that it overlaps itself—Israel's entire history takes place from Genesis to Nehemiah; the rest of the books overlap that same time period.)

Let the following portals take you into God's Word. Where you go from there is up to you. There's nothing overwhelming—nothing scholarly or formal—about the following chart. Just a few launch pads for a rockin' good time with God.

PENTATEUCH

GENESIS

A history book, Genesis lends itself to a study based on time, geography, or any of the awesome personalities you'll encounter. Not only is Genesis a record of mankind's beginnings, you'll also find the genesis of most of the Bible's major themes.

GROUND COVERED:

Genesis takes us from Creation to Jacob's family move to Egypt.

GENESIS 1-3

Dissect the anatomy of temptation, and track the consequences of sin. Have students put everything they learn on a pocket-sized card, and challenge them to not leave home without it (especially on Friday and Saturday nights).

GENESIS 1-11

Find the first mentions of subjects and themes that run throughout the entire Bible, such as obedience and disobedience, grace, covenant, and nations.

GENESIS 12-46

Keep a running list of everything God reveals about himself when he makes contact with Abraham, Isaac, and Jacob.

GENESIS 39

As you follow Josephs' story, note the phrase that goes something like this: "The Lord was with him." Draw parallels between the circumstances around that phrase and the circumstances surrounding your students. Teach them to claim the same promises.

| GENRE | BOOK BASICS | PORTALS FOR IN-DEPTH STUDY |

PENTATEUCH

EXODUS

Here we catch our first glimpse of what it takes to be a holy people whom God can use. Embrace the details; draw what you see in Exodus, such as the tabernacle and priestly garments.

GROUND COVERED:

Exodus spans from Jacob's family (now the nation of Israel) in Egypt to God filling the movable tabernacle with his glory before the people head to the Promised Land.

EXODUS 6-8,10,14, 16, 29, 31

The purpose of all the incredible events in Exodus can be found in the little phrase, "Know that I am God." Find the various people this phrase was directed to and what actions will lead to our *knowing*. Challenge students to make their lives a tool God can use to help others know that he is God.

EXODUS 32-34

The golden calf incident was a watershed moment. Follow the dialogue between God (what he said and did) and Moses in this tense back-and-forth scene. Students will appreciate seeing God's softer side displayed.

| GENRE | BOOK BASICS | PORTALS FOR IN-DEPTH STUDY |

PENTATEUCH

LEVITICUS

Welcome to the book most often cited as "That's where I lost it" by those who've tried to read straight through the Bible. Here's the good news: Leviticus can take on new life when we simply track the key phrase (and its variations): "Be holy, because I am holy."

GROUND COVERED:

All of the action takes place at Mount Sinai.

LEVITICUS 11, 19-21

Instances where Israel is told to "be holy" serve as outline anchors for this difficult book. In fact, the difficulty of Leviticus can give students new appreciation for what Jesus has done for them and breathe new life into the "sanctify" verses of the New Testament.

GENRE	BOOK BASICS	PORTALS FOR IN-DEPTH STUDY

PENTATEUCH

NUMBERS

What begins as the chronicle of an 11-day journey to the Promised Land becomes the chronicle of a 40-year sojourn in the wilderness brought about by a fateful decision in Numbers 14.

GROUND COVERED:

Numbers covers Israel's departure from Mount Sinai, her wilderness wanderings, and the final stop before the Promised Land.

NUMBERS 13

Notice how the details of the spy scene give a window into human nature: How easily we suffer from a lack of faith despite God's promises. How easily we look backward when the way forward is laden with giants.

GENRE	BOOK BASICS	PORTALS FOR IN-DEPTH STUDY

PENTATEUCH

DEUTERONOMY

This book sets up the remainder of the Old Testament, giving significant insight as to why Israel is either enjoying peace or enduring oppression for the rest of her days.

GROUND COVERED:

All of the action takes place on the plains of Moab in preparation for moving into the Promised Land.

DEUTERONOMY 4-11, 28

This book's juxtaposition of blessing for obedience versus consequences for disobedience lays the groundwork for the rest of the Old Testament (and also for our lives).

DEUTERONOMY 28-31

Explore God's heart for the things "written in this book." Use this as a catalyst for taking God's Word more seriously in your student ministry.

GENRE	BOOK BASICS	PORTALS FOR IN-DEPTH STUDY

HISTORY

JOSHUA

This book represents the pinnacle of Israel's obedience as they drive out the "-ites" (rather, *most* of the "ites") and take possession of the Promised Land.

GROUND COVERED:

Joshua picks up just outside the Promised Land and ends with Israel enjoying peace within its borders as the reward for obeying God.

COMPARE NUMBERS 33:51-56 WITH JOSHUA 9 AND 12-16

Contrast what God told Israel to do with what Israel actually did. This vivid example of partial obedience will show your students that there's no such thing as "mostly obedient." It's all or nothing with God.

GENRE	BOOK BASICS	PORTALS FOR IN-DEPTH STUDY

HISTORY

JUDGES

Israel cycles from defeat to victory to defeat again, their downfall explained by the key phrase, "Everyone did what was right in his own eyes" (Judges 21:25, NASB). Judges offers a great picture of the spiritual cycles in our own lives.

GROUND COVERED:

Judges covers roughly 335 years, approaching the time of Samuel, the last judge.

JUDGES 2-4

These chapters dramatically display the vicious cycle that runs throughout the book: falling away, oppression, repentance, restoration, and peace. Seeing this cycle can give students insight into their personal "commit-fail-commit" cycles. It can also spark a great evaluation of your student ministry as you find where you are in the cycle.

GENRE	BOOK BASICS	PORTALS FOR IN-DEPTH STUDY

HISTORY

RUTH

Ruth is a love story that takes place during the time of the judges.

GROUND COVERED:

The action occurs during the period covered by the book of Judges.

RUTH 1-4

The contents of Ruth are like the stuff of a great movie. In fact, invite your students to make a digital short film of Ruth's story. This will help them live the plight of Naomi, the unselfishness of Ruth, and the redemption displayed in the acts of Boaz.

GENRE	BOOK BASICS	PORTALS FOR IN-DEPTH STUDY

1 SAMUEL

Chronicling the transition from the last judge of Israel, Samuel, to the first king, Saul, this book is a great lesson on the consequences that can result from a vacuum of godly spiritual leadership.

GROUND COVERED:

1 Samuel covers 94 years, from the birth of Samuel to the death of Saul.

1 SAMUEL 8

This powerful chapter documents Israel's insistence on being like the other nations (talk about peer pressure!) and introduces one of the first documented substitutes for God—a king. God's people have been making substitutes ever since. Follow the dialogue between Israel, Samuel, and God in this chapter, and compare it to God's foretelling of this moment in Deuteronomy 17:14-20. Then discuss any substitutes for God that you and your students have locked in on.

GENRE	BOOK BASICS	PORTALS FOR IN-DEPTH STUDY

2 SAMUEL

Watch the rise, fall, and restoration of King David.

GROUND COVERED:

2 Samuel picks up just after David's reign begins and closes just before he dies.

2 SAMUEL 6

The return of the Ark of the Covenant under David's reign is loaded with teachable moments, including the sacredness of the Ark, the importance of God's presence, and the value of celebration. And students will have a lot of fun with Michal's reaction to David's celebration.

GENRE	BOOK BASICS	PORTALS FOR IN-DEPTH STUDY

1 KINGS

This book begins with one kingdom and ends with two. Subtitle: Lessons on How *Not* to Lead a Kingdom.

GROUND COVERED:

The action extends from the reign of Solomon over one kingdom to the reigns of Jehoshaphat in Judah and Ahaziah in Israel.

1 KINGS 3

Learn from King Solomon, shortly after he assumed his reign, why wisdom is always a good thing to ask for when you're requesting things from God. In the same chapter, see this wisdom in action as Solomon makes one of the gutsiest calls of all time.

GENRE	BOOK BASICS	PORTALS FOR IN-DEPTH STUDY

HISTORY

2 KINGS

The consequences of disobedience outlined in Deuteronomy come to fruition in 2 Kings. The northern kingdom is conquered by Assyria; then the southern kingdom is conquered by Babylon.

GROUND COVERED:

The book opens with the two kingdoms divided and closes with the two kingdoms gone.

2 KINGS

It's amazing how many of Israel's and Judah's kings are described as doing evil in the sight of God. Spiritual leadership is no guarantee of immunity from temptation. Search the word *evil*, and track what each king did that was so bad in God's eyes.

GENRE	BOOK BASICS	PORTALS FOR IN-DEPTH STUDY

HISTORY

1 CHRONICLES

1 and 2 Chronicles serve as a spiritual editorial on the events in 2 Samuel and 1 and 2 Kings, describing many of the same events from a more God-focused perspective.

GROUND COVERED:

With special emphasis on David's reign, 1 Chronicles includes a genealogy documenting the entire history of Israel (and the world), from Adam to the return of God's people from exile.

1 CHRONICLES 17

Track God's response to David when he expresses his desire to build God a house.

GENRE	BOOK BASICS	PORTALS FOR IN-DEPTH STUDY

HISTORY | **2 CHRONICLES**

This book parallels 1 and 2 Kings, with emphasis on Judah's few good kings who brought reform and revival to the land.

GROUND COVERED:

2 Chronicles opens during Solomon's reign, documents the kings of Judah through that nation's fall, and closes with Cyrus' announcement that the Jewish people can return to Jerusalem. | **2 CHRONICLES 14-20, 23, 27, 29-32, 34-35**

These chapters document the handful of revivals Judah enjoyed. Look for the actions and prayers of the leaders, and process with your students how these reveal what God desires from us before he will bring spiritual revival and awakening. |

GENRE	BOOK BASICS	PORTALS FOR IN-DEPTH STUDY

HISTORY | **EZRA**

Through the prophets, God told his people that they would return from Babylon to their land after 70 years. Ezra records how God made good on that promise.

GROUND COVERED:

The book begins with the first two waves of captives leaving Babylon and ends with God's people reestablishing life and spiritual order in the land. | **EZRA 9-10**

After God's people returned to their land, their obedience to and reverence for God were high. These chapters provide a great model of what a group of people can do when they realize they've drifted from God's plan. Find the trespasses, the *uh-oh* moments, the response of the leaders, and the response of the people. |

GENRE	BOOK BASICS	PORTALS FOR IN-DEPTH STUDY

HISTORY

NEHEMIAH

Whereas Ezra was a catalyst for restoring life and spiritual order after the exile, Nehemiah was a catalyst for restoring physical order as he rebuilt the walls around Jerusalem.

GROUND COVERED:

The book takes place after the exile and records the final action in the Old Testament.

NEHEMIAH 7-10

These chapters provide a great how-to for those who have seriously blown it and want to recover lost ground with God. Note the attention to God's Word and appreciation for God's mercies.

GENRE	BOOK BASICS	PORTALS FOR IN-DEPTH STUDY

HISTORY

ESTHER

One of two books without a direct reference to God (Song of Solomon is the other), Esther shows a great picture of God's providence. Meet a brave young woman who was at the right place at the right time to save God's people.

GROUND COVERED:

The entire book takes place during the time of Ezra.

ESTHER 4

Fear. Apprehension. Anxiety. These are just a few of the things we might feel when God calls us to a task. Chapter 4 of Esther offers a great example of someone who overcame these emotions.

GENRE	BOOK BASICS	PORTALS FOR IN-DEPTH STUDY

POETRY

JOB

Job begins with a strange conversation between God and Satan—a conversation that unexpectedly involves a man of integrity named Job.

GROUND COVERED:

Job likely lived prior to or around the time of Abraham, going by key references in the book, such as measuring wealth by livestock.

JOB 40-42

Explore the back-and-forth exchange between God and Job. See what you and your students can learn about God and how Job handled this test of his faith.

GENRE	BOOK BASICS	PORTALS FOR IN-DEPTH STUDY

POETRY

PSALMS

So far God has been teaching us. Now it's our turn to write back to God. From anguish to praise, Psalms has every human emotion and a wealth of information about God.

GROUND COVERED:

The 150 psalms cover a span of roughly a thousand years, from the time of Moses (Psalm 90) to the return of the exiles (Psalm 126).

PSALM BY PSALM

Need an easy Bible study? Grab a psalm—any psalm—and look for these things:

1. What you learn about the writer of the psalm.

2. What you learn about God.

3. Any promises from God that speak to human needs or emotions.

GENRE	BOOK BASICS	PORTALS FOR IN-DEPTH STUDY

POETRY

PROVERBS

Often called the most practical book in the Bible, Proverbs helps us see what righteous living is supposed to look like.

GROUND COVERED:

Most of the proverbs were written by Solomon, during the events covered in 1 Kings.

PROVERBS BY THEME

Pick a topic—any topic—and Proverbs probably has a few practical verses about it. Here are a few words and phrases to get you going:

- wisdom/prudence/understanding
- integrity/honesty
- thoughts/motives
- righteousness
- work
- mouth/tongue
- dissension/temper/hatred
- rich/poor
- discipline/correction/instruction
- pride/humility

GENRE	BOOK BASICS	PORTALS FOR IN-DEPTH STUDY

ECCLESIASTES

Solomon's grand experiment of trying everything under the sun brought him back to what's really important: fearing and obeying God.

GROUND COVERED:

Ecclesiastes likely covers the late years of Solomon's life, recorded in 1 Kings.

ECCLESIASTES 4

The backdrop of hopelessness in this chapter offers a striking contrast to the hope we find in Christ. Compare the oppression, discontent, and loneliness of Ecclesiastes 4 with Jesus' messages of freedom (Luke 4:18-19), contentment (Luke 18:18-23), and unity (John 17:20-21).

GENRE	BOOK BASICS	PORTALS FOR IN-DEPTH STUDY

SONG OF SOLOMON

The only PG-13 book in the Bible, Song of Solomon is a great metaphor for the love between God and His people.

GROUND COVERED:

The action takes place during the reign of Solomon, recorded in 1 Kings.

SONG OF SOLOMON

This entire book can serve as a basis for your sex and dating series. Consider this breakdown:

Dating/courtship: Chapters 1-2

Marriage: Chapters 3-4

The give-and-take of love: Chapters 5-6

Deepening, adoring love: Chapters 7-8

GENRE	BOOK BASICS	PORTALS FOR IN-DEPTH STUDY

ISAIAH

The "mini-me" book of the Bible, Isaiah contains 66 chapters; its first 39 chapters prophesy justice and judgment, while the last 27 prophesy hope in the Messiah. Pretty cool!

GROUND COVERED:

Isaiah ministered during the era of 2 Kings.

ISAIAH 1, 11, 12

Contrast the spiritual condition of God's people in Isaiah 1 with the restoration promised them in Isaiah 11-12. For some additional play-by-play on Isaiah the prophet, check out 2 Kings 19 and 20.

The word *salvation* shows up more in Isaiah than in all the other prophets combined. Search this word in Isaiah, and lead your students on a rich journey through passages that describe Christ in great detail.

GENRE	BOOK BASICS	PORTALS FOR IN-DEPTH STUDY
PROPHECY	**JEREMIAH** He didn't have a fun job, bringing an unpopular prophecy of judgment for which he was beaten and isolated from his people. But every word of Jeremiah's prophecy either came true...or will. **GROUND COVERED:** Jeremiah prophesied to Judah during the time of 2 Kings, just before and into the Babylonian exile.	**JEREMIAH 13, 18, 24** Through Jeremiah, God used an array of vivid object lessons to show Judah just how badly they had trashed their relationship with him. These object lessons are made-to-order studies that can help your students not only see the situation in Jeremiah's day, but also evaluate their relationship with God in the present day.

GENRE	BOOK BASICS	PORTALS FOR IN-DEPTH STUDY
PROPHECY	**LAMENTATIONS** Aptly named, this book is a lament from Jeremiah over Jerusalem's destruction. **GROUND COVERED:** The prophecy takes place during Judah's exile in Babylon, in the era of 2 Kings and Jeremiah.	**LAMENTATIONS 2-3** God's judgment on Jerusalem was so harsh that it looked like God was the enemy (which lines up with something said way back in Numbers 33:56). Watch as Jeremiah's astonishment at God's judgment morphs into gratitude for his faithfulness.

GENRE	BOOK BASICS	PORTALS FOR IN-DEPTH STUDY
 PROPHECY	**EZEKIEL** Ezekiel was made famous by the dry bones analogy, but the book is more than a skeleton song. Ezekiel reiterates the judgment God's people had brought on themselves, but brings a message of hope and promised restoration. **GROUND COVERED:** The book takes place during the Babylonian exile, between the times of 2 Kings and Ezra.	**EZEKIEL 37** Use Ezekiel's most famous scene (the valley of the dry bones) as a portal into this great book. Explore the preceding chapter (Ezekiel 36) to determine Israel's spiritual condition. Discover just what God was saying through the picture of dry bones. Challenge students to examine areas where they could use similar restoration.

GENRE	BOOK BASICS	PORTALS FOR IN-DEPTH STUDY

DANIEL

During the darkest days of the Jewish people—no land, no temple—God revealed his master plan for an eternal kingdom, bringing hope to those in exile.

GROUND COVERED:

The action takes place during the Babylonian exile, between the times of 2 Kings and Ezra.

DANIEL 1-2

Daniel's actions in these first two chapters model how youth can live godly lives in an ungodly culture. Daniel and his friends provide some practical approaches that can be easily imitated.

GENRE	BOOK BASICS	PORTALS FOR IN-DEPTH STUDY

HOSEA

Hosea ministered during the days just before Assyrian captivity. His marriage to a harlot illustrates God's faithfulness in stark contrast to Israel's unfaithfulness.

GROUND COVERED:

Hosea ministered to Israel during the time leading up to the Assyrian captivity, which is covered in 2 Kings.

HOSEA 1-2

It's an incredible object lesson—Hosea's marriage to a harlot illustrates God's unconditional love for adulterous Israel. God drives his point further home through the naming of Hosea's children. Discover what God was saying through these names, and then look for the restoration in Hosea 2.

GENRE	BOOK BASICS	PORTALS FOR IN-DEPTH STUDY

JOEL

Joel brings a "get right with God or get left to your enemies" message, using a recent plague of locusts to illustrate what Judah can expect if she doesn't get in step with God.

GROUND COVERED:

Joel's writings give no specific date references, but all signs point to a pre-exilic time period (during the time of 2 Kings).

JOEL

Search for the phrase "day of the Lord" in Joel. Find out everything you can about that "day," and note what you learn about the traits of God that are found around that phrase in Joel.

GENRE	BOOK BASICS	PORTALS FOR IN-DEPTH STUDY
	### AMOS Amos was on the scene during Israel's salad days, when the nation prospered. Unfortunately, these weren't her most spiritual days—a point Amos tried to get across. ### GROUND COVERED: The book takes place before the Assyrian captivity (during the time of 2 Kings).	### AMOS 2 In Amos 1, Amos brings a word of judgment against some of Judah's and Israel's neighbors. In Amos 2, the sights are set on Judah and Israel. Make a list of the wrongs of God's people and draw parallels to how those might show up in our lives today.

GENRE	BOOK BASICS	PORTALS FOR IN-DEPTH STUDY
	### OBADIAH What started as a scuffle between Esau and Jacob in Genesis became a theme that ran throughout the Old Testament as Israel continued to deal with Esau's descendants, the Edomites. Here Obadiah brings a word against them. ### GROUND COVERED: The action takes place during the time of 2 Kings.	### OBADIAH The reasons for Edom's judgment are great warnings for God's people today. The phrase "you should not" is a good clue to look for.

GENRE	BOOK BASICS	PORTALS FOR IN-DEPTH STUDY

JONAH

We know the fish story, but that's often about it. Jonah is a story of faith, in that his message was intended to bring the Ninevites to repentance and salvation. Jonah didn't want their repentance; he wanted to see God destroy them.

GROUND COVERED:

The action takes place during the time of 2 Kings.

JONAH 3

Once we get past the fish story, there's much more to learn from this book. Notice in Jonah 3 the response of a pagan people to an unpopular message from God. Let this serve as a reconnaissance mission to help your students understand the mindset of unbelievers around them.

GENRE	BOOK BASICS	PORTALS FOR IN-DEPTH STUDY

MICAH

Prophesying mostly against Judah, Micah gave a few nods to Israel as well. Micah railed against the nation's rampant injustice, which stood in stark contrast to God's merciful justice.

GROUND COVERED:

Micah takes place during the time of 2 Kings.

MICAH 6-7

Micah 6:8 may be the most famous verse from the minor prophets and can serve as a summary statement for following God. As you use this verse as a gateway into the back and forth dialogue between Micah and God, you'll see what really ticks God off.

GENRE	BOOK BASICS	PORTALS FOR IN-DEPTH STUDY

NAHUM

Jonah's message to Nineveh 150 years earlier sparked reform, but it was long gone by Nahum's time. Another of the few prophecies in Scripture directed to the Gentile nations, Nahum decreed that Nineveh's time was up.

GROUND COVERED:

Nahum takes place during the time of 2 Kings.

NAHUM 1

In this introduction to Nahum's message to Nineveh, we see key traits of God, as well as benefits for following him.

GENRE	BOOK BASICS	PORTALS FOR IN-DEPTH STUDY
	### HABAKKUK Habakkuk must have been shocked ("You're going to do what?!") when he heard how God planned to deal with the wickedness of his people—by conquering them with people who were even more wicked. ### GROUND COVERED: Habakkuk takes place during the time of 2 Kings.	### HABAKKUK This prophecy is unique in that it doesn't address a people, but instead records an exchange between Habakkuk and God. In asking God for an explanation, Habakkuk reflects the hearts of many believers today. This leads him to pray one of the most incredible prayers in Scripture, Habakkuk 3:17-19.

GENRE	BOOK BASICS	PORTALS FOR IN-DEPTH STUDY
	### ZEPHANIAH The nation of Judah experienced occasional revival and reform. Zephaniah's presence was likely a catalyst for one of these reforms. ### GROUND COVERED: Zephaniah takes place during the time of 2 Kings.	### ZEPHANIAH 3 As you dissect this chapter, notice how it's a microcosm of nearly every message from an Old Testament prophet: judgment and then restoration.

GENRE	BOOK BASICS	PORTALS FOR IN-DEPTH STUDY
	### HAGGAI We all need a Haggai— someone to encourage us to get rid of the distractions and persist in completing God's work. ### GROUND COVERED: Haggai takes place during the time of Ezra, after the return of the exiles from Babylon.	### HAGGAI As you explore these chapters, look for the parallels between the faith journeys of teenagers today and of the people then. Draw parallels between Haggai's encouraging words and the encouragement needed today.

GENRE	BOOK BASICS	PORTALS FOR IN-DEPTH STUDY

PROPHECY

ZECHARIAH

This book is a lesson in how to give spiritual encouragement without sparking a guilt trip. Zechariah motivated the Jewish people to complete the temple for a bigger reason than themselves: The Messiah is coming!

GROUND COVERED:

Zechariah takes place during the time of Ezra, after the return of the exiles from Babylon.

ZECHARIAH 14

Explore this chapter with your students, looking for every detail about the new era Zechariah speaks of.

GENRE	BOOK BASICS	PORTALS FOR IN-DEPTH STUDY

PROPHECY

MALACHI

How soon they forget. Back from captivity for only a few years, God's people slide into the same patterns that sent them into captivity. Malachi is the last recorded word from God until those hopeful words from a voice in the wilderness: "Repent, for the kingdom of heaven is near."

GROUND COVERED:

Malachi takes place during the time of Nehemiah.

MALACHI 4

Use this last chapter of the Old Testament to learn as much as you can about the benefits of the coming Messiah.

GENRE	BOOK BASICS	PORTALS FOR IN-DEPTH STUDY

BIOGRAPHY

MATTHEW

To leave no doubt that Jesus is the King foretold in the Old Testament, Matthew opens with Jesus' Jewish lineage and continues the king theme throughout his Gospel.

DATE LIKELY WRITTEN:

AD 60s

MATTHEW 5-7

The Sermon on the Mount in Matthew could be one of the most effective studies you could do with your students. Each section of the sermon (beatitudes, salt/light, and so on) is a made-to-order session.

GENRE	BOOK BASICS	PORTALS FOR IN-DEPTH STUDY
BIOGRAPHY	**MARK** Mark portrays the "serving" side of Jesus—the way he ministered to the needs of people as he preached and taught throughout the land. **DATE LIKELY WRITTEN:** AD 57-67 (the earliest Gospel)	**MARK 7-8** Perhaps one of the most human pictures of Jesus is that of him sighing. Mark's is the only Gospel to record this. Find these instances in Mark 7 and 8, and explore everything going on in these scenes.

GENRE	BOOK BASICS	PORTALS FOR IN-DEPTH STUDY
BIOGRAPHY	**LUKE** Detail was Luke's thing, in that he set out to give us an orderly account of Jesus' ministry. A Gentile, Luke wrote with Gentiles in mind, specifically Greeks. **DATE LIKELY WRITTEN:** AD 60-65	**LUKE 15-16** These two chapters present parables that only Luke recorded for us. As you explore these with your students, keep track of *what* Jesus said about heaven and his Kingdom, as well as *who* he said it to.

GENRE	BOOK BASICS	PORTALS FOR IN-DEPTH STUDY
BIOGRAPHY	**JOHN** In contrast to an orderly account, John takes a more thematic approach. His Gospel includes many details not found in the other three Gospels. **DATE LIKELY WRITTEN:** AD 85-95 (the latest Gospel)	**JOHN 13-17** John's is the only Gospel to record what's known as Jesus' farewell address. Knowing that these are Jesus' final words to the guys who would carry on the work of the Kingdom, explore these words of Jesus with the same urgency that he conveyed when he first spoke them.

GENRE	BOOK BASICS	PORTALS FOR IN-DEPTH STUDY

ACTS

A portrait of God's church in its purest form, Acts gives a great framework for understanding how God mobilizes his people in the era of his Spirit.

DATE LIKELY WRITTEN:

AD 61

ACTS 1-2, 8, 13

These chapters reveal the growth of Christianity as foretold by Jesus: to Jerusalem, to Judea, to Samaria, and to the ends of the earth. Use these chapters to show students what can happen when we operate with the power of the Holy Spirit, as promised in Acts 1:8.

GENRE	BOOK BASICS	PORTALS FOR IN-DEPTH STUDY

ROMANS

The Bible's *tour de force* explanation of what faith in Christ is all about, Romans is the book where the New Testament pivots from *what* Jesus did (the Gospels) to *why* (the letters).

DATE LIKELY WRITTEN:

AD 55-57

ROMANS 12

This one makes the Top 5 Favorite Chapters list of many believers. Let your students experience why as you give them a chance to make it their fave, too.

GENRE	BOOK BASICS	PORTALS FOR IN-DEPTH STUDY

1 CORINTHIANS

There's a lot we can learn from a letter to a church struggling with divisions on the inside and a pagan culture on the outside.

DATE LIKELY WRITTEN:

AD 54-56

1 CORINTHIANS 11

Paul's instructions regarding the Lord's Supper contain details we should never neglect. Study these instructions with your students, and then put them into practice by experiencing the Lord's Supper together.

GENRE	BOOK BASICS	PORTALS FOR IN-DEPTH STUDY
LETTER	**2 CORINTHIANS** After his first letter to these folks, false teachers emerged seeking to discredit Paul and his message. This called for a follow-up letter from Paul and assurance of his calling as an apostle. **DATE LIKELY WRITTEN:** AD 55-56	**2 CORINTHIANS 5** Paul's teaching on reconciliation in this chapter can serve as a portal to the larger message of reconciliation that runs throughout Scripture. Explore the *who, what, how,* and *why* of reconciliation with your students.

GENRE	BOOK BASICS	PORTALS FOR IN-DEPTH STUDY
 **LETTER**	**GALATIANS** Paul reserved some of his strongest and most colorful words to denounce certain practices that had filtered into the Galatian churches—practices that put God's grace at risk. **DATE LIKELY WRITTEN:** AD 49 (ties with James for possible earliest New Testament book)	**GALATIANS 3** Study with your students the very chapter that may have launched the Reformation, sparked by Martin Luther's study of it. Today's church may not sell indulgences, but we're still easily "bewitched" by the temptation to live by flesh and works, rather than grace and faith.

GENRE	BOOK BASICS	PORTALS FOR IN-DEPTH STUDY
 **LETTER**	**EPHESIANS** Not only do you find most of the big themes of the Christian faith in this small book, you'll also find practical ways to live out the big themes. **DATE LIKELY WRITTEN:** AD 60-61	**EPHESIANS 5** Many of Paul's letters follow a pattern that goes something like this: *Because Jesus has done this for us, here's what we need to do.* Ephesians is a classic example of this pattern. Observe Ephesians 1-3 (what Jesus has done for us) before exploring Ephesians 5 (what we need to do in response).

GENRE	BOOK BASICS	PORTALS FOR IN-DEPTH STUDY

PHILIPPIANS

Peace. Unity. Affliction. Humility. Joy. In the middle of it all—the good and the bad—Paul learned to be content, and he explains to the Philippians just how to do it. (Hint: It has to do with Christ.)

DATE LIKELY WRITTEN:
AD 61-62

PHILIPPIANS 2

Paul's description of Jesus' actions captures the essence of what it means to follow Christ. As you unpack this passage with your students, explore ways to follow the instruction in Philippians 2:5: "Your attitude should be the same as that of Christ Jesus."

GENRE	BOOK BASICS	PORTALS FOR IN-DEPTH STUDY

COLOSSIANS

As time went on and people tried to describe the Jesus phenomenon to those who hadn't heard, they sometimes added to or subtracted from the pure message of the gospel. Paul's letter makes it clear that Christ is all we need.

DATE LIKELY WRITTEN:
AD 60-61

COLOSSIANS 2

This could be one of the most valuable Bible chapters for teenagers to "get," as it exhorts them to stay away from hollow worldly philosophies and empty religious rules.

Teach your group to memorize the order of Galatians, Ephesians, Philippians, and Colossians once and for all with a mnemonic such as "**G**o **E**at **P**op **C**orn." It will save them hours of page flipping over the course of a lifetime.

GENRE	BOOK BASICS	PORTALS FOR IN-DEPTH STUDY

1 THESSALONIANS

Paul loved these guys and hoped to see them again. Meanwhile, he wrote this letter to encourage them to continue in their steady growth and in their hope of Jesus' return.

DATE LIKELY WRITTEN:
AD 50-51

1 THESSALONIANS 4

A major theme of the New Testament is this: *Jesus is returning, so constantly do what you want to be caught doing when he returns!* This chapter captures the essence of this theme and offers some great instructions on how to live with one another until Jesus returns.

GENRE	BOOK BASICS	PORTALS FOR IN-DEPTH STUDY

LETTER

2 THESSALONIANS

A misunderstanding regarding Jesus' return sparked this letter that gives great information and hope about that very return.

DATE LIKELY WRITTEN:
AD 50-51

2 THESSALONIANS 2

This chapter may raise more questions than it answers, which could be the start of an amazing journey as you explore Jesus' return with your students. Next stop, Revelation!

GENRE	BOOK BASICS	PORTALS FOR IN-DEPTH STUDY

LETTER

1 TIMOTHY

It's good for us that Timothy faced a few challenges in leading the church at Ephesus. It sparked this letter from Paul that provides a framework for church structure and leadership.

DATE LIKELY WRITTEN:
AD 62-63

1 TIMOTHY 4

1 Timothy 4:12 is the go-to youth leadership passage, which means your teenagers may be overly familiar with it. But use this verse as a gateway into the rest of the chapter, helping them see why this needed to be said and what Paul was asking of Timothy.

GENRE	BOOK BASICS	PORTALS FOR IN-DEPTH STUDY

LETTER

2 TIMOTHY

There may not be a better manual for ministry than 2 Timothy. In this ministry manual, we see God's prime instruction to his ministers: Guard the gospel. Why? Because attacks will surely come.

DATE LIKELY WRITTEN:
AD 63-67

2 TIMOTHY 3

This chapter helps us see why the pastoral epistles (1 Timothy, 2 Timothy, and Titus) were necessary. As you explore this chapter with your students, look for the spiritual atmosphere described, along with instructions regarding things learned.

GENRE	BOOK BASICS	PORTALS FOR IN-DEPTH STUDY

LETTER

TITUS

This small letter makes a huge contribution toward helping us understand what a biblically functioning faith community should look like.

DATE LIKELY WRITTEN:

AD 62-63

TITUS

Looking to establish (or grow) a student leadership team? Make this short book required reading. Work with students to apply the instructions in Titus to the student ministry setting.

The *T* collection: Have your students noticed that all of the New Testament books beginning with *T* are grouped together? Another nice flip-through time-saver.

GENRE	BOOK BASICS	PORTALS FOR IN-DEPTH STUDY

LETTER

PHILEMON

As Paul goes to bat for a runaway slave, we see a practical picture of grace.

DATE LIKELY WRITTEN:

AD 60-61

PHILEMON

As you explore this one-chapter book, list today's situations that parallel the subject of this letter.

GENRE	BOOK BASICS	PORTALS FOR IN-DEPTH STUDY

LETTER

HEBREWS

Jewish believers were feeling the heat for following Christ. This letter affirmed to them (and to us) why Jesus offers the better way and is worth the persecution.

DATE LIKELY WRITTEN:

AD 64-68

HEBREWS—*BETTER*

A great way to get a handle on Hebrews is to search for the key word *better* (in most English versions) and see what you learn whenever it shows up.

GENRE	BOOK BASICS	PORTALS FOR IN-DEPTH STUDY
LETTER	### JAMES James is packed with practical instructions on how to live the Christian faith. By simply *doing* the instructions in James, you'll never have to ask what God's will is for your life. **DATE LIKELY WRITTEN:** AD 45-55 (ties with Galatians for possible earliest New Testament book)	### JAMES 3 The Bible talks a lot about the tongue, but James 3 contains the biggest, most colorful collection of tongue-related instructions and descriptions. Explore every detail—analogies, warnings, commands, and teachings.

GENRE	BOOK BASICS	PORTALS FOR IN-DEPTH STUDY
LETTER	### 1 PETER Suffering shouldn't surprise us. In fact, describing persecution and suffering, Peter doesn't say *if*, but *when*. But he assures us that the blessings are worth the suffering. **DATE LIKELY WRITTEN:** AD 63-64	### 1 PETER 4 Have your students find and mark the *why* and *what* of suffering. This chapter does as good a job as any in the Bible at explaining why bad things happen to good people.

GENRE	BOOK BASICS	PORTALS FOR IN-DEPTH STUDY
LETTER	### 2 PETER Like many New Testament letters, this one was written to refute false teaching. Peter backed up the need to adhere to truth with the reminder that Jesus is coming soon. **DATE LIKELY WRITTEN:** AD 63-64	### 2 PETER 1 This first chapter is a great apologetic message from one of Jesus' closest followers—not only for the gospel but for the inspiration of the Scriptures. Explore with your students the list of spiritual virtues that are guaranteed to keep them spiritually fruitful.

GENRE	BOOK BASICS	PORTALS FOR IN-DEPTH STUDY

LETTER

1 JOHN

In this letter John elaborates on several of the themes he explored in his Gospel.

DATE LIKELY WRITTEN:
AD 85-95

1 JOHN 4

You'll notice that one word shows up more often than the number of verses in the chapter. That's good info to know—and to obey.

GENRE	BOOK BASICS	PORTALS FOR IN-DEPTH STUDY

LETTER

2 JOHN

Even the strongest and most resolute among us can fall if we don't follow one of the simplest of all commands from God: Love one another.

DATE LIKELY WRITTEN:
AD 85-95

2 JOHN

Compare the false teachings being put forth about Jesus with the false teachings about Jesus swirling around today. Students will see that there's not much difference, making the instructions in this book timelier than they may have thought.

GENRE	BOOK BASICS	PORTALS FOR IN-DEPTH STUDY

LETTER

3 JOHN

This is the smallest book in the Bible, cut short due to high hopes of a face-to-face visit. It provides insight into the life of the early church.

DATE LIKELY WRITTEN:
AD 85-95

3 JOHN

For a short book, this letter mentions a lot of names. Doing a few short character sketches on these people will give you a window into early church life.

GENRE	BOOK BASICS	PORTALS FOR IN-DEPTH STUDY
LETTER	**JUDE** The threat from false teachers was so imminent that Jude changed the subject of his letter to warn his readers of teaching that had already slipped in. **DATE LIKELY WRITTEN:** AD 65-80	**JUDE** Jude's imagery is similar to John's in Revelation. But one of the most striking characteristics of Jude's letter is his use of threes. Look for things grouped in sets of three as you explore this one-chapter book.

GENRE	BOOK BASICS	PORTALS FOR IN-DEPTH STUDY
PROPHECY	**REVELATION** This prophecy from John comes in the form of a letter written to seven churches, offering the hope of incredible things to come. **DATE LIKELY WRITTEN:** AD 90-95	**REVELATION 1-3** Each message to one of the seven churches touches on a key aspect of church life. Every student ministry could benefit from the warnings and blessings in these messages.

What Am I Doing in Student Ministry That Will Outlast Me?

As we were putting the finishing touches on the manuscript for *Unleashing God's Word in Youth Ministry*, I got a call from a guy named Tim, a youth worker in our area. New to youth ministry, Tim explained that he'd just become the interim youth pastor of a thriving student ministry in town. One of his first official acts in the position was to meet with his student leadership to take stock of the ministry: What do the students want? What do they need?

Many things were tossed on the table, but the "want" that stuck in Tim's mind was this: "We want to know how to study our Bibles."

Perhaps the reason it stuck in Tim's mind was that it also stuck in his knees. Tim felt more than a little shaky in regard to the responsibility of helping his students with that desire. So he called me.

Scanning the shelves of a Christian bookstore or the pages of Amazon.com, we in youth ministry often come up empty when it comes to finding cohesive tools to help us deliver the depth students crave, particularly if it involves the Bible.

So we cut and paste. We borrow and steal. Or we fill the gap with other things.

These techniques can work in a pinch—even get us by for a few years. But to use a well-worn analogy, this *modus operandi* won't teach students how to fish. And we're not ministering out of our own pool of depth with Christ. We're siphoning off someone else's.

My major purpose in writing this book was to give us in youth ministry a tool that provides a specific, intentional starting point for helping students go deeper with God through his Word.

The other day I read an article by John Ortberg in the latest issue of *Leadership* journal (Winter 2008, pp. 37–40) about the importance of "the Book" in ministry. Ortberg's intro noted that you don't hear much these days about Philistines or Moabites or Amalekites—nations and tribes from Old Testament days that were similar in size to Israel. Those nations and tribes are no more, but the Jewish people live on. Israel's distinguishing feature in contrast to those nations? Not their wealth or power or size.

It was God's Word. God's story. The Scriptures.

As you'd expect, Ortberg's article made many convicting and eloquent points. But here's the one that struck me the most: Using the process of physical healing as an analogy, Ortberg notes that experts emphasize how important it is for the healing agent (i.e., a doctor) to believe that healing will actually happen.

In other words, you have to believe that it will work.

Ortberg points out a similar dynamic with Scripture: "The Scriptures really are used by God in a unique way to change lives. But those of us who teach them must be gripped by this conviction. It cannot be faked or forced. It comes as a gift."

As I think about it, this is my personal goal for this book: That it will help all of us in student ministry to trust that the Scriptures will do what God says they will do, and that the way we teach and disciple, whether it's an approach advanced by this book or something completely different, will flow from this conviction and trust.

Not long ago I bumped into a former student from one of our Bible studies. In fact, Sarah was part of that first Bible study in Colossians I described in chapter one. Now a public school teacher, she's well into her adult life. Rushing through the frozen food aisle, we hurried to catch each other up on our lives (it had been several years since we'd seen each other). Then Sarah paused and made a point to say, "I find myself thinking a lot about our Bible studies. I want you to know how much I appreciate what you and Dana taught me."

I'm tearing up as I type those words.

Sarah had been right there, front-and-center, at all the great things you do in youth ministry: Ski trips, work camps, wacky icebreakers. She could have mentioned many things she appreciated about that youth ministry (though I happen to know she was *not* a fan of the wacky icebreakers).

But to me she captured, without knowing it, the essence of the journey that started with the question: *What am I doing in student ministry that will outlast me?*

I don't expect this book to have answered all your questions about teen Bible study or to have covered every scenario (or even most scenarios) that can pop up when you pull out a Bible with students.

I don't imagine that you'll adopt every idea or approach I've put forth.

But I do pray that it can help set you on a journey—the journey that culminates in all the fruit and benefit that comes from pouring into your students' lives something you know will outlast you: God's Word.

Appendix A

The Equipping Gifts

In Chapter 11 we looked at five leadership positions and their corresponding spiritual gifts given by God for the equipping of his people: *apostles, prophets, evangelists, pastors,* and *teachers.*

Within the body of Christ there are widely varying views about spiritual gifts—and our purpose here is not to settle any long-standing debates regarding the viability and use of every spiritual gift mentioned in Scripture. I suggest that you do your own inductive study on spiritual gifts, basing your conclusions not on what I say or what others say, but under the guidance of the Holy Spirit. You'll be wowed by what you see—and your insights will fire you up to help your students experience God's call on their lives.

In the meantime here are a few observations on the five equipping gifts outlined in Ephesians 4.[65]

Apostleship

This gift is listed first among the gifts appointed by God in 1 Corinthians 12:28 and Ephesians 4:11. The Greek word for *apostle* means "to send, one sent, ambassador." Some see apostleship as a gift given by Jesus to just a few people (the Twelve Apostles and later Paul) for a select period of time. However, because the Bible names others as apostles, many believe this gift continues today. (See Acts 14:14; Romans 16:7; 1 Thessalonians 1:1, 2:6.)

Examples

Apostles are sent from God as witnesses to others (see Matthew 10:1-7 and Acts 2:42-43). Like Paul and the Twelve, today's apostles might be missionaries and/or church planters. Just as the work of the New Testament church was built upon the foundation of the apostles of old (Ephesians 2:19-22), so today's ministries and churches are built on the solid work of gifted planters and launchers.

Description

If you have this gift, you would likely feel comfortable being sent out as an ambassador of the gospel to a place where there is little or no Christian presence. You get excited about sharing Christ with people of other cultures or nations.

Prophecy

The gift of prophecy is given by the Spirit (1 Corinthians 12:10) and appointed by God (1 Corinthians 12:28). The Greek word for prophecy means "to speak forth"—specifically, to speak forth what God is saying in his Word. Set apart as a gift that should be greatly desired in the church because it brings edification (1 Corinthians 14:2-5), prophecy is to be used in proportion to the gifted person's faith (Romans 12:6).

Examples

Acts 13:1 lists several prophets at the church in Antioch. In Acts 13:5 and 13:43-49, we see two prophets, Barnabas and Paul, proclaiming the Word of God. Acts 21:9 describes Philip's daughters as prophetesses. 1 Corinthians 14:24-25 tells us of the powerful effect this gift can have on unbelievers.

Description

Prophecy is not fortune telling. Many Bible prophets did predict future events, but this was because they were simply relaying the word God had spoken to the people. If you have this gift, you likely feel comfortable leading talks and devotionals or giving sermons that proclaim God's Word. The effect of your gift is that others are strengthened, encouraged, comforted, convicted by God's Word, and equipped for his service (1 Corinthians 14:3-4, Ephesians 4:11-13).

Evangelism

Ephesians 4:11-13 tells us that evangelists and other gifted leaders are appointed in the church to build up the body of Christ. Note that all believers are told to spread the Good News about Jesus; it's clear, however, that some will be especially gifted in this area.

Examples

In Acts 8:26-40, Philip followed God's Spirit to help the Ethiopian know and believe in Jesus through a one-on-one witnessing situation. Philip also proclaimed Christ to the multitudes in Acts 8:5-8, and Paul preached the gospel to countless people. The basics of the gospel, found in 1 Corinthians 15:1-5, are what every evangelist must know and be able to communicate.

Description

The gift of evangelism is the ability to share about Jesus Christ with confidence and clarity, whether one-on-one or in groups. Those with this gift are typically described as having a broken heart for the lost.

Pastoring (also called "Shepherding")

Ephesians 4:11-12 lists *pastor* as one of the gifted leaders given for the purpose of building up the body so that believers become mature and Christlike. The Greek word for *pastor* means "a shepherd; one who tends herds or flocks." Shepherds feed, guide, and care for the flock. This gift involves both teaching and looking after the spiritual health of other people.

Examples

Jesus used the shepherd analogy in John 10:1-18 to illustrate his care for the flock. Acts 20:28 says that God's Spirit made certain people overseers to shepherd and care for the church.

Description

Shepherds are to live as examples for others to follow (1 Peter 5:2-4). It's important to note that while the majority of 21st century Americans view *pastor* solely as an office in the church, the New Testament broadens that definition and helps us understand that the gift of shepherding is given to many in the church, not just the pastor.

Teaching

Teaching is listed with other gifts as given according to God's grace (Romans 12:6-7) and appointed by God (1 Corinthians 12:28-29).

Examples

Apollos, Priscilla, and Aquilla were teachers (Acts 18:24-26). Peter and John couldn't stop teaching, even when they were ordered not to (Acts 4:18-20; 5:28). Paul taught publicly and from house to house (Acts 20:20).

Description

Teachers must have a thorough knowledge of Scripture, be instructed in the way of the Lord, speak with fervor, and accurately teach the things of Jesus (Acts 18:24-26). Jesus instructed all believers to teach others to obey what he commanded (Matthew 28:19-20), but the person with this gift would have a special ability (combined with a diligent personal Bible study life) to communicate truth so that others understand.

Appendix B

How We Got the Bible

Then He opened His mouth and taught them, saying:

MATTHEW 5:2 (NKJV)

When Jesus opened his mouth, everything that came out was the Word of God. Instead of saying, "Turn in your Bibles..." Jesus could simply say, "Turn to me and listen." Thus was the transmission of Scripture for the two to three years of Jesus' ministry.

But how did the words Jesus spoke get into our Bibles for us to read?

To track the history of Jesus' words—from verbal transmission to a printed book you and I can experience—is to track the history of humankind's quest for the things of God. Sometimes the person who carried the baton was an early church leader, desperate for the people to know God and understand his Word for themselves. Sometimes it was a believer who risked death to preserve the Bible—and thus the entire transmission process—so that generations after him could remain in intimate contact with the story of the universe.

The history of the Bible is a picture of God's sovereign rule and his presence in creation.

Jesus' Bible

The Gospel accounts contain more than 50 references to Old Testament Scripture. So how did this come about? Were Jesus and the guys carrying around pocket Old Testaments?

That may not be far from the truth, though the Scriptures of the day certainly weren't pocket-sized.

After the Babylonian Exile of the Jews, tradition has it that Ezra championed the task of collecting the writings that now make up the Old Testament of the Christian Bible. Even by the time of Ezra, one set of Hebrew writings had already been collected and was referred to throughout Israel as the Book of the Law. Eventually this group of books, comprised of the five books of Moses—Genesis through Deuteronomy—came to be known as the Torah.

Added later to the Book of the Law were the Prophets (historic books, such as Joshua, as well as prophetic books, such as Jeremiah) and the Writings (poetry books, such as Psalms).

As the Jewish people began to settle in communities, a great need arose for the wider dissemination of these sacred writings.

Enter the scribes.

Scribes get a bad rap in the New Testament, mostly because of their hostile interaction with Jesus. By Jesus' day the scribes had become more like lawyers and less like copyists. But before the coming of the Messiah, they served an essential function in getting the Old Testament to us today.

With the invention of the printing press centuries away, any copying of Scripture had to be done by hand. And copying these sacred writings wasn't for the faint of heart. Just look at some of the stringent regulations placed on the scribes:

1. They could use only clean animal skins to write on and to bind manuscripts.

2. Each column of writing could have no less than 48 and no more than 60 lines.

3. The ink had to be black and of a special recipe.

4. They had to verbalize each word aloud while they were writing.

5. They had to wipe the pen and wash their entire bodies before writing the word *Jehovah*—every time they wrote it.

6. There had to be a review within 30 days, and if as many as three pages required correction, the entire document had to be redone.

7. The letters, words, and paragraphs had to be counted, and the document became invalid if two letters touched each other. The middle paragraph, word, and letter must correspond to those of the original document.

8. All old and worn documents had to be buried with ceremonial pomp. (This is why we have none of the original documents today.)

9. The documents could be stored only in sacred places.

10. As no document containing God's Word could be destroyed, each was stored or buried in a *genizah*, a Hebrew term meaning "hiding place." These were usually kept in a synagogue or sometimes in a Jewish cemetery.[66]

Within a few centuries of this era in Jewish history, Alexander the Great swept the land, bringing with him the language and culture of the Greeks. Soon many Jews were speaking Greek, growing rusty with the Hebrew language or forgetting it altogether. By then anything read aloud from the sacred text was barely understood at best, boring at worst.

So a campaign was launched in roughly 300 BC for the translation of the Hebrew writings into the more common Greek language.

Tradition has it that six elders were selected from each of the 12 tribes of Israel. The 72 men were sequestered on the island of Pharos in the harbor of Alexandria. There these scholars translated the Pentateuch (the first five books of what is now the Old Testament) in 72 days, a timeframe that curiously matched the number of men selected for the project. Proponents of this work saw this coincidence as giving credence to the divinity of the effort.

Stories circulated that each elder did his work in a separate room, having no contact with the others—and that all of the men produced identical manuscripts. (Historians have since found evidence that the stories may have been propaganda—an overzealous marketing department, perhaps?—but we recognize their zeal for a divine process.)

The work of the elders came to be known as the Septuagint, Latin for 70, which represented the number of elders who worked on the project, minus a couple.

From this time to roughly 100 BC, the books of the Prophets and the Writings were gradually added to the Septuagint. This was likely the "Bible" that Jesus and the New Testament writers used.

Not only did Jesus and the apostles have the Septuagint, they had access to other Hebrew writings (copied by the scribes in the same painstaking manner), as well as to the Targums, which were Aramaic translations and interpretations of the Hebrew writings.[67] Interestingly, fragments of these writings still exist, dating back to the first century AD and containing excerpts from Genesis, Exodus, Leviticus, Numbers, Deuteronomy, and the Minor Prophets.

Oral Tradition

For the first 20 to 30 years after Jesus was on the earth, his teachings and actions were communicated by word of mouth, beginning with the apostles.

Before you start picturing the telephone game and how information is easily distorted, remember that in New Testament days word of mouth was the primary means of communication. Story was revered. It was the fabric of the culture. What folks lacked in literacy, they made up for in memorization.[68] We can trust that the transmission of God's Word from spoken form to written was both accurate and reliable. Why?

Anywhere from 20 to 30 years is actually a short amount of time for oral transmission. During that period, many eyewitnesses of Jesus' ministry were still alive and able to refute any inconsistencies in the retelling of these stories.

During Jesus' life and ministry, the apostles had already begun telling people about him and spreading his message. The fact that many already knew this information would have helped preserve its integrity after Jesus' departure.[69]

Author and pastor Mark Roberts points out that the reverence Jesus' followers had for his words motivated them to preserve them accurately. We get a strong sense of this from their writings:[70]

Therefore everyone who hears *these words of mine* and puts them into practice is like a wise man who built his house on the rock. (MATTHEW 7:24, ITALICS ADDED)

Heaven and earth will pass away, but *my words* will never pass away. (MARK 13:31, ITALICS ADDED)

The Spirit gives life; the flesh counts for nothing. The *words I have spoken to you* are spirit and they are life. (JOHN 6:63, ITALICS ADDED)

"You do not want to leave too, do you?" Jesus asked the Twelve. Simon Peter answered him, "Lord, to whom shall we go? You have the *words of eternal life.*" (JOHN 6:67-68, ITALICS ADDED)

If you remain in me and *my words* remain in you, ask whatever you wish, and it will be given you. (JOHN 15:7, ITALICS ADDED)

Written Tradition

Interestingly, the writing of what is now the New Testament didn't begin with a Gospel, but rather with Paul's letters. It's believed that Galatians was the first New Testament document, written around AD 49-50.

The first Gospel written was probably Mark's, between AD 57 and 67.[71]

Every book of the New Testament was written within 60 years of Jesus' ministry. In the world of ancient documents and literature, a time frame this short is almost the equivalent of a play-by-play commentary on real-time events.

But the world was hungry for the message of Jesus. One original of each letter wouldn't do. Copies were needed—and while there was no ready method of mass production, there *was* a professional scribe industry. The letters of Paul and the other apostles were soon systematically hand-copied for wider distribution.

Oral and Written—The Overlap Years

By AD 100 to 150, any eyewitnesses to Jesus' ministry had passed on. But the friends of those eyewitnesses stepped up to the plate.

Not only did these friends continue to tell the stories of Jesus and his disciples, thus continuing the oral transmission, they also wrote about the writings of the eyewitnesses.

The writings of Papias, the bishop of Hierapolis (a location near Colossae), lead one to believe he knew several of Jesus' followers personally.[72] He also wrote of Mark, a traveling companion of Peter who "wrote accurately all that Peter recorded of the words and deeds of the Lord, though not in strict order."[73]

Polycarp, the bishop of Smyrna, was reported by other church leaders to have known the apostle John. Polycarp wrote a letter (the original of which still exists today) to the Philippian church quoting from many New Testament letters.[74] A contemporary of Polycarp, Basilides quoted from New Testament letters and made reference to writings "in the gospels."[75] And Clement of Rome, bishop of the church of Rome at the end of the first century, wrote a letter to the church in Corinth containing several references to Paul's letters as well as to the book of Hebrews.[76] Some scholars speculate that this could have been the Clement whom Paul referenced in Philippians 4:3, but most say this is unlikely given that Clement was a popular name.[77]

Canonization of the Bible

By AD 100 many other letters and writings about Jesus were circulating, including those of Papias, Polycarp, and Clement. Between AD 150 and 300, some people were attempting to bring all of these spiritual writings into a cohesive work; these were the first efforts toward determining which of the writings were authoritative and worthy of canonization. The work of early church fathers like Tertullian and Origen birthed a list of letters and books that closely resembles the 27 books of the New Testament.

And so the councils began.

With the spread of Christianity had come variations in beliefs and doctrines. Church leaders began to pull together other leaders from across the land to discuss and decide key issues in an attempt to provide standards and doctrines to a dispersed people.

The first of these councils was held in Nicea (today's Turkey) and named, unimaginatively, The Council of Nicea. This council gave us the first uniform Christian doctrine, called the Nicene Creed.

Subsequent councils ratified the discussions and decisions at Nicea. But before long, attention began to turn toward a uniform written code that believers could trust for guidance. It was apparent that the church needed more than a list of letters and books—perhaps something with a little more authoritative heft.

With the advent of the codex (a book bound in volume form, as opposed to a scroll), this need for an approved canon of Scripture grew still more urgent. By the end of the first century, the Gospels had begun to circulate as a cohesive codex. So had Paul's letters. Questions had begun to arise as to which books should be bound together and accepted as sacred Scripture by the church.

In AD 397 the eighth of 14 councils was convened in Carthage, Africa (aptly named the Eighth Council of Carthage). This council ratified a decision made at the Council of Hippo four years earlier, giving us the official canon of 27 New Testament books.

First Non-Greek Translations

You'll recall from the book of Acts that Antioch began to emerge as an epicenter of the early church; Antiochians were even the first to use the word *Christian* to describe Christ's disciples (Acts 11:26).

Apparently the momentum in Antioch didn't stop where the book of Acts left off. The gospel took such root in Antioch that need arose for the Gospel writings to be translated into the region's mother tongue, Syriac. The first Syriac translation, later called the Peshitta, was completed between AD 300 and 400 and represents one of the first serious collections combining both Old and New Testament writings—although not in today's order, nor containing all of today's books.

At the same time the Syriac versions of Scripture were being translated, the Latin language was spreading throughout other parts of the Roman Empire. As it did, local regions took it upon themselves to translate Scripture from Greek into Latin. For a time, the Scriptures were read aloud in Greek during public worship and then translated into Latin. Manuscripts were even prepared with two parallel columns—one in Greek, the other in Latin.[78]

Soon there was a groundswell of Latin Scriptures. Because of different regional dialects, these versions varied greatly from one to another, leading to considerable confusion. Even Augustine weighed in, writing in *On Christian Doctrine*, "For in the early days of the faith, everyone who happened to gain possession of a Greek manuscript and thought he had any facility in both languages, however slight that might have been, attempted to make a translation."[79]

Finally Pope Damasus (AD 305-384) commissioned his favorite church historian, Jerome, to produce a definitive Latin version using the common, literary form of Latin, as opposed to the more formal Ciceronian Latin. Using the best Greek manuscripts available, along with the Septuagint and the Hebrew writings, Jerome oversaw what's known as the Vulgate—the title taken from *vulgata*, which means "common."

The impact of the Vulgate cannot be overstated. The proliferation of the Latin language had paved the way for the widespread dissemination of this Bible. And while Latin is now considered a dead language (officially used only in Vatican City), it has greatly influenced many of today's modern languages—60 percent of our English words have been derived from Latin.[80] And many of today's theologically "heavy" words come directly from Jerome's Vulgate: *regeneration, salvation, propitiation, reconciliation, Scripture, sacrament,* and many others.[81]

The Vulgate was the Bible for a long, long time—perhaps too long a time.

Strikingly, what Jerome set out to accomplish—the creation of a uniform manuscript that all could read and understand—became a nearly insurmountable obstacle because eventually, no one spoke Latin.

At least the masses—the common people, that is—didn't speak Latin.

Darkness

As the Roman Empire disintegrated, each conquering people brought in its own language—the languages of the Lombards, the Goths, the Saxons, and so on. Latin became the language of the elite and spiritual hierarchy.

By AD 500 the Bible had been translated into hundreds of languages. But because the Vulgate was so highly esteemed, by AD 600 religious leaders forbade successive generations from translating it into any language other than Latin—successfully snuffing out the many translations that had already been produced.

Thus Latin became the official language of religion, taught only to priests no matter their native language. And so the world slid into the darkest of ages, with its only source of Light inaccessible to the masses, the common people—you and me.

Reformation

And then, a flicker.

Throughout the Middle Ages there were several small-scale efforts to translate the Bible into the common language. But it was John Wycliffe (circa 1320-1384) who confronted the church hierarchy and took the first bold strides toward bringing the Scriptures into the language of the ordinary people.

For Wycliffe this meant English.

Wycliffe and his team were not Hebrew or Greek scholars but renowned Latin scholars. Therefore they translated from Jerome's Vulgate. They completed their first version in 1382. Revised in 1388, Wycliffe's Bible created immense curiosity among its readers, launching an irresistible tide of hunger for God's Word.

Still there was no printing press. So copies had to be made by hand. As Ken Connolly writes in *The Indestructible Book*, "It took ten months to reproduce one copy of the Bible, and the cost of a copy was between £30 and £40. It was reported that two pennies could buy a chicken, and four a hog. £40 was 9,600 pennies—an enormous amount of money. [Some people] provided a load of hay for the privilege of having the New Testament to read *for one day*. Some would save for a month in order to purchase a single page."[82]

Before long the popularity of Wycliffe's translation caught the unwanted attention of church leaders who tried to halt it. They succeeded in persecuting and martyring many proponents of Wycliffe's Bible, but they didn't kill its momentum. (Wycliffe himself died of a stroke before he could be martyred.)

God's Word was now in the hands of the people, and there would be no turning back. Despite a massive effort to burn every copy of Wycliffe's Bible, a successful stealth effort to continue copying it—again, by hand—continued. In fact, nearly 200 copies of Wycliffe's versions have survived to this day.

Wycliffe's watershed Bible represented the first crack in a door that was soon to be blown wide open. A few years later, William Tyndale continued the spread of God's Word by offering the first English translation from the Greek and Hebrew languages, leapfrogging over Jerome's Latin Vulgate.

Using the historic, newly released Greek New Testament compiled by Erasmus in 1516 (a work which evolved into the *Textus Receptus* and later served as the basis for the King James Bible), Tyndale released his English Bible in 1526. In 1536 he was martyred for his work, "mercifully" strangled rather than burned at the stake.

While all of this was happening in England, events were percolating in Germany as well. Martin Luther, an Augustinian monk, had experienced a spiritual awakening—gripped by the truth that the just live by faith, not by paying indulgences and other abuses of the church.

As he challenged the church hierarchy, Luther, like Tyndale, saw the great need for the Bible to be placed in the hands of the people and understood in their own language. While sequestered in Wartburg Castle, he translated Erasmus' Greek New Testament into German and released it in 1522. A few years later, he added the Old Testament—and within the next 14 years, Luther's Bible underwent 377 editions.[83]

The widespread dissemination of Luther's Bible was assisted by something else that had been percolating in Germany—the invention of the printing press by Johannes Gutenberg. What took Tyndale months to produce could now be made in a matter of days.

The English Trail

Throughout the 16th century several historic Bibles were produced, each contributing a feature still in use today.

In 1535 Myles Coverdale produced the first complete printed Bible in English (the Coverdale Bible). This was the first Bible to use the order of the Latin Vulgate for the Old Testament (an order followed by all English versions since) and to print the Apocrypha separately in an appendix.[84]

In the mid-1500s English Protestant scholars fled to Switzerland to avoid persecution from the Catholic Church. Gathering in Geneva, they set out to produce a new English translation with explanatory notes and commentary. This came to be known as the Geneva Bible—a Bible that introduced several innovations: verse references, which became the basis for all subsequent English versions, and italics for words not in the original language text. Maps, tables, and chapter summaries were also included.

These innovations made the Geneva Bible widely popular. Revised annually between 1560 and 1616, this was the Bible used by Shakespeare, John Bunyan, Cromwell's army, the Puritan pilgrims, and even King James himself.[85]

In fact, it was King James' dislike for and disagreement with the explanatory notes in the Geneva Bible that spurred him to commission a new translation. By 1604 it was widely held that the current English translations were in need of correction and revision. James I of England, who had a personal interest in biblical study and translation, commissioned the most ambitious English translation project yet.

The project involved a team of translators representing the best scholarship of the day. The king devised a set of 14 rules for the translators. Using Erasmus' Greek New Testament, along with an edition of the Masoretic Text (a Hebrew translation of the Old Testament dating back to the ninth century) for Hebrew language, the translators also had other English versions at their disposal for when these versions employed a better English word.

The first edition of the King James Bible was released in 1611, but contained so many typos that a new edition was released the same year. Two of the more notable typos: Matthew 23:24 printed "strain at a gnat" instead of the intended "strain out a gnat," (which is how the verse still reads today) and omitting *not* from Exodus 20:14 so that the seventh commandment read, "Thou shalt commit adultery."[86]

It wasn't until the early 1800s that Bible translation and printing moved across the Atlantic to America's shores. Charles Thomson published the first Bible in the United States. As a secretary to the Continental Congress for 15 years, Thomson had had a front-row seat at the American Revolution. It was he who had delivered the news to George Washington that he had been elected America's first President. Thomson translated the Old Testament into English from an edition of the Septuagint; he used a version of Erasmus' *Textus Receptus* to translate the New.

Noah Webster, of dictionary fame, also produced an English version of the Bible, revising the King James Version into more current language.

Modern Versions

By the mid-1800s a new era of biblical study began to emerge as several prominent Greek manuscripts, as well as new manuscript study, came to the forefront. Significant codices such as *Alexandrinus, Sinaiticus,* and *Vaticanus*—Greek manuscripts of all or most of the Bible dating back to the fourth and fifth centuries—had been discovered and were producing a wealth of fresh study.

New translation work began and resulted first in the English Revised Version from Great Britain and in its U.S. counterpart, the American Standard Version (forerunner to the Revised Standard Version and New American Standard Version).

In 1897 a remarkable discovery in Egypt brought great insight to Bible translators. British archaeologists happened upon an ancient Egyptian garbage dump containing timeworn papyri of grocery lists, bills, and letters—all written in Greek. What struck them was that the Greek dialect used in the discarded papyri differed significantly from the Greek of the same era that had been preserved in libraries and museums.

The Greek of the garbage dump was the everyday language of the common Greeks—not of the highly literate or artful. It also matched the Greek of the New Testament—a startling discovery, revealing that the sacred writings had been written in the common, everyday language of the people, not in lofty spiritual-speak.[87]

Why shouldn't our modern translations be the same way? some wondered. So the first half of the 20th century saw an increase in modern-language translations, including the Moffatt Translation and the Goodspeed-Smith "American" Bible. The movement also paved the way for more recent versions, such as *Good News for Modern Man, The Living Bible,* and *The Message.*

In the late 1960s a transdenominational team of more than 100 scholars set out to produce a new, contemporary translation of Scripture based on the best available scholarship—"an accurate translation, suitable for public and private reading, teaching, preaching, memorizing, and liturgical use."[88] The resulting New International Version released in 1978 and became one of the best-selling modern-English translations of all time.

Around the turn of the millennium we witnessed an explosion of new Bible versions and translations, brought about by two dynamic streams: Increased scholarship based on the latest discovered ancient manuscripts and a continued demand for the Word of God in contemporary language. These trends have given us many modern, readable translations that also offer a high degree of accuracy and faithfulness to the original languages.

A Final Note on Modern Versions

More than 500 English versions of the Bible have been produced since Wycliffe's first English Bible in 1382. Dozens of modern versions are available today, not to mention the hundreds of niche Bibles, those with branding and packaging based on categories such as age, gender, occupation, hobby, or stage of life.

Finding a Bible to buy isn't a problem. Finding the Bible translation that meets your and your students' needs can be a bit more challenging.

Take a few minutes to get familiar with some of the major translation philosophies in use today. Bible publishers typically include descriptions of a Bible's translation philosophy in its opening pages. Examine the following definitions to get a running start.

Then consult the following chart for helpful information on the top-selling Bible versions as of this writing. Use this in choosing a Bible for your personal use or for your students. Obviously this information is in constant flux as new translations are released. Most Bible publishers' Web sites contain similar information that can help you decide which translation best suits your purposes.

Formal Equivalence

The phrase *formal equivalence* signifies an effort by translators to create a word-for-word translation from the original languages, sometimes at the expense of a more fluid-sounding text. Examples include the New American Standard Version and the King James Version. Versions that strive to be word-for-word are recommended for deeper adult study.

Dynamic Equivalence

Dynamic equivalence signifies an attempt by translators to create what some have called a thought-for-thought translation. Thought-for-thought renderings typically read more fluidly, letting the expression of the translated language win out over a higher degree of literalness. Examples include the New Living Translation and Today's New International Version. These versions are helpful for deeper study with teenagers.

Paraphrase

A paraphrase is generally one person's rendition of a translation, striving for high readability and sometimes even colloquial language. Examples include *The Living Bible* and *The Message*. Paraphrases are great for casual reading and for gaining another perspective on a passage you've already studied.

BIBLE TRANSLATION	READING LEVEL BY GRADE	READABILITY	TRANSLATION PHILOSOPHY	COMMENTS FROM THE PUBLISHERS
English Standard Version (ESV); Crossway Bibles	8	A literal style, but more readable than the King James Version.	word-for-word	The ESV is an "essentially literal" Bible translation that combines word-for-word precision with literary excellence, beauty, and readability.
Holman Christian Standard Bible (HCSB); B&H Publishing Group	6	A highly readable, accurate translation written in modern English.	balance of word-for-word and thought-for-thought	After several years of preliminary development, Holman Bible Publishers, the oldest Bible publisher in America, assembled an international, interdenominational team of 90 scholars, all of whom were committed to biblical inerrancy, to produce this translation.
King James Version (KJV); various publishers	12	Difficult to read due to 17th-century English vocabulary and word order.	word-for-word	Now outdated in language, the KJV was a vast undertaking of historic proportions. It was developed by a committee of scholars who built on the labors of many generations of Bible translators.
New American Standard, Updated (NASB); various publishers	11	Formal style but more readable than the King James Version.	word-for-word	A highly respected formal translation of the Bible, the purpose of the work was to update the American Standard Version into more current English. Published in 1971, the NASB was updated in 1995, making the "most literal now more readable."

BIBLE TRANSLATION	READING LEVEL BY GRADE	READABILITY	TRANSLATION PHILOSOPHY	COMMENTS FROM THE PUBLISHERS
New Century Version (NCV); Thomas Nelson	3	Contemporary language with down-to-earth vocabulary.	thought-for-thought	The NCV is one of the easiest transla-tions of the Bible to understand. It accurately communi-cates the messages found in the original languages of biblical manuscripts, using the kinds of terms we use every day.
New Interna-tional Version (NIV); Zonder-van	7.8	An accurate and smooth-reading version in mod-ern English.	balance of word-for-word and thought-for-thought	The purpose in translation was to "produce an accurate translation, suitable for public and private reading, teaching, preaching, memoriz-ing, and liturgical use."
New King James Ver-sion (NKJV); Thomas Nelson	8	Its modern English makes the NKJV easier to read than the King James, yet it retains the familiarity of the KJV's 17th cen-tury sentence structure.	word-for-word	A modern language update of the origi-nal KJV, the NKJV retains much of the traditional language and sentence struc-ture without the Old English *thees*, *thous*, and other archaic words.
New Living Translation (NLT); Tyndale House	6.3	A readable translation that uses vocabulary and language structures commonly used by the average American.	thought-for-thought	The NLT is a dy-namic equivalence translation based on the work of 90 Bible scholars and a smaller team of Eng-lish stylists who went back to the original languages and sought to produce the clos-est equivalent of the message in contem-porary English.

BIBLE TRANSLATION	READING LEVEL BY GRADE	READABILITY	TRANSLATION PHILOSOPHY	COMMENTS FROM THE PUBLISHERS
The Message; NavPress	4.3	An easy-to-read, modern-language paraphrase from the Greek and Hebrew texts.	paraphrase	*The Message* was paraphrased from the original languages using the rhythms and idioms of contemporary English. With no formal language and no verse numbers, *The Message* is a refreshingly unique Bible-reading experience.
Today's New International Version (TNIV); Zondervan	7.8	A highly readable, accurate translation written in modern English.	balance of word-for-word and thought-for-thought	TNIV continues the legacy of the NIV, communicating the Bible's timeless truth in today's language. Over the last three decades, words and language have changed at an unprecedented pace. The TNIV ensures that God's unchanging message will continue to be expressed clearly to an emerging generation of readers.

NOTES

Chapter 1

1. Josh McDowell and David H. Bellis, *The Last Christian Generation* (Holiday, Fla.: Green Key Books, 2006), 13.

2. Jon Walker, Southern Baptist Council on Family Life Report to Annual Meeting of the Southern Baptist Convention 2002, http://www.sbcannualmeeting.net/sbc02/newsroom/newspage.asp?ID=261 (accessed February 17, 2008).

3. "Most Twentysomethings Put Christianity on the Shelf Following Spiritually Active Teen Years," *Barna Update* (Ventura, Calif.: Barna Group, September 11, 2006), http://www.barna.org/FlexPage.aspx?Page=Barna Update&BarnaUpdateID=245.

4. Christian Smith, *Soul Searching: The Religious and Spiritual Lives of American Teenagers* (New York: Oxford University Press, 2005), 89.

Chapter 2

5. Peter C. Scales, Dale A. Blyth, James J. Conway, Michael J. Donahue, Jennifer E. Griffin-Wiesner, and Eugene C. Roehlkepartain, *The Attitudes and Needs of Religious Youth Workers: Perspectives From the Field* (Minneapolis: Search Institute, 1995), 15.

6. Search Institute is unlikely to repeat the survey because it has expressed that it's too difficult to get youth workers to respond. Imagine that.

7. R. Laird Harris, Gleason L. Archer, and Bruce K. Waltke. *Theological Wordbook of the Old Testament, Volume 2.* (Chicago: Moody Press, 1980), 943.

8. Ibid., 872-873.

9. "Most Adults Feel Accepted by God, But Lack a Biblical Worldview," *Barna Update* (Ventura, Calif.: Barna Group, August 9, 2005), http://www.barna.org/FlexPage.aspx?Page=BarnaUpdate&BarnaUpdateID=194.

10. "Discipleship Insights Revealed in New Book by George Barna," *Barna Update* (Ventura, Calif.: Barna Group, November 28, 2000), http://www.barna.org/FlexPage.aspx?Page="BarnaUpdate&BarnaUpdateID=76.

11. "Teenagers' Beliefs Moving Farther From Biblical Perspectives," Barna Update (Ventura, Calif.: Barna Group, October 23, 2000), http://www.barna.org/FlexPage.aspx?Page=BarnaUpdate&BarnaUpdateID=74.

12. The Barna Group, (Ventura, Calif.: Barna Group, www.barna.org, Barna by Topic, "Born Again Christians," 2007) http://www.barna.org/FlexPage.aspx?Page=Topic&TopicID=8.

13. The Barna Group, (Ventura, Calif.: Barna Group, www.barna.org, Barna by Topic, "Born Again Christians," 2007) http://www.barna.org/FlexPage.aspx?Page=Topic&TopicID=8.

Chapter 3

14. Spiros Zodhiates, *The Complete Word Study Old Testament* (Chattanooga, Tenn.:

   AMG Publishers, 1994), 2302 (referencing Strong's 571).

15. Ibid., 2317 (referencing Strong's 2617).

16. *Report Card 2002: The Ethics of American Youth,* (Los Angeles:, Josephson Institute of Ethics, 2002). This was the last year this organization made a religious distinction in their research other than by teenagers attending religious schools.

17. "Teens Evaluate the Church-Based Ministry They Received as Children," *Barna Update,* (July 8, 2003), http://www.barna.org/FlexPage.aspx?Page=BarnaUpdate&BarnaUpdateID=143.

18. Smith, *Soul Searching,* 131.

19. Ibid., 133.

20. Ibid., 137.

21. Gary M. Burge, "The Greatest Story Never Read," *Christianity Today,* August 9, 1999, 45-48.

22. George Gallup Jr., "Central Challenges to Churches: Overcoming Biblical Illiteracy," *Emerging Trends,* vol. 19, no. 2 (February 1997), 1.

Chapter 4

23. A recent Barna study indicates that nearly half of all Americans who have accepted Jesus Christ as their Savior did so before reaching the age of 13 (43 percent) and that two out of three born-again Christians (64 percent) made that commitment to Christ before their 18th birthdays. The Barna Group notes that these figures are consistent with similar studies it has conducted during the past 20 years. ("Evangelism Is Most Effective Among Kids," *Barna Update*, October 11, 2004), http://www.barna.org/FlexPage.aspx?Page=BarnaUpdate&BarnaUpdateID=172.

24. Spiros Zodhiates, *The Complete Word Study New Testament*. (Chattanooga, Tenn.: AMG Publishers, 1991), 1344.

25. Ibid., 850.

26. Ceslas Spicq, translated by James D. Ernest. *Theological Lexicon of the New Testament*, Volume 2. (Peabody, Mass.: Hendrickson Publishers, 1996), 285.

27. Sonja Steptoe, "How to Get Teens Excited about God," *Time*, November 1, 2006, http://www.time.com/time/nation/article/0,8599,1553366,00.html.

28. Smith, *Soul Searching*, 267.

Chapter 5

29. Dan Kimball, *The Emerging Church*, (Grand Rapids, Mich., Zondervan, 2003), 26.

Chapter 6

30. Eugene Peterson, *Eat This Book: A Conversation in the Art of Spiritual Reading*. (Grand Rapids, Mich., Wm. B. Eerdmans Publishing Company, 2006), 4.

Chapter 7

31. This is a simplified description of *lectio divina*, a practice that has generated volumes of writing. For a more detailed description, check out *The Sacred Way: Spiritual Practices for Everyday Life* by Tony Jones (Zondervan, 2004).

32. context. Dictionary.com Unabridged (v 1.1). Random House, Inc. http://dictionary.reference.com/browse/context (accessed: February 17, 2008).

Chapter 8

33. Peterson, *Eat This Book*, 87-88.

34. Ibid., 53.

Chapter 9

35. Spicq, *Theological Lexicon of the New Testament*, Volume 2, 595.

36. Kara Powell, "What Type of Students Are We Developing? The State of Our Seniors," Fuller Theological Seminary, The College Transition Project, http://www.cyfm.net/article.php?article=What_Type_of_Students_Are.html#_ftn2 (accessed February 17, 2008).

37. Smith, *Soul Searching*, 38.

Chapter 10

38. Our Name, Solomon's Porch, http://www.solomonsporch.com/aboutus_page_group/ourname.html (accessed February 17, 2008).

Chapter 11

39. Spicq, *Theological Lexicon of the New Testament*, Volume 2, 271-274.

40. See 1 Peter 4:10-11 for the reason why many people divide the spiritual gifts into two broad categories: "speaking gifts" (which deal primarily with communicating God's Word) and "serving gifts" (which are less oriented toward speaking and sometimes involve a hands-on or behind-the-scenes type of service in the body of Christ).

41. See Appendix A for an overview of the gifts outlined in Ephesians 4. Or better yet, do a study of your own. Then compare your conclusions with mine.

Chapter 13

42. Sonja Steptoe, "In Touch With Jesus," *Time*, October 31, 2006, http://www.time.com/time/magazine/article/0,9171,1552027-1,00.html.

43. "Most Twentysomethings Put Christianity on the Shelf Following Spiritually Active Teen Years," *The Barna Update* (Ventura, Calif.: Barna Group, September 11, 2006), http://www.barna.org/FlexPage.aspx?Page=BarnaUpdate&BarnaUpdateID=245.

44. Sonja Steptoe, "How to Get Teens Excited about God," (November 1, 2006) http://www.time.com/time/nation/article/0,8599,1553366,00.html.

45. Colleen Carroll, *The New Faithful* (Chicago: Loyola Press, 2002), 10.

46. Ibid., 15.

47. Tony Jones, *Postmodern Youth Ministry* (Grand Rapids, Mich.: Zondervan, 2001), 26-27.

48. Brian McLaren, *A Generous Orthodoxy* (Grand Rapids, Mich.: Zondervan, 2004), 159.

49. Rob Bell, *Velvet Elvis* (Grand Rapids, Mich.: Zondervan, 2005), 185.

50. Ibid., 67-68.

51. Jones, *Postmodern Youth Ministry*, 211.

52. Powell, "What Type of Students Are We Developing? The State of Our Seniors", Fuller Theological Seminary, The College Transition Project, http://www.cyfm.net/article.php?article=What_Type_of_Students_Are.html

Chapter 14

53. Publishers of other Bible translations, such as NIV and NASB, have recently produced exhaustive concordances of those versions. For the NIV, a new numbering system known as the G/K system was introduced by Edward Goodrick and John Kohlenberger. Many G/K concordances and other Bible study tools include a conversion table for converting a Strong's number to a G/K number and vice versa. However, most newer Bible study tools are still connected to the Strong's numbering system. Not every Bible version has an exhaustive concordance, and not every concordance provides a Greek or Hebrew dictionary. Strong's has both a Greek and a Hebrew dictionary with a brief definition for every entry. Finally, most online tools use Strong's, which is why I use it in these examples.

54. Spiros Zodhiates, *The Complete Word Study New Testament with Greek Parallel*. (Chattanooga, Tenn.: AMG Publishers, 1992).

55. A great variety of word study dictionaries are available. Some I've found most helpful are:

Vine's Expository Dictionary of Biblical Words, Thomas Nelson

The Complete Word Study New Testament, AMG Publishers

The Complete Word Study Old Testament, AMG Publishers

Expository Dictionary of Bible Words, Zondervan

Mounce's Complete Expository Dictionary of Old and New Testament Words, Zondervan

If you know the Greek alphabet, one of the most comprehensive word study dictionaries is *Theological Dictionary of the New Testament, 10 volumes*, Wm. B. Eerdmans Publishing Company.

56. Other helpful commentaries include *New Testament Commentary*, Baker Books, and The *Expositor's Bible Commentary*, Zondervan.

57. Leon Morris, *The Gospel According to John: New International Commentary on the New Testament*, (Grand Rapids, Mich.: Wm. B. Eerdmans Publishing Company, 1995), 580.

58. Zodhiates, *The Complete Word Study Old Testament*, 2326-27.

59. For further insight you could do a Greek word study on the New Testament's use of *atonement*.

Chapter 15

60. Michael Yaconelli, *Messy Spirituality: God's Annoying Love for Imperfect People*, (Grand Rapids: Zondervan, 2002), 14. See also Genesis 9:21-23.

61. Jill Goldsmith, "People Who Need People," *Variety*, July 9, 2006, http://www.variety.com/article/VR1117946434.html?categoryid=18&cs=1.

Chapter 16

62. Irving L. Jensen, *Enjoy Your Bible*. (Minneapolis: World Wide Publications, 1969), 115.

63.

| 10 | 11 | 12 | 13 | 14 |

1	2	3
4	5	6
7	8	9

Chapter 17

64. Farnaz Fassihi, *The Wall Street Journal*, "Two Junior Analysts Charted the Capture Of Saddam Hussein," December 18, 2003.

Appendix A

65. Because of the wording in the Greek, many consider pastor/teacher to be one spiritual gift or position rather than two distinct gifts or positions. For our purposes I am treating them as two separate gifts.

Appendix B

66. Ken Connolly, *The Indestructible Book* (Grand Rapids, Mich.: Baker Books, 1996), 16.

67. Joel B. Green, Scot McKnight, I. Howard Marshall, Eds., *Dictionary of Jesus and the Gospels*. (Downers Grove, Ill.: InterVarsity Press, 1992), 442.

68. Mark D. Roberts, "The Telephone Game and Oral Tradition: Section B," *Are the New Testament Gospels Reliable? Further Thoughts*, posted July 24, 2006, http://www.markdroberts.com/htmfiles/resources/gospelsreliable-more.htm (accessed February 17, 2008).

69. Green, et al., *Dictionary of Jesus and the Gospels*, 246.

70. Roberts, "The Telephone Game and Oral Tradition: Section B."

71. Green, *et al.*, *Dictionary of Jesus and the Gospels*, 514.

72. F.F. Bruce, *The Canon of Scripture* (Downers Grove, Ill.: InterVarsity Press, 1988), 126.

73. Connolly, *The Indestructible Book*, 30-32.

74. Green, *et al.*, *Dictionary of Jesus and the Gospels*, 935-936.

75. Bruce, *The Canon of Scripture*, 122.

76. Ibid., 132.

77. Gordon D. Fee, *Paul's Letter to the Philippians: The New International Commentary on the New Testament* (Grand Rapids, Mich.: Wm. B. Eerdmans Publishing Company, 1995), 395.

78. Bruce M. Metzger, *The Bible in Translation: Ancient and English Versions* (Grand Rapids, Mich.: Baker Books, 2001), 30-31.

79. Saint Augustine, "2.16" in *On Christian Doctrine*. Cited by Metzger, Ibid., 31.

80. Martha Wheelock and Deborah Wheelock Taylor, foreword to *Wheelock's Latin*, 5th edition, by Frederic M. Wheelock and Richard A. Lafleur, (New York:HarperCollins, 1995), x.

81. Metzger, *The Bible in Translation*, 30.

82. Connolly, *The Indestructible Book*, 78.

83. Ibid., 98.

84. Metzger, *The Bible in Translation*, 60.

85. Ibid., 66.

86. Ibid., 78.

87. Peterson, *Eat This Book*, 142-144 and Metzger, *The Bible in Translation*, 105.

88. "New International Version: Notes," Zondervan Home > Bible Translations > Stats & History > New International Version, http://www.zondervan.com/Cultures/en-US/Translations/Stats (accessed February 17, 2008).